Contents

Unit 5: Amazing animals 34–41

Get talking	A guessing game: Animals / Talking about animals
Vocabulary	Adjectives: *small, strong, hairy, clever, heavy, big, dangerous*
Grammar	Comparatives / *as … as* / Superlatives
Reading	A newspaper text: Saved by a pig / Gaming cards / A magazine article: The most amazing animals in the world
Listening	The animal quiz
Writing	A creature from Atlantis
Pronunciation	/dʒ/ /tʃ/
MORE!	A song 4 U: Teatime in Atlantis / A poem: Shark in the park Kids in NYC 1: Homework first
Everyday English	*It depends. Ready? Can you do me a favor? Hang on.*

Unit 6: Where's the post office? 42–49

Get talking	Giving directions / Acting out a dialogue
Vocabulary	Directions / Buildings
Grammar	Directions (Prepositions of place)
Reading	Dialogues: Asking the way / Story time: Missing tourist finally found!
Listening	Dialogues: Asking the way
Writing	A text message: How to get to my house
MORE!	A Song 4 U: This is where you go
Developing speaking competencies	The Twins 2: The way to the station (around town / interrupting politely / checking understanding)

Unit 7: Outdoor adventure 50–55

Get talking	Describing a picture / Making plans
Vocabulary	Places
Grammar	*have to – don't have to*
Reading	Story time: Treasure hunt
Listening	A treasure hunt
Writing	An email home from a youth camp
Pronunciation	*have to*
MORE!	The Story of the Stones 3: The new girl
Everyday English	*I'm off now. Too late! Poor you! Hang on.*

Unit 8: We might go out 56–61

Get talking	Intentions / Acting out a dialogue / Plans for the weekend
Vocabulary	*watch a DVD, do your homework, do the shopping, stay at a friend's house, tidy your room, have a party, play basketball, do nothing*
Grammar	*going to* (negative) / Grammar chant (*not going to*) / *might – might not*
Reading	Messages / Story time: William, the worrier
Listening	Dialogues: Weekend plans
Writing	A party invitation
Pronunciation	*going to*

UNIT 1 Welcome back

You learn
- about the present simple (revision)
- about the past simple (revision)
- about school subjects

You can
- talk about daily routines
- talk and write about your holidays
- talk about school subjects

A song 4 U

CD1 1/2

1 Listen and sing.

Where did you go?

Hey, hey, hey!
Where did you go for
your holiday?

Did you go to Paris?
And did you go to Rome?
Did you go to Lisbon?
Or did you stay at home?

I didn't go away
on a holiday.
I was glad to stay
at home.

Were you on a cruise ship?
Were you at a spa?
Were you in the jungle?
Did you travel far?

I didn't go away
on a holiday.
I was glad to stay
at home.

Did you see the North Pole?
Did you see Madrid?
Did you go Down Under?
Tell me what you did.

I didn't go away
on a holiday.
I was glad to stay
at home.
Yeah, I was glad to stay
at home.

② CHOICES

A Read about Jacob from New Zealand. Then write the times.

My name's Jacob. I live in Queenstown on the South Island of New Zealand. I usually wake up at 7.30. I wash, get dressed and have breakfast with my mum and dad. At ten past eight, my mum drives me to school. I play with my friends there. School starts at 8.45. I really like school. My teacher takes us on a lot of trips – I like that best. School ends at 4 o'clock. Then I usually go to rugby practice with my friends. I get home at 6 o'clock. Then I go for a quick walk with my dog. At 8 o'clock, we have dinner. After dinner, I watch TV or read a bit. I usually go to bed at 9.30.

1 Jacob wakes up at .... 7.30 a.m. ....
2 Jacob goes to school at ....
3 Jacob's lessons start at ....
4 Jacob gets home at ....
5 Jacob goes to bed at ....

B Read about Abeeku from Ghana. Then cover up the text and write notes in the boxes. Check with a partner.

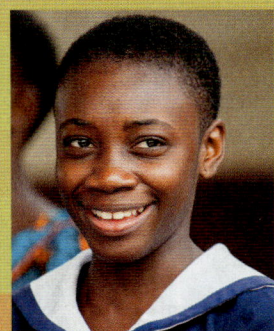

My name's Abeeku and I go to school in a village 200 kilometres from Accra in Ghana. I usually wake up early in the morning, around 4 a.m., so I can study a bit and do my household chores*. People here get up early because it is better to do your chores when it is not so hot. First, I say my morning prayers. Then I sweep the house, wash, make breakfast and put on my school uniform. I always get to school around 6.30 a.m. As soon as I get to school, I sweep my classroom – this is what I and my friends do every day. At 7 a.m., we all meet in assembly, where we usually hear some important information. Our first lesson starts at 7.30 a.m., and lasts for 80 minutes. Every day, we have five lessons. We have a break at 10.10 a.m. and we start again at 10.40 a.m. The older kids have more lessons, of course. But when we finish, I don't go home right away. I stay for private classes with one of our teachers. I get home at about 3.30 p.m. I have my lunch, then go for water for the house. After that, I help my mum to prepare food for our supper. I do my homework after supper. I usually go to bed at 10 p.m.

VOCABULARY: *household chores – Aufgaben im Haushalt

4 a.m.	6.30 a.m.	7.30 a.m.	3.30 p.m.	10 p.m.
Abeeku wakes up				

Get talking Talking about your day

3 Work in pairs. Talk about your daily routines.

> I wake up at … . I go to school at … .

Vocabulary School subjects

4 Listen and number the school subjects. Say which subject you like best.

☐ Maths ☐ English ☐ Geography ☐ History

☐ Science ☐ Music ☐ Art

☐ Information Technology (IT) ☐ French ☐ Design and Technology ☐ Physical Education (PE)

CD1 4 SbX

5 Oliver is from England. Here is his timetable. Listen and complete.

	Monday	3	6	8	Friday
9 – 9.55 a.m.	English	Maths	Science	French	11 ....
10 – 10.55	1	English	History	Science	IT
BREAK					
11.15 – 12.10	Design and Technology	4	Maths	9	History
LUNCH					
1 – 1.55 p.m.	Maths	Science	7	English	12 ....
2 – 2.35	Art	French	....	10	English
2.40 – 3.15	2	5	....	Music	Geography

WB p. 4, 5 CYBER Homework  1

Story time

6 Read the story.

SbX

First day at school

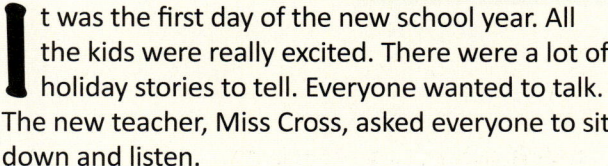

It was the first day of the new school year. All the kids were really excited. There were a lot of holiday stories to tell. Everyone wanted to talk. The new teacher, Miss Cross, asked everyone to sit down and listen.

"OK," she said. "Who wants to tell me about their holidays?"

Twenty arms went up in the air.

"Let's start with Sara," said Miss Cross.

We didn't hear any other stories in that lesson. Sara's family always go somewhere exciting for their holidays. This year was the same.

"My family – that's me, my mum, my dad and my five-year-old brother Michael – went to Australia," she said. "We went to North Queensland. It was really beautiful and we had a great time swimming in the sea and playing on the beach."

"Boring!" said Andrew Wilson.

"Sh!" said Miss Cross. Sara went on.

"One day, my brother was near the sea on his own. When he came back, he had a beautiful shell in his hand. He showed it to us."

"So what?" said Andrew Wilson.

"Well, I saved my brother's life."

"I don't believe you," said one boy.

"How?" shouted another.

"My brother looked in the shell. He told us there was a strange blue and yellow thing inside. He started to put his fingers inside. He wanted to pull it out. Then I remembered about the blue-ringed octopus."

"The what?" Andrew Wilson asked.

"The blue-ringed octopus – I read about it before we went. It lives in the sea, near Australia and Japan. It's small, but it's really poisonous. It can kill you with one bite. I hit my brother's hand and the shell fell onto the sand. Then we saw a small blue and yellow octopus come out of the shell. Of course, we didn't touch it."

"We don't believe you," said lots of the students.

"There's no octopus that's so dangerous," said Andrew Wilson.

"There's one way to find out," said Miss Cross. "Let's check on the internet!"

7 **How many of these tasks can you do?**

Circle T (*True*) or F (*False*).

1 It's the last day of the school year.   T / F
2 The children were excited.   T / F
3 Not many children wanted to tell their holiday stories.   T / F

Choose the correct answer.

4 How many people are there in Sara's family? ☐ 3 ☐ 4 ☐ 5
5 Where did Sara's brother find the shell? ☐ in the sea ☐ on the beach ☐ behind some rocks
6 What did Sara remember about the octopus?
   ☐ it's only from Australia ☐ it's not very big ☐ it lives in shells

Answer the questions.

7 How can a blue-ringed octopus kill a person? ....
8 How did Sara save her brother's life? ....
9 Why does Miss Cross tell them to go onto the internet? ....

  8 **Check your answers with a partner. Then listen to the story.**

 **9** **Read the webpage for the blue-ringed octopus.**

The blue-ringed octopus is very dangerous. It lives in the sea from Japan down to Australia. It lives for about two and a half years. The blue-ringed octopus has blue rings on its body and on its eight arms. It's about the size of a golf ball. It's dark yellow, but when you attack it, it turns bright yellow. The rings turn bright blue. The blue-ringed octopus hunts during the day. It eats fish. It bites the fish and kills them with its poison. The blue-ringed octopus also uses the poison to kill attackers. The poison is so strong and dangerous that it can kill a person. There is no medicine against the poison.

10 **Complete the questions with the question words in the box. Then write the answers to the questions.**

| How |
| What |
| Where |
| When |
| How |
| What |

1 .... does the blue-ringed octopus live?

....

2 .... long does it live?

....

3 .... many arms has it got?

....

4 .... colour is it?

....

5 .... does it hunt?

....

6 .... does it eat?

....

  11 **Listen to the poem. Then read it.**

The furious octopus

The octopus, the octopus
is sometimes very furious.
You shake his first arm and you see
some octo-ink right on your knee.
You shake the others – two to eight –
and suddenly it's much too late
to get away.

The octopus, the octopus
is getting really furious.
He covers you in ink so black.
It's on your head and legs and back.
And then he hugs you really tight.
Believe me, this is quite a sight:
you and the eight-armed octopus.
It's furious, so furious.

(12) CHOICES

Writing for your Portfolio

Tricia is from Brighton in the UK. Read her email to you.

From: tricia_p05@mailconnect.com

Subject: My summer holidays

REPLY

Hi,
This year my family stayed at home. I got up late every day. In the mornings, I usually watched TV.
After lunch, I played volleyball or went swimming. In the evenings, I played on my computer.
I sometimes went to the cinema. It was the perfect holiday.
Bye,
Tricia

A **Write an email answer to Tricia (30–35 words). Tell her about your holidays.**
Write about:

- the place (*I was in … / We went to …*)
- who was with you (*My parents, my …*)
- what the weather was like (*It was sunny / …*)
- how good it was (*The holidays were good / …*)

B **Write your answer to Tricia (70–80 words). Tell her:**

- where you went
- who you went with
- how long you stayed
- what you did all day
- who you met
- what interesting things you did
- why you enjoyed / did not enjoy your holidays

SbX # GRAMMAR

Present simple (revision)

Du verwendest das Present simple, um über Tatsachen zu sprechen.

*The blue-ringed octopus **eats** fish.*

*When you **attack** it, it **turns** bright yellow.*

*The octopus **doesn't hunt** at night.*

*I **do** my homework after supper.*

*Our first lesson **starts** at 7.30 a.m.*

*I **don't believe** you.*

Past simple (revision)

Mithilfe des Past simple berichtest du über Ereignisse und Situationen in der Vergangenheit.

Bei regelmäßigen Verben (regular verbs) hängst du ein -ed an das Verb:

*play – We **played** on the beach.*

*show – He **showed** it to us.*

Einige Verben haben unregelmäßige Formen im Past simple:

*go – We **went** to Australia.*

*read – I **read** about it before the holiday.*

UNIT 2 — Did we catch them?

You learn
- about past simple questions
- about past simple negation (revision)
- more irregular verbs

You can
- ask questions about the past
- use negation (*Verneinung*)
- understand a sketch
- write a dialogue

Vocabulary

1 Listen and look at the picture. Then write the numbers next to the words. How many can you remember?

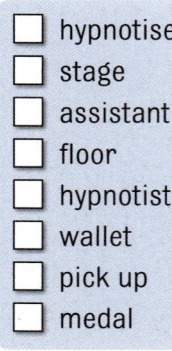

- [ ] hypnotise
- [ ] stage
- [ ] assistant
- [ ] floor
- [ ] hypnotist
- [ ] wallet
- [ ] pick up
- [ ] medal

Time for a sketch

2 Read the sketch.

"Pronto!"

The characters

Charles Granger, a hypnotist
Vivien Tate, his assistant
Roger Allen, a man at the show
Claire Grimes, his girlfriend

Inspector Lime
Sergeant Lewis
a doctor at the hospital

SCENE 1

A show with Charles, a hypnotist, on stage. With him is his assistant Vivien. In front of them there are tables with people sitting at them.

Charles And now, ladies and gentlemen, we need a man for a little experiment. What about you, sir?

Roger No, thank you.

Claire Oh, come on, Roger. Maybe it's fun. Please do it.

Roger Oh, alright.

 WB p. 11, 12, 13

 CYBER Homework 3 Revision

Charles Come up here, sir.

(Roger walks on stage. Applause.)

What's your name?

Roger I'm Roger.

Charles Please have a seat, Roger. I'm going to hypnotise you. Look at this medal. I'm going to swing it. You follow it with your eyes – that's all.

Roger And then?

Charles And then I'm going to give you some commands. And you are going to do what I say.

Claire Tell him to do the washing-up every day!

(Laughter.)

Charles Right, here we go. You only hear what I say. You only follow my commands.

(He hypnotises Roger.)

Good! Stand up! Stand on one leg. Hop around. Very good. Jump down to your friend. Kiss her hand. Very good. Come back here again. Give me your watch. Thank you, very good. When I say "Pronto" – you wake up again. You don't remember anything, of course! One, two, three – "Pronto".

Roger What happened? What did you do? Did you hypnotise me? What did I do?

Charles It's alright. You gave me your watch.

Roger I didn't. *(He checks.)* I did. Give it back to me.

Vivien Here you are, sir. Thank you, sir.

Charles Applause for the gentleman.

(Applause.)

SCENE 2

After the show, Charles and Vivien are alone.

Vivien Did it work?

Charles Of course it did. I gave Roger the secret commands.

Vivien So, we're going to be rich?

Charles Very rich, baby, very rich.

Vivien Do you think he can break into the museum?

Charles Yes, he can. He's very strong.

Vivien Did you tell him to throw the jewels in the bushes?

Charles I did. We pick up the jewels. The police pick up Roger.

(They both laugh.)

SCENE 3

In a room of the museum. In the background there is a broken window. There is broken glass everywhere.

Inspector Lime	Come on, Lewis. Tell me the facts.
Sergeant Lewis	Somebody broke into the museum, took the Deng Jewels and jumped out of the window.
Inspector Lime	Jumped out of the window? Why didn't he use the door?
Sergeant Lewis	The alarm went off when he broke in and the security guards came.
Inspector Lime	I see. Any clues?
Sergeant Lewis	Yes, we found blood under the window, but no thief.
Inspector Lime	Ah, what have we got here? A wallet!
Sergeant Lewis	Don't touch it, sir.
Inspector Lime	But my hands are clean!
Sergeant Lewis	I know, sir. But we need the fingerprints. The thief's fingerprints. Not yours!
Inspector Lime	Ah, yes. Hm, hm. Sorry, errm. And just look at all the mess around here.
Sergeant Lewis	Don't walk around in it, sir.
Inspector Lime	You're right. My shoes are getting dirty.
Sergeant Lewis	No, the footprints, sir.
Inspector Lime	Am I making footprints? Well, the museum people can clean them up.
Sergeant Lewis	Not your footprints, sir. The thief's footprints. I have to go now, sir. See you at the station.
Inspector Lime	Yes, yes. Good man. Off you go.

SCENE 4

Sergeant Lewis is at the door of Claire's house.

Sergeant Lewis   I'm trying to find Mr Allen. I've got his wallet. This address was in it.

Claire   Oh yes, he's my boyfriend.

Sergeant Lewis   I see. Can I talk to him?

Claire   Is it about the accident? He's still in hospital. And he can't remember what happened.

Sergeant Lewis   An accident? Tell me more about it.

SCENE 5

In a room at the hospital.

Sergeant Lewis   Sir, can you hear me?

Claire   He can't hear you.

Sergeant Lewis   Sir, please, talk to me. It's very important.

(The door opens, and a doctor comes in.)

Doctor   What are you doing here? This man is in shock.

Sergeant Lewis   I'm from the police, sir.

Doctor   I don't care. I want you out now. Pronto!

(Suddenly Roger sits up and starts walking stiffly towards the door.)

Doctor   Hey, what's going on? Don't get out of bed!

Claire   Goodness me, you said "Pronto". That's what the hypnotist said.

Sergeant Lewis   The hypnotist? Tell me more.

SCENE 6

In Inspector Lime's office at the police station.

Inspector Lime	Look at the paper, Lewis!
Sergeant Lewis	Why, sir?
Inspector Lime	It says "Inspector Lime solves another case! Jewels back at the museum." Let me read it to you.
Sergeant Lewis	No, sir. Thank you, sir.
Inspector Lime	Alright. I like that. "Inspector Lime solves another case!" Where did you catch them, Lewis? The paper doesn't say.
Sergeant Lewis	The hypnotist and his friend were already on a plane to Singapore. I phoned the police in Singapore this morning and they arrested them an hour ago.
Inspector Lime	Fantastic! We did an excellent job!
(He takes the newspaper.)	
	"Inspector Lime solves another case!" I like that!

THE END

3 **How many of these tasks can you do?**

Choose the correct answer.

1 Charles hypnotises ☐ Roger. ☐ Claire. ☐ Inspector Lime.
2 What does Roger give to Charles? ☐ his wallet ☐ a kiss ☐ his watch
3 Who gives Roger the secret commands? ☐ Charles ☐ Vivien ☐ Charles and Vivien

Complete the sentences.

4 Roger steals the jewels from the ....
5 Sergeant Lewis finds Roger's address in ....
6 When the doctor says "Pronto" Roger ....

Answer the questions.

7 Why is Inspector Lime happy with the newspaper story? ....
8 Why do you think that Sergeant Lewis doesn't want to hear the newspaper story?
....
9 Where are the criminals at the end of the story? ....

   4 **Check your answers with a partner. Then listen to the sketch.**

Get talking Talking about the past

5 **Ask your partner about yesterday. Use the verbs in the box to form questions.**

play	do	read	go	go	help	have	watch

… your homework?   … your brother/sister with the dishes?

… to the cinema?   … a video game?

… TV?   … for a run?

… a book?   … a good time?

Did you go to the cinema?

Grammar chant Past simple

6 **A chant. Listen and repeat.**

What did you do?
Did you steal anything?
Did you take my ring?
Did you hypnotise me?
Did you take my key?

No, I didn't.
You're wrong.
It was really
Harry Strong.

7 CHOICES

Writing for your Portfolio

A **Use the phrases in the box to complete the dialogue. There is one phrase you can't use. Write the dialogue in your exercise book (I = Inspector, W = Witness).**

| he didn't |
| did I |
| did he |
| did he |
| did you see |
| did you |

I What ¹.................................... ?

W I saw a man with a large bag in his hands.

I What ².................................... do?

W He threw the bag into the bush over there.

I And then?

W Then he walked away.

I ³.................................... look nervous?

W No, ⁴.................................... . He looked very calm.

I Why ⁵.................................... call the police then?

B **Somebody broke into a shop and stole an expensive watch. An inspector (I) is asking a witness (W). Write the dialogue (60–70 words).**

GRAMMAR

Past simple negation (revision)

*The thief **didn't take** everything.*
*The inspector **didn't catch** the thief.*
*I **didn't do** it.*

Wichtig: Kein *did* oder *didn't* mit *was, were* und *could*!
*Roger **wasn't** at home.*
*Vivien and Charles **weren't** on a plane to Paris.*
*Sergeant Lewis **could not** talk to Roger.*

Past simple questions

***Did** you **hypnotise** me?*
***Did** you **read** the newspaper?*

Wichtig: Kein *did* oder *didn't* mit *was* und *were*!
***Was** Roger a thief?*
***Were** Charles and Claire on their way to Singapore?*

Complete. Write *did* or *didn't*.

So bildest du die Verneinung im Past simple: person + [1]............................ + *base form* of the verb.

So bildest du Fragen im Past simple: [2]............................ + person + *base form* of the verb.

More irregular verbs

break – **broke**	find – **found**	take – **took**	catch – **caught**
give – **gave**	get – **got**	have – **had**	say – **said**

MORE fun with Fido!

Tonight I can sleep in your bed.

Aaah, time for bed.

Now, what did I do wrong?

BOOT!

HYPNOSIS FOR BEGINNERS

 WB p. 15, 16

 CYBER Homework 5

The Story of the Stones 1

It's only a dream

1 Match the names to the characters.

Darkman
Sarah
Sunborn
Daniel
Emma

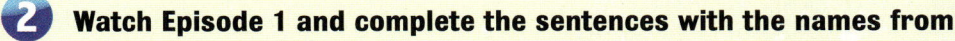

 2 Watch Episode 1 and complete the sentences with the names from **1**.

1 .... makes a promise.
2 .... has three dreams about Darkman.
3 .... dreams she is on a rope.
4 .... says they have to speak to Sunborn.
5 .... thinks Darkman is dead.

3 Write a message to Sunborn from the children.

....
....
....
....

Everyday English

4 Watch Episode 1 again. Complete the sentences with the words in the box.

I mean	Oh, come on	I promise

Daniel Yeah, let's get in touch with her.

Sarah [1].. .
They're only dreams.

Darkman I'll get them.
[2].................................... .

Daniel It's the third time this week.

Sarah Me too. [3]........................... ,
I have almost the same dream.

UNIT 3 How embarrassing!

You learn
- how to use *one / ones*
- how to use *why – because*
- about online behaviour

You can
- ask why something happened
- give reasons
- use the internet responsibly
- write a picture story

SbX **1 CHOICES**

THE PARTY THAT WASN'T A SURPRISE (by Alan S., 12)

At the end of the last school year my friends and I wanted to organise a surprise party for Mr Harris, our English teacher. He had a job at a new school. So we wanted to say thank you and goodbye. We made a big cake and we bought a big box of chocolates, too.

Two days before the party I wrote an email to the kids from my class. I said, "Don't forget! The party for Mr Harris is a SURPRISE! So don't tell him!" Then I pressed SEND. The next day at school my friends told me about my mistake. I had sent* the email to them and I had sent it to Mr Harris, too!

VOCABULARY: *had sent – hatte geschickt

MUM'S MISTAKE (by Sophie K., 13)

A few months ago my best friend Karen's dad needed to go to hospital for an operation. She was really worried. When I told my mum about the operation, she asked me for Karen's email address. She wanted to send her a message to wish the family luck. The next time I saw Karen, she wasn't very happy. "I'm a bit upset with your mum's message," she said. I was really confused, but then she showed me the message. "Dear Karen. I hope the operation is a success. We are all thinking of you. LOL Mrs Beeton." When I got home, I asked Mum, "Why did you write LOL in your message to Karen?" "Because I wanted to send her lots of love." "Mum," I explained, "LOL doesn't mean 'lots of love', it means 'laugh out loud'." My mum was so embarrassed and phoned Karen immediately to say sorry. Luckily the operation was a success. Now we can all laugh at my mum's embarrassing mistake.

A Read Alan's story. Then match the questions and answers. There is one extra answer.

1 What did Alan's class plan for their teacher?
2 What did they want to give him?
3 What did Alan write in his email?
4 What mistake did he make?

- [ ] He sent the email to Mr Harris, too.
- [ ] A big box of chocolates, and a cake.
- [ ] He made a mistake.
- [ ] He wrote, "Don't tell Mr Harris about the party!"
- [ ] They planned a surprise party.

B Read Sophie's story. Then answer the questions.

1 Who is Karen?
....
2 Why did Sophie's mum want to write to Karen?
....
3 Why was Sophie confused?
....
4 What three words did Sophie's mum want to write?
....

WB p. 19, 20 CYBER Homework 6 Revision

 CD1 12 **2** Listen to the story *Modern art* and circle T (*True*) or F (*False*).

1 Mrs Smith had a new job in a shop. T / F
2 The director went to check on Mrs Smith's work. T / F
3 The floor was still dirty. T / F
4 Part of the modern sculpture was missing. T / F
5 The jacket with five roses was missing. T / F
6 The jacket with the roses was part of a sculpture. T / F

3 Think of the stories in and . Who do you think said these sentences?

1 What an old jacket!
2 Oh no! I didn't take his address out.
3 I can't believe that she wrote that.
4 What's the matter, you look upset?
5 There's something missing here.
6 Oh no! I must phone her immediately.

I think Alan / Karen / Sophie / Sophie's mum / the cleaning lady / the director of the museum said, "…"

 CD1 13 **4** Listen to the dialogue. Then act it out.

SbX

Richard	Dad?
Dad	What is it?
Richard	Can I have another T-shirt?
Dad	Why? What's wrong with the blue one?
Richard	Nothing, but I want my extra large one. The one that has got an alien on it.

Dad	Sorry, I can't give you that one.
Richard	Why not?
Dad	I put it in the washing machine. And now it's extra small.
Richard	Oh, Dad!

Sounds right /w/

 CD1 14 **5** Listen and repeat.

Why and **wh**y and **wh**y!
Why is it always **wh**y?
Why not ask me **wh**en,
or **wh**ere or **wh**at or who?
It's something you could do.

6 **Read the webpage.**

Online dos and don'ts

Why was 14-year-old Jacob so upset when he opened the door of his house? Because there were about a hundred young people in the garden for his birthday party. Some of them he knew. Most of them he didn't know.

Why were they there? Because Jacob posted his invitation on Facebook. But why did so many people turn up? Because Jacob didn't check who could see his postings. So not only his real friends turned up, but also friends of his friends.

Jacob was lucky because one of his neighbours called the police and the people went away. The garden was a mess, but the house was fine.

Jacob made a terrible mistake. Jacob is not the only one to make such a mistake. There are lots of stories about something going wrong because of wrong behaviour on the web. So here are some important tips for when you go online:

- Think before you post something and check who can see it.
- Think about what you write or what sort of pictures you send. You never know how many people can read your text or look at the picture. Your best friend could send it on to his or her best friend and so on. Do you really want that?
- Don't give your passwords to anyone. And don't post your real name and home address online.
- When you hear something bad about someone, don't pass it on to other people. Maybe it's not true.
- When someone bullies you online, talk to an adult.

7 **Match the answers to the questions.**

1 Why were there lots of people in Jacob's garden?
2 Why was Jacob upset?
3 Why was Jacob lucky?
4 Why is it a good idea to check who can see your postings?
5 Why is it not a good idea to give your password to other people?
6 Why is it a good idea to talk to an adult?

- [ ] Because a neighbour called the police.
- [ ] Because you don't want everyone to know your plans.
- [ ] Because they can help when someone bullies you.
- [ ] Because he posted his invitation on Facebook.
- [ ] Because you don't want other people to use it.
- [ ] Because lots of people turned up for his birthday.

Get talking Giving reasons

8 **Work in pairs. Talk to your partner about the following: a TV series, a school subject, a book, a CD. Make short dialogues. Use words from the box.**

exciting	fun	cool	interesting	funny	great	boring
bad	too long	confusing	scary	difficult	silly	awesome

A Do you like Science?
B Yes, I do.
A Why do you like it?
B Because it's exciting.

A Do you like Science?
B No, I don't.
A Why not?
B Because it isn't interesting.

WB p. 18, 21

⑨ CHOICES

Writing for your Portfolio

A Look at the pictures. Write a story (30–40 words). You can use the words below to help you.

This morning Tom was ...
He looked ... and saw ...
He ran ...
His friends ... because ... slippers*.

2 SCHOOL BUS

VOCABULARY
*slippers – Hausschuhe

B Look at the pictures. Write a story (70–80 words). Add a good title.

❶ **❷** 8:45 **❸** SCHOOL BUS STOP **❹** 9:15

 GRAMMAR

one / ones

Wenn du über gleiche Dinge sprichst, aber das Nomen nicht immer wiederholen möchtest, dann kannst du das Nomen durch **one** oder **ones** ersetzen.
*I needed an email with everyone's address in it so I used the **one** Mr Harris sent.*

Complete with *one* or *ones*.

Du verwendest [1]..................... , wenn du ein Nomen im Singular nicht wiederholen willst.
Du verwendest [2].................... , wenn du ein Nomen im Plural nicht wiederholen willst.

Which one would you like?

why – because

Why were the people there? – **Because** Jacob posted his invitation on Facebook.
But **why** did so many people turn up? – **Because** Jacob didn't check who could see his postings.

The Twins 1
DEVELOPING SPEAKING COMPETENCIES

Language function
- apologising (*sich entschuldigen*)

Speaking strategy
- expressing dismay (*Missfallen ausdrücken*)

The bike tour

Vocabulary Mistakes

CD1 15

1 Look at the photos. Match them with the mistakes. Listen and check.

- [ ] send a text message to the wrong person
- [ ] break someone's camera
- [ ] eat someone's chocolate
- [ ] lose someone's pen

CD1 16

2 Watch or listen to the dialogue. Then read it. Why does Leo say sorry?

Leo Lucy, I'm really sorry. I made a terrible mistake.

Lucy What did you do?

Leo Well, you told me to invite Emily Clarke … for the bike tour.

Lucy And?

Leo I wanted to text her, but I sent the message to Emily White.

Lucy What? You know I don't really like her. She's a bit boring.

Leo I know. I feel really bad about it.

Lucy You fool. She's so boring.

Leo I'm sorry. It was a mistake. I know.

Lucy But how could you do that?

Leo Hang on a minute. Here's her answer: *Great idea. Thanks. See you both near the old castle at two. Say hi to Lucy.*

Lucy Oh, no!

3 Complete the sentences with *Lucy*, *Leo* or *Emily*.

1 .... invited the wrong person for a bike tour.
2 .... got an invitation to go on a bike tour with Lucy and Leo.
3 .... knows what .... thinks about Emily White.
4 .... thinks that Emily White is boring.
5 .... tells .... that she will join them.
6 When .... hears that she is not happy at all.

WB p. 24

Useful phrases Apologising

(4) **Write the sentences that Leo uses to apologise to Lucy. Then check with (2).**

1 sorry / really / I'm   ....

2 about / I / really / bad / it / feel ....

(?) **What do you think? Answer the questions.**

- Do they meet Emily White?   • What happens on the bike tour?

Mobile homework

Watch part 2 of the video. Use a verb from the box and your own ideas to complete the sentences.

meet	stop	apologise	have	ride

1 Lucy and Leo .... near ....

2 The three kids .... their bikes ....

3 They .... next to ....

4 Emily .... a surprise ....

5 In the end, Lucy ....

Speaking strategy Expressing dismay

(5) **Try to complete the phrases. Check with the dialogue in (2).**

1 **Leo** I sent the message to Emily White.
   Lucy W.............................. ?

2 **Leo** I know. I feel really bad about it.
   Lucy You f.................... . She's so boring.

3 **Leo** I'm sorry. It was a mistake. I know.
   Lucy But h.................... c.................... y.................... d.................... that?

(6) CHOICES

A **Work in pairs. A apologises to B for a mistake. B shows dismay.**

send / text message
break / mobile phone
lose / pen
eat / ice cream

A I sent the text message to Pam, not to Paula. I'm so sorry.

B How could you do that?

B **ROLE PLAY: Look at the situations from A. Choose one. Work in pairs and extend it into a longer dialogue. Take 2 or 3 minutes to practise it. Don't write it down. Act it out in class.**

UNIT 4 Halloween

You learn
- Halloween words
- how to use *should / shouldn't*

You can
- talk about Halloween
- create an ending to a story
- make suggestions (*Vorschläge*)
- write an email based on a mind map

Vocabulary Halloween

CD1 17
SbX

1 Listen and look at the picture. Then write the numbers next to the words.

- ☐ apple bobbing
- 1 a ghost
- ☐ a pumpkin
- ☐ a haunted house
- ☐ a vampire
- ☐ a witch

A Song 4 U

CD1 18/19

2 Listen and sing.

When they come after you

We are brave, we are strong.
Here's our Halloween song:

We aren't scared of witches.
We smile at every ghost.
We do not fear the zombies.
In fact, we like them most.

*But what will you do
when they come after you?*

We are brave, we are strong.
Here's our Halloween song:

We say hello to pirates
and wizards are our friends.
We do not fear the vampires
that fly until night ends.

*But what will you do
when they come after you?*

We are brave, we are strong.
Here's our Halloween song:

We love the Halloween
  monsters.
We think they are alright.
It's all a great big party.
A party for a night.

WB p. 25   CYBER Homework 9 Revision

3 Read the webpage about Halloween. Who do you think has the most fun and why?

The question was: Do you have any Halloween traditions or fun things to do? Your answers were:

George, USA, aged 11
My mum gets a scary film from the DVD shop. We change the house into a haunted castle and then we invite friends for a Halloween party. My brother and I have got a CD of scary noises, and when our friends walk up the stairs in the dark, we play it. After a tour of the house we eat popcorn and watch the film.

Megan, Ireland, aged 14
We always have a party. Everyone wears a mask. We're vampires, witches and ghosts. And we also play apple bobbing. There are lots of apples in a bowl of water and you try to take them out with your mouth. You can't use your hands. It's difficult, but fun. I often win the game because I'm a vampire. And with my vampire teeth it's easy to get the apple.

Steve, UK, aged 12
Me and my brothers usually go out on Halloween. We knock on people's doors and say "Trick or treat". People sometimes give us a treat; sweets, etc. But if they don't, we play a trick on them. Last year our neighbour Mr Eliot didn't give us a treat, so we put some vampire stickers on his front window.

Henry, Canada, aged 11
Every year we take a pumpkin to school. We cut off the top and take out everything inside. Then we cut a scary face in it. Finally, we put a candle inside the pumpkin. This year my pumpkin face was the best. It was so scary that the teacher said: "Let's keep it for our Halloween party at school." I was very proud. Henry – Master of Horror!

4 Read the sentences below. Which of the four texts on the webpage in **3** do they go with? Write the names: *George, Megan, Steve* or *Henry*.

1 That's really scary, well done! All we need now is a candle. ....

2 My clothes are really wet. I must get another T-shirt! ....

3 Wait for me before you start the film! ....

4 Can I borrow your knife, please? ....

5 Those pictures look really scary! ....

6 This is unfair. Your teeth are so long. ....

7 Wow, that's a lot of sweets. ....

8 What was that? Did you hear that? What an awful sound! ....

5 **Read the story.**

Trick or treat

"We shouldn't go in there," I said. "And you shouldn't be a baby," said Jim. "Come on."
Jim walked up the long drive. We followed. An old man opened the door. He wasn't very happy to see us. "Trick or treat?" Jim asked. The old man looked at us. "Go away," he said. "Go away – now!" He closed the door. "Come on," I said. And we walked to the gate. At the gate Jim stopped. "That man was mean," he said. "We should play a mean trick on him." "OK," I said. "Let's make ghost noises." "No," said Jim. "We should play a really mean trick on him." "Let's throw a stone at his window," said Kerry. "No," said Jim. "Let's put superglue in his door lock." "I think we should go home," I said. But it was too late.

Last Halloween, I went trick-or-treating with my twin sister Kerry. "Larry and Kerry, don't go too far away," our mum said. But we didn't listen and soon we were on the other side of town. There we met a boy about the same age as us. He told us his name was Jim. He said he wanted to go trick-or-treating with us. "There are some really good houses in this street," he told us. So we went with him.

At the end of the street was a really big old house with a big gate and a long drive up to the front door. We stopped and looked at it. It was the kind of house you see in horror films. "Let's try this house," said Jim.

6 **How many of these tasks can you do?**

1 Larry *tells* / *doesn't tell* his mum where they are going.
2 The kids *know* / *don't know* Jim.
3 The big house is *old* / *new*.

4 Larry thought the house was like one from ....
5 Jim calls Larry .... because he doesn't want to go into the house.
6 The old man tells the children .... and then shuts the door.

7 Why does Jim want to play a trick on the old man? ....
8 What trick does Kerry want to play on the old man? ....
9 What trick does Jim want to play on the old man? ....

7 **Check your answers with a partner. Then listen to the story.**

WB p. 26, 27, 28   CYBER Homework **10**

Get talking Creating an ending to a story

8 Work in pairs. Think of an ending to the story.

CD1 22 **9** Now listen to the end of the story.

10 Complete Sarah's list of suggestions for going trick-or-treating. Write *should* or *shouldn't*.

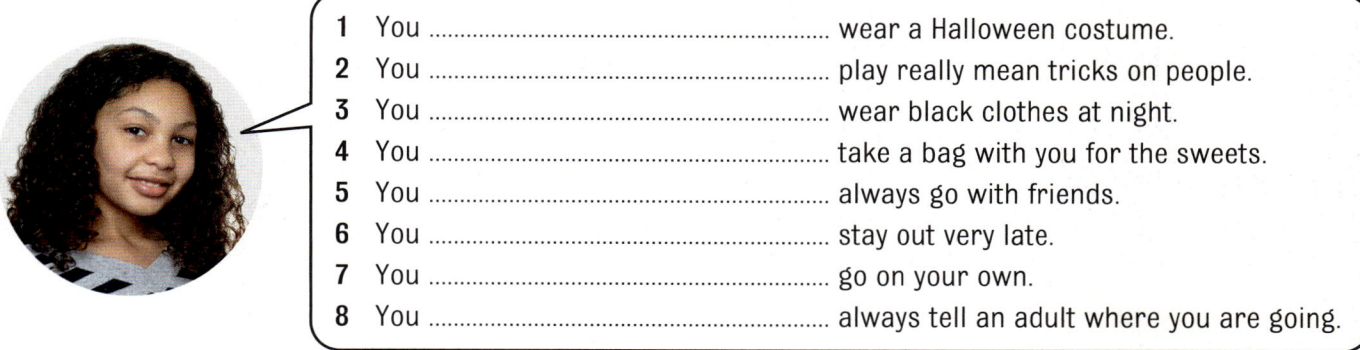

1	You	....	wear a Halloween costume.
2	You	....	play really mean tricks on people.
3	You	....	wear black clothes at night.
4	You	....	take a bag with you for the sweets.
5	You	....	always go with friends.
6	You	....	stay out very late.
7	You	....	go on your own.
8	You	....	always tell an adult where you are going.

Sounds right *should – shouldn't*

CD1 23 **11** Listen and check. Then say the sentences in **10** yourself.

Writing for your Portfolio

12 Read Sarah's email to you. Then answer her in an email.

From: sarah_clarkson@mailconnect.com
Subject: Halloween party!

REPLY

Hi there,
Mum says I can have a Halloween party ☺ (and U R the first I'm inviting),
but I don't really know how to plan it. I have some ideas, but you're much
better at that than I am.
So can you send me a few ideas? Please.
C U

Here are some ideas for your email:

plenty of food · very loud music · costumes · games · should · Party · shouldn't · ... · good music · popcorn · very wild games · something to drink · too many sweets

13 Listen to the poem. Then read it.

I'm not so keen on Halloween

I'm not so keen
on Halloween.
When my friends meet
for trick or treat,
I'm not the one
who thinks it's fun
to run around
as witch or ghost.

What scares me most
is other kids
who hunt for treats,
who look for sweets.
They don't play tricks
but just give kicks
to get their treats,
to get your sweets.

SbX ## GRAMMAR

 should – shouldn't

Lies die Beispielsätze.

*We **should go** home – it's late.*
*We **shouldn't go** in there – it's dangerous.*
*What **should** I **do**?*

 **Complete the sentences with *should* or *shouldn't*.**

Wenn du sagen willst, was jemand tun sollte,
dann verwendest du [1]................................. .
Wenn du sagen willst, was jemand nicht tun sollte,
dann verwendest du [2]................................. .
Wenn du um Rat fragst, dann verwendest du
ebenfalls [3]................................. .

Bildung: *should / shouldn't + base form* of the verb.

We should take our umbrellas.

MORE fun with Fido!

Trick or treat!

A bone?

Why didn't they like my treat?

 **WB p. 30**  **CYBER** Homework **11**

The Story of the Stones 2

We're all in danger

1 Look at the pictures from Episode 1 and put them in the correct order.

 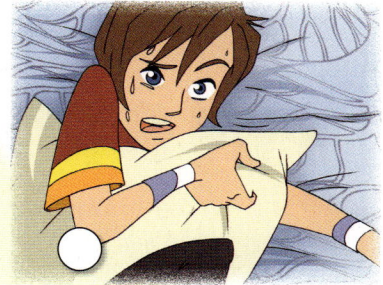 

2 Can you remember who morphs into each of these animals? Write the names.

❶

❷

❸

....

DVD **3** Watch Episode 2 and answer the questions. Circle a, b or c.

1 Who is Darkman's master?
   a) The Black Knight   b) Demon Eyes   c) The Lord of the Fire

2 What does Darkman's master want?
   a) the belt and stones   b) a spaceship   c) the three stones

3 Which Lord wanted all the stones?
   a) The Lord of the Earth   b) The Lord of the Fire   c) The Lord of the Water

4 Who is trying to find the stones?
   a) Sunborn   b) Darkman   c) The Lords

Everyday English

DVD **4** Watch Episode 2 again. Complete the sentences and match them with the person who said them.

Here you are	get it	How can that be

1 .... ? He's dead, isn't he?   ☐ Emma

2 Only your stones can protect you now. ....   ☐ Sarah

3 But I still don't .... Why didn't Darkman die?   ☐ Sunborn

UNIT 5 Amazing animals

You learn
- about comparatives and superlatives
- about amazing animals
- words to describe animals

You can
- compare things
- talk about animals
- write about an imaginary animal

 Read the text.

Saved by a pig

August 5th, 2004 was a hot day in Worcester. Judith Crowe, her 5-year-old son Jeff and their little pig Bacon went swimming in the river near their home. Bacon was a very good swimmer. In fact, he was better than Jeff.

Judith and her son played and swam in the water for an hour. All the time Bacon was with them. Then Jeff's mother got out of the water to get a towel. "Stay here for a minute," she said. When she turned round, she saw Jeff in the middle of the river. The water was deeper and more dangerous there. He was in trouble.

Jeff's mother jumped into the water and started to swim. But Bacon was faster than Judith and got to the boy first.

The little boy put his arms around the pig. But he was bigger than the pig and he was heavier. The boy and the pig both disappeared under the water.

Jeff's mother didn't know what to do. Then suddenly she saw the little pig again. Jeff was on the pig's back. Her son was safe.

2 **How many of these tasks can you do?**

1 Judith is Jeff's mother   T / F
2 Bacon is Jeff's hen   T / F
3 They went swimming in a river.   T / F
4 .... was near their house.
5 Bacon was a .... than Jeff.
6 Judith left Jeff in the water to ....
7 Where was Jeff when he got into trouble? ....
8 Who got to Jeff first? ....
9 Why did Jeff and Bacon under the water? ....

3 **Check your answers with a partner.**

Vocabulary Adjectives

SbX **4** **Match the pictures with the adjectives. Write the numbers.**

☑ small   ☐ strong   ☐ hairy   ☐ clever   ☐ heavy   ☐ big   ☐ dangerous

❶   ❷   ❸   ❹   ❺   ❻   ❼

➤ WB p. 32, 33   CYBER Homework 12   Revision

Get talking   A guessing game

5 Choose one of the animals. Make sentences using comparatives. Your partner guesses what animal it is. Use the words in the box in **4** to help you.

A It's bigger than a mouse.

B Is it a guinea pig?

A No, it's heavier than a guinea pig.

B Is it a rabbit?

A That's right.

SbX **6** Read the gaming cards for these animals from Atlantis.

ANIMALS OF ATLANTIS
THE RUCKLE
The Ruckle was very exotic. It was half land animal and half bird, but it didn't fly. It was as big as a rabbit. It was very friendly and many Atlantians had them for pets.

ANIMALS OF ATLANTIS
THE BUGBOY
The Bugboy was a small reptile. It was as small as a mouse, but it was as dangerous as a snake. In fact, it was as poisonous as a blue-ringed octopus. Every year, hundreds of people died from its bite.

ANIMALS OF ATLANTIS
THE SNAPKLE
The Snapkle was a kind of dragon. It lived in the mountains outside of Atlantis. It was as big as an elephant. But it wasn't as beautiful as an elephant. In fact, it was very ugly.

ANIMALS OF ATLANTIS
THE HIPCOP
The Hipcop wasn't as friendly as the Ruckle, but it was also a popular pet. It was as clever as a chimpanzee.

7 Read the cards again and circle T (*True*) or F (*False*).

1 Atlantians had Ruckles in their homes. T / F
2 The Ruckle was bigger than a rabbit. T / F
3 The Bugboy was very dangerous. T / F
4 The Bugboy was a kind of octopus. T / F
5 The Snapkle was bigger than an elephant. T / F

6 The Snapkle wasn't a beautiful animal. T / F
7 The Hipcop was friendlier than the Ruckle. T / F
8 The Hipcop wasn't as clever as a chimpanzee. T / F

WB p. 33, 35, 36

8 Look at the pictures and write four sentences using *as … as* and *not as … as*.

The yellow car is not as expensive as …

5 metres
1930
£35,000
100 kph*

4 metres
1930
£30,000
100 kph

VOCABULARY: *kph – short for "kilometres per hour"

Sounds right /dʒ/ /tʃ/

CD1 25

9 **Listen and repeat.**

His name's **J**im,
I'm more beautiful than him.
He's a **ch**impanzee,
and he's as big as me.

CD1 26

10 **Read the magazine article. Complete it with the missing numbers from the box. Then listen and check.**

| 150 | 2 | 8 | 3 | 110 | 1 | 3 |

The Estuarine crocodiles of South East Asia are the longest crocodiles in the world. They can be .... metres long – as long as two cars together!

a

d

The bumblebee bat from Thailand is the smallest mammal in the world. It is .... centimetres long and weighs .... grams.

b

The world's most poisonous snake is the taipan. It lives in the deserts of Australia. It can be more than .... metres long.

The most Amazing Animals in the world

The most dangerous animal in the world is the mosquito. It can carry malaria. Every year more than .... million people worldwide die from malaria.

e

c

The biggest animal on land or in the sea is the blue whale. It's also the heaviest. It weighs .... tons.

f

The fastest land animal in the world is the cheetah. It can run very fast – more than .... kph.

WB p. 32, 35, 36

CYBER Homework 13

11 Whose eye is it? Match the eyes and the animals.

 antelope
 giraffe
3 rhino
2 ostrich
6 chimpanzee
5 dolphin

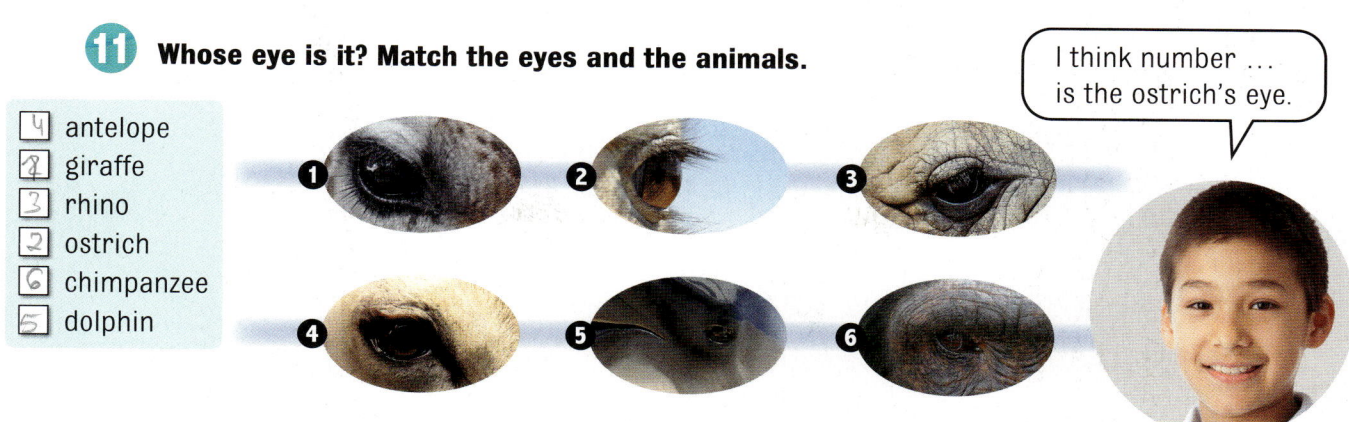

I think number … is the ostrich's eye.

CD1 27 **12** Listen and check.

13 Put the animals in order. Write 1, 2 and 3 in the boxes.

The animal quiz

ANIMALS

❶ Which is the tallest?
a ☐ a giraffe
b ☐ an ostrich
c ☐ an elephant

❷ Which is the longest?
a ☐ an anaconda
b ☐ a whale shark
c ☐ a crocodile

❸ Which is the fastest?
a ☐ a lion
b ☐ a rabbit
c ☐ an antelope

❹ Which is the most intelligent?
a ☐ a dolphin
b ☐ a pig
c ☐ a chimpanzee

❺ Which is the heaviest?
a ☐ a rhino
b ☐ a blue whale
c ☐ an elephant

Get talking Talking about animals

CD1 28 **14** Discuss your answers with a partner. Then listen and check.

A I think the elephant is the tallest.

B I don't think so. I think the …

WB p. 32, 34, 36

A song 4 U

15 **Listen and sing.**

Teatime in Atlantis

It's teatime in Atlantis
and everyone is there.
They drink and sing
and you can hear
them really everywhere.

The Hipcop and the Ruckle
went for a cup of tea.
They sat down on a sofa.
Guess what!
Who did they see?

It's teatime in Atlantis …

The Bugboy and the Snapkle,
the Huffump and his son,
they had ten cups of orange tea
and had a lot of fun.

It's teatime in Atlantis …

CD1 31

16 **Listen and say the poem.**

Shark in the park by Roger McGough

Ever see*
a shark
picnic
in the park?

If he offers
you a bun,

run.

VOCABULARY: *ever see – short for "Have you ever seen … ?"

Writing for your Portfolio

SbX

17 **Read about the Huffump.**

The Huffump was a kind of shark. It lived in the sea around Atlantis. It was as big as a whale and it was very dangerous. It had a really big mouth and more than 4,000 teeth. Every year it killed and ate more than 200 Atlantians. The Atlantians were very scared of swimming in the sea.

18 **Design your own animal from Atlantis. Make up a name for the creature and write a text of 50–70 words about it.**

WB p. 33

GRAMMAR

 ## Comparatives

Wenn du zwei Dinge vergleichst, die verschieden sind, dann verwendest du das Wort *than*. An die englischen Eigenschaftswörter mit einer Silbe (*fast, slow, deep, old, …*) hängst du -er an.
*He's old**er than** me.   She's fast**er than** me.*

An die englischen Eigenschaftswörter mit zwei Silben, die auf -y, -le und -ow enden (*happy, simple, slow, …*) hängst du ebenfalls -er an.

Bei manchen Eigenschaftwörtern verändert sich jedoch die Rechtschreibung:
hot, big, fat, etc. – *It's hot**ter** today than yesterday.*
heavy, angry, hungry, etc. – *Joe's heav**ier than** me.*

Wenn das Eigenschaftswort mehr als zwei Silben hat (*dangerous, difficult, interesting, …*), dann verwendest du *more + adjective.*
*The book is **more interesting than** the film.*

Ausnahmen:

good – **better**	*He was **better than** Jeff.*
bad – **worse**	*I'm bad at football, but he's **worse than** me!*

 ## as … as

Wenn du sagen willst, dass zwei Dinge / Tiere / Personen gleich groß, klein usw. sind, dann verwendest du *as … as*:
*It was **as** small **as** a mouse.*
*It was **as** dangerous **as** a snake.*

Wenn du sagen willst, dass ein/e Ding / Tier / Person nicht so groß, klein usw. ist wie ein/e andere/s Ding / Tier / Person, dann verwendest du *not as … as*:
*It was **not as** friendly **as** the Ruckle.*

Superlatives

Wenn du ausdrücken willst, dass etwas am größten, schwersten, schnellsten usw. ist, hängst du -est an das Adjektiv an:
fast, slow, deep, old, etc. – *The cheetah is **the** fast**est** mammal in the world.*

Bei einigen Adjektiven ändert sich die Schreibung:
hot, big, fat, etc. – *The blue whale is **the** big**gest** animal in the world.*
heavy, angry, hungry, etc. – *The blue whale is **the** heav**iest** animal in the world.*

Bei Adjektiven, die aus drei oder mehr Silben bestehen, verwendest du *the most + adjective*:
dangerous, interesting, etc. – *The mosquito is **the most dangerous** animal in the world.*

Ausnahmen:

good – **the best**	*She's **the best** player in the team.*
bad – **the worst**	*It's **the worst** restaurant in town.*

Kids in NYC 1

Homework first

Before you watch

1 Write the words under the pictures.

bedroom
living room
hall
kitchen

1 .... 2 .... 3 .... 4 ....

2 What order do you think these pictures come in the DVD? Write 1–4.

Watch the story

3 Check your answers to **2**.

4 Complete the sentences.

1 Steve is in the ....
2 Steve and Jenny want ....
3 Steve's .... isn't done.
4 Jenny did the Geography ....
5 Jenny wants to ring her sister to ....

5 Complete the dialogue.

need
see
listen
want
remember
get
do
think

Jenny Clare? Hi, it's me. ¹............................... , can you ²............................... me a favor?

Clare It depends. What do you ³............................... ?

Jenny I ⁴............................... my Geography homework – it's in my school bag.
Can you ⁵............................... it?

Clare Where is it?

Jenny In my room, I ⁶............................... .

Clare Hang on then. Jenny? I'm in your room, but I don't ⁷............................... your bag.

Jenny I'm really sorry, Clare, but I ⁸............................... now – I left it in the kitchen.

6 Answer the questions.

1 Where's Jenny's Geography homework? ....

2 Does Clare find the bag in the bedroom? ....

3 Where does Clare find the bag? ....

4 Why does Steve say "This isn't right"? ....

Everyday English

7 Complete the dialogues.

Note:
favor = American English
favour = British English

It depends.   Ready?   Can you do me a favor?   Hang on

Listen. ¹...

Can you just read me the answers to the Geography homework?

2 ....

Where is it?

In my room, I think.

³............................... then.

OK. ⁴...............................

You learn
- to understand directions
- how to use prepositions of place
- words for buildings

You can
- ask the way
- give directions
- write a text message with directions to your place

Vocabulary Directions

1 Gretta the witch is explaining to Sir Florestan, a knight, how to get to the dragon's place. Listen and follow the way. Write *D* where the dragon lives.

 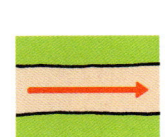 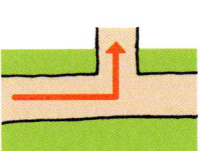 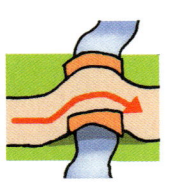 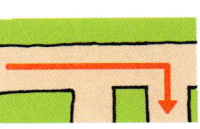

go past the tree   go straight ahead   turn left   cross the bridge   take the second right

WB p. 40   CYBER Homework 15 Revision

Vocabulary Buildings

2 Listen and look at the pictures. Then write the numbers next to the words.

10 bank	12 police station	5 chemist's	3 post office	7 tourist office	1 railway station
2 church	M supermarket	9 cinema	6 restaurant	8 music shop	4 hospital

❶ 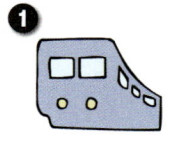 **❷**  **❸**  **❹**  **❺** 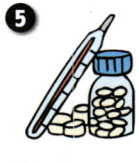 **❻**

❼  **❽**  **❾**  **❿**  **⓫**  **⓬**

❸ CHOICES

A Read the dialogue and draw the sign for the post office in the map.

DIALOGUE 1

Woman	Excuse me, where's the post office?
Man	The post office? Go straight ahead. Go past the supermarket.
Woman	Alright. And then?
Man	Then take the first left.
Woman	OK.
Man	Go past the bank. The post office is next to it.

You are here

B Read the dialogue and draw the sign for the cinema in the map above.

DIALOGUE 2

Boy	Excuse me.
Woman	Yes, dear?
Boy	Can you tell me where the Odeon cinema is?
Woman	The Odeon? Well, let me think. It's in Hill Road.
Boy	How do I get there?
Woman	Go straight on, take the second right and go past the police station.

Boy	OK, past the police station …
Woman	Then there's a little park in front of you. Go through the park. Turn right, then left, and then right again. The cinema is behind the large music shop.
Boy	Thank you.
Woman	Not at all.

4 Listen to two more dialogues and draw the other two signs on the map in **❸**.

Get talking Giving directions

 ⑤ **Work in pairs. Student A works with the map here, student B works with the map in the Workbook (page 43).**

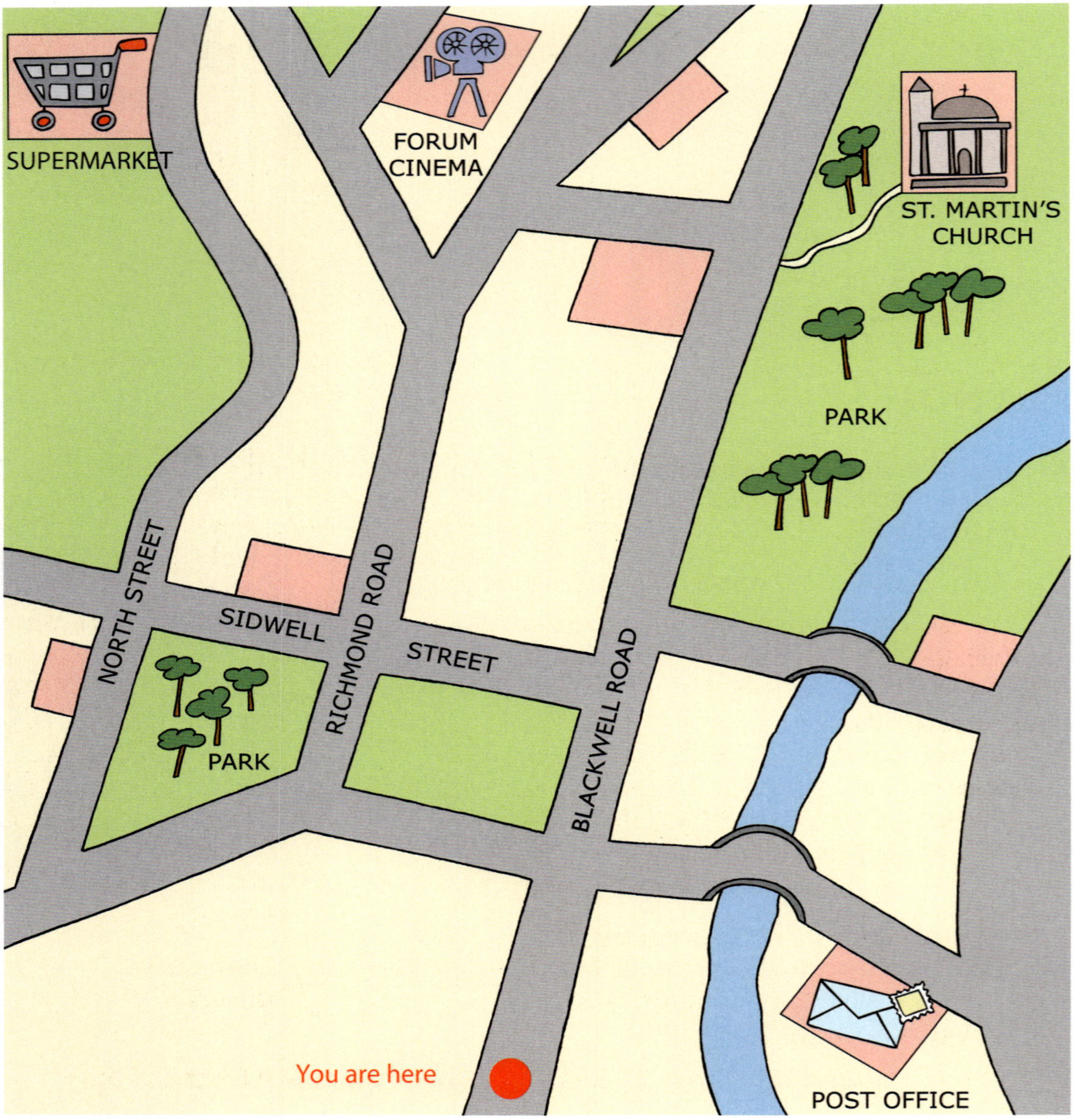

SUPERMARKET

FORUM CINEMA

ST. MARTIN'S CHURCH

PARK

NORTH STREET

SIDWELL

RICHMOND ROAD

STREET

BLACKWELL ROAD

PARK

You are here

POST OFFICE

You ask your partner the way to the tourist office, the restaurant, the police station and the bank.

A Excuse me, how do I get to the tourist office? (Excuse me, I'm trying to find … / Excuse me, I'm looking for …)

B That's easy. Take the …

> WB p. 42, 43

CYBER Homework **16**

Story time

6 Read the story.

SbX

Missing tourist finally found!

Romanian tourist found safe and well after three days.

Mr Vasile Belea (63) from Romania came to London three days ago. He wanted to have a holiday with his son's family. His son picked him up from the airport and they went into London by underground. When they changed trains at Stockwell Station, Mr Belea's son, Radu, jumped on the next train and the doors closed. Mr Belea was too slow and the doors closed in front of him.

"I came back right away," Radu Belea said, "but Dad wasn't there. So I looked around the station, and then I went to the next stop again, but I really couldn't find him."

We know now that Mr Belea went back into the street and tried to ask a policeman for help. When he finally found one, the policeman was very friendly, but he didn't understand a word Mr Belea said to him. And Mr Belea didn't know a word of English! So he walked around and hoped to see his son somewhere, but, of course, he didn't. He asked another policeman and another – they were all very friendly, but they didn't understand him and he didn't understand them. Mr Belea had only £17 in his pockets, he didn't know where his son lived, and he couldn't talk to people. When it got dark, he sat in a bus stop and spent the night there. In the morning, he started walking again. When he was cold, he went into a shopping centre. He stayed there most of the time, and in the evening he went to a bus stop again.

After two days and nights like this he saw a man reading a newspaper. On the cover of this newspaper he saw a picture: It was him!

Mr Belea had one pound left. So he bought a newspaper and with the newspaper he went to a police station. He showed the paper to a policeman there, and after half an hour, Mr Belea was back with his son's family.

"We're so glad to have him back," his son said. "And I think it's great that the paper helped so much. They put an extra large photo of my dad on the cover. I really want to thank everybody for their help."

7 How many of these tasks can you do?

1 Mr Vasile Belea is ☐ English. ☐ British. ☑ Romanian.

2 Vasile Belea was in London
☐ on business. ☐ for a conference. ☑ for a holiday with his son's family.

3 Mr Belea got lost
☑ on the underground. ☐ on a bus. ☐ in a shopping centre.

4 The policeman didn't speak ..... *romanian* ..... .

5 Vasile Belea only had a little .... on him.

6 Vasile Belea did not know his son's *adress* ....

7 Where did Vasile Belea spend the nights? *In the bus stop/station* ....

8 Why did Vasile Belea buy the newspaper? *to show it to the police* ....

9 Why was the paper a big help? *because the police now realised what was the problem*

  CD2 4/5 **8** Check your answers with a partner. Then listen to the story.

 WB p. 41

This is where you go

CD2 6/7

9 ... sing.

A Song 4 U

... want to go to Newtown?
... en simply go ahead.
Just cross the bridge
and don't forget
to stop when lights are red.

*Right and left and straight ahead,
this is where you go.
Right and left and straight ahead,
that's what you need to know.*

You want to go to Market Square?
Then take the second right.
Then turn left
and left again.
That's Market Square alright.

Right and left and straight ahead ...

You want to find the cinema?
Go past the music shop,
and opposite
the restaurant
take a few steps more and stop.

Right and left and straight ahead ...

10 Put the dialogue in the correct order. Compare with your partner. Then act it out.

☐	**Jasmine**	The Carlton? The film's at the Odeon. Hurry up!
☐	**Jasmine**	I'm in front of the cinema, too. The Odeon cinema.
1	**Jasmine**	Hey, Ron, where are you?
☐	**Jasmine**	Go up Broad Street and turn left after the bank.
☐	**Ron**	What's the quickest way?
☐	**Ron**	I'm in front of the cinema.
☐	**Ron**	Right. See you in five minutes.
☐	**Ron**	Oh dear. Wrong cinema. I'm in front of the Carlton cinema.

WB p. 45

Writing for your Portfolio

11 Your friend is coming to visit you.
She sent you a text message.
Send her a text message with
directions to your house.
(Write 40–60 words.)

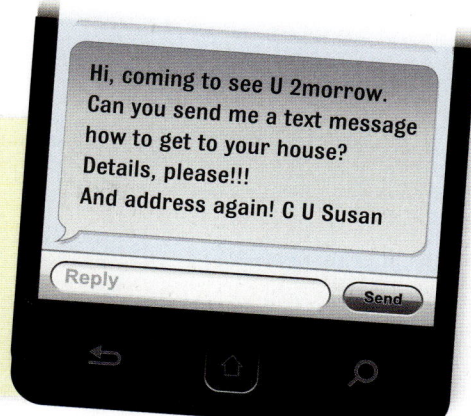

Hi, coming to see U 2morrow.
Can you send me a text message
how to get to your house?
Details, please!!!
And address again! C U Susan

Reply   Send

SbX GRAMMAR

Directions (Prepositions of place)

So sagst du jemandem, wie er/sie an ein bestimmtes
Ziel gelangen kann:

Go straight ahead.   *Turn left / right.*
Take the first left / second right.   *Cross the bridge / street.*
Go past the post office.   *Walk up the hill* **as far as** *the church.*

opposite

So sagst du jemandem, wo ein bestimmtes Ziel zu
finden ist:

The cinema is **behind** *the shopping centre.*
Next to *the bank, there's the post office.*
The restaurant is **opposite** *the church.*
There's a little park **in front of** *you.*
On the corner *of the next street, there's a large bank.*
It's just **round the corner**, *beside the bank.*

round the corner   **in front of**

MORE
fun
with
Fido!

Excuse me, do you know where the nearest lamp post is?

Straight on, and take the first left.

Thanks.

DEVELOPING SPEAKING COMPETENCIES

Language function
- interrupting politely (*jemanden höflich unterbrechen*)

Speaking strategy
- checking understanding (*nachfragen, ob man etwas richtig verstanden hat*)

The way to the station

Vocabulary Around town

CD2 8 **1** **Match the places and the pictures. Then listen and check.**

| bridge | bus stop | fountain | traffic lights | statue | clock tower |

1 ....

2 ....

3 ....

4 ....

5 ....

6 ....

CD2 9 **2** **Watch or listen to the dialogue. Then read it. What items from 1 do Lucy and Leo mention?**

Tourist	Excuse me.
Leo	Yes?
Tourist	I'm sorry to bother you, but can you tell me the way to the railway station?
Leo	Sure, no problem.
Lucy	Can you see that bus stop over there?
Tourist	Yes.
Lucy	Go past it and take the second left.
Tourist	Second left.
Lucy	Yes, the second left. Then go straight ahead and turn left at the traffic lights.
Tourist	Sorry?

Lucy	Straight ahead and then left at the traffic lights. The railway station is at the end of the road.
Tourist	So that's second left after the bus stop, then left at the traffic lights.
Lucy	That's right. You can't go wrong.
Tourist	Thank you.

WB p. 45

③ Cover up the dialogue in **②**. Try to complete the directions. Then check.

Walk past the ¹.................................. and then take the ².................................. left. Go straight ahead until you get to some ³.................................. lights. Turn ⁴.................................. . The ⁵.................................. is at the end of the road.

Useful phrases Interrupting politely

④ Write the words in the correct order to make sentences. Then check with the dialogue in **②** to find a good answer to the phrases.

1 me / excuse   ....
2 sorry / bother / I'm / to / you   ....

? What do you think? Answer the questions.

• The tourist asks Leo for directions. Why does Lucy tell him the way?   • What happens next?

Mobile homework

Watch part 2 of the video and complete the sentences with *Lucy* and/or *Leo*.

1 .... is angry with ....
2 .... gives the directions to the next tourist.
3 .... tells the tourist to follow the man.
4 .... laugh at the end.

Speaking strategy Checking understanding

⑤ Complete. Check with the dialogue in **②**.

Lucy   Then go straight ahead and turn left at the traffic lights.
Tourist   ¹.. ?
Lucy   Straight ahead and then left at the traffic lights. The railway station is at the end of the road.
Tourist   ².. second left after the bus stop, then left at the traffic lights.
Lucy   That's right. You can't go wrong.

⑥ CHOICES

A Work in pairs. Use the prompts.

> A Take the third right. Then take the second left and then the first right.

> B Sorry?

first / second / third right
first / second / third left

A Give directions. → B Check understanding.

B ROLE PLAY: Work in pairs. Then swap roles.

Student A: You are a tourist. Where do you want to go? Ask student B the way. Interrupt politely and check his/her directions.

Student B: Give student A directions. Make sure he/she understands.

UNIT Outdoor adventure

You learn
- words for places
- how to use *have to* / *don't have to*

You can
- make/suggest a plan
- write an email home from a youth camp
- describe a picture

Vocabulary Places

CD2 10

SbX

1 Listen and look. Then write the numbers next to the words.

☐ hill	☐ stars	☐ valley	☐ sea	☐ motorway	☐ town	☐ forest	☐ sun
☐ fields	☐ lake	☐ road	☐ village	☐ mountain	☐ river	☐ moon	☐ beach

2 Work in pairs. Look at the picture above for half a minute. One of you closes the book. Ask and answer questions.

Student A

Where	's are	the	village? sea? lake? … fields? …

Student B

On the right-hand side.
On the left-hand side.
In the middle.
In the top right-hand corner.
In the bottom left-hand corner.
Next to the …

 WB p. 47, 48

 CYBER Homework 18 Revision

Get talking Making plans

3 Listen and complete the dialogue.

A Let's ¹.................................. on Monday.

B Canoeing? I'm not sure.

A Well, you don't have to come along. I'll go alone, then.

B Wait a minute. I think I'll join you.

A Great. But bring ².................................. ! And you have to ³.................................. a life jacket in the boat all the time.

B Of course. I know that.

Build a tree house!
When: Thursday 3 p.m.
Don't be late!
Bring a hard hat!

Go for a picnic!
When: Sunday 12 a.m.
Bring your own food and drink!
Clean up the picnic area after the picnic!

Go rock climbing!
When: Friday 11 a.m.
Bring warm clothes and good shoes.
Read the camp guide carefully.

Visit the waterfalls!
When: Saturday 2 p.m.
Don't be late!
Wear an anorak near the waterfalls.

4 Work in pairs. Look at the notices above and act out dialogues.

A Let's visit/go/build … .

B … I'm not … .

A Well, you don't … .

B Wait … .

A Great. But … . And you … . .

Sounds right *have to*

5 Listen and repeat.

A I can't stay here, I **have to** go.

B You **have to** go? But why?

A I **have to** move to London!

B I **have to** say goodbye.

6 Listen to Emma and Harry talking about a treasure hunt. Take notes.

	When?	What did you find?	Where did you find it?
Emma			
Harry			

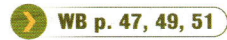

Treasure hunt

When Dad said that Gillie and I could go to an adventure holiday camp, I wasn't too excited. I didn't want to go on a holiday camp with my nine-year-old sister! But Gillie really loved the idea. So I couldn't say no. But the camp was great! Lots of new friends and Gillie was OK, too (most of the time ☺). What I liked most about the camp were the surprise activities: wild water canoeing, rock climbing, a visit to the waterfall – these things were never boring! No wonder – Rick, Pamela, Laura, Jack and Ron (our guides) were fantastic. Especially Ron! He was really cool. One Friday, Gillie was very excited: "Chris, come quickly, there's a geo-caching treasure hunt with Ron tomorrow. Quick, only 20 kids can go!" "Geo-caching???" I thought. I had no idea what it was – but I didn't want to ask. I was fourteen. And she was nine, you know! "Geo-caching? Not a bad idea," I said. When we wrote our names on the list, I saw this note:

GEO-CACHING TREASURE HUNT!
WHEN: WEDNESDAY 1 P.M.
BRING: GOOD SHOES, A SNACK
AND A BOTTLE OF WATER.
DON'T FORGET: ONE OR TWO
SMALL THINGS FOR THE CACHE!
WRITE YOUR NAME ON THE LIST –
ONLY 20 KIDS CAN GO!
SEE YOU!
RON

I went to speak to Ron later to find out more about geo-caching and this was what I learnt: for geo-caching you need a GPS unit. The camp guides tell you where you can find the 'treasure'. But they don't say things like "go through the forest until you come to a little pond" etc. They only tell you the coordinates of the place (for example 1.27 mi S: GCG8V5), and you put them in your GPS and off you go! Oh, there's something else: The treasure is usually several small things in a box (the so-called 'cache'!). You can take out as many as you want. But for every treasure you take out, you have to put in something new.

The next day we started our geo-caching hunt. We looked for three hours, and we looked everywhere, behind every tree, under every stone, in every hole in the ground. Nothing! "Let's go back!" I said. Then suddenly Gillie shouted "Here it is!" She had her hand in a hole in the ground and when she took her hand out, I knew that it wasn't a cache! In her hand, my nine-year-old sister Gillie had a handful of old coins!

WB p. 48, 50

Back at the camp, we showed the coins to Ron. He laughed. "Old coins? Ha, ha, ha! Good joke! They're not old. But give them to me!" Ron was very nice. He gave me a DVD and my sister a bar of chocolate for the coins! Later in the evening, Gillie showed me a coin. "I didn't give him this one," she said. "I wanted to keep it." "Silly idea," I thought. But I didn't say much. After all, she was only nine.

Two days later, there was a visit to a museum in a town near our camp. Ron went, so of course Gillie and I went along, too. We saw lots of interesting things.

Gillie suddenly shouted. "Look! The coins! The coins! They look like my coins!" Gillie was very excited. She looked at the coin in her hand. It looked exactly like the old Roman coins behind the glass window.

There was a man in uniform at the other end of the room. When Ron saw him, he got very nervous. "Be quiet, you silly girl!" he shouted. But the man in the uniform saw the coin. "Where did you find this coin?" he asked. "In the forest," Gillie said. "But not only this one. We found lots of them. And Ron has got them all. Ron has got them!"

Gillie pointed at Ron. Suddenly he did not look very cool any more. He turned around and ran away! Then things happened very quickly. The man in the uniform phoned the police. Two very friendly police officers came and took us to the police station in a car. "These coins are Roman coins. They're very old," one of them said.

"And when you find old coins, you have to give them to the museum. Nobody can keep them! We're going to find this young man, Ron. He has to give the coins to the museum!" Two days later the police found Ron. They took the coins away from him. They are now behind glass in the museum. And next to them is a little sign:

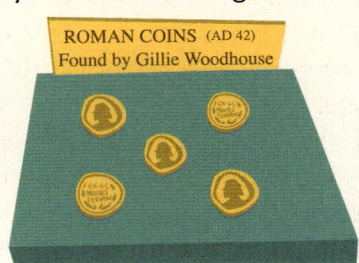

ROMAN COINS (AD 42)
Found by Gillie Woodhouse

Gillie is very proud of this. Well, after all, she is only nine …

 8 **How many of these tasks can you do?**

1 Chris was excited by the idea of a holiday camp.   T / F
2 Chris changed his ideas when he got to the camp.   T / F
3 Ron was a guide at the camp.   T / F
4 For geo-caching you do not need ☐ a map.   ☐ a GPS unit.   ☐ small objects.
5 Gillie found the treasure ☐ under the ground.   ☐ behind a tree.   ☐ under a stone.
6 Gillie gave Ron ☐ all the coins.   ☐ the coins and a DVD.   ☐ nearly all the coins.
7 How did Gillie find out that her coins were really old coins? ....
8 Why was the man at the museum upset? ....
9 What happened to the coins? ....

 CD2 14/15 **9** **Check your answers with a partner. Then listen to the story.**

>> WB p. 48, 50

10 Samantha is at a youth camp. Read her email to her mum.
Which paragraph (1, 2 or 3) talks about

a) what she did yesterday? ☐ **b)** the rules of the camp? ☐
c) all the different things you can do at the camp? ☐

From: sam06@hello.uk

Subject: Youth camp

REPLY

Hi Mum,
[1] The camp is really great! There are lots of things to do here like football and volleyball, for example. We can go horse riding too. We can go swimming in the river – it's fantastic! We never get bored.
[2] Yesterday I went on a great canoeing trip! We went down the river for two hours and then we had a picnic. Jack, our guide, made a fire and we sang songs and played games.
[3] Everything is great, but of course there are rules. We have to go to bed at ten.
We have to help in the kitchen. We have to make our beds. But we don't have to wash up – that's good. I hope you and Dad are well. See you soon.
Love,
Sam

11 CHOICES

A Imagine you are at the same youth camp as Samantha. Write an email of 30–40 words to a friend. Write about:

• what sports you can do   • what sport you played yesterday

B Imagine you are at a different youth camp. Write an email to your parents (100–120 words). Write about:

• what the camp is like   • what you did yesterday
• how you like it there   • what you are going to do tomorrow
• what you can do there   • what you like best
• the rules in the camp   • what you don't like

 SbX **GRAMMAR** *have to – don't have to*

You have to wear a helmet!

You **have to** *wear a life jacket. You* **don't have to** *come along.*

Complete the rule with *have to* **or** *don't have to.*
Mit [1]... sagst du, dass etwas **notwendig** ist.
Mit [2]... sagst du, dass etwas **nicht notwendig** ist.

 WB p. 51, 52, 53

 CYBER Homework 20

The new girl

1 Match the sentence halves to complete the summary of Episode 2.

1 The children tell Sunborn	☐ Darkman is alive.
2 The children learn that	☐ to the children.
3 Sunborn tells the children	☐ about their dreams.
4 Sunborn gives the stones	☐ into animals.
5 The children morph	☐ the story of the stones.

2 Look at the picture from Episode 3 and say what you can see. What do you think happens in this episode?

DVD **3** Watch Episode 3 and put the sentences in order to tell the story.

☐ The children hear a cry for help.
☐ The children learn the new girl's name is Gillian.
☐ The tiger rescues the girl.

☐ The children talk about their dreams.
☐ Emma morphs and jumps in the river.
☐ Daniel thinks it's a trap.

Everyday English

DVD **4** Watch Episode 3 again. Match the pictures with the expressions.

I'm off now.
Too late … !
Poor you!
Hang on.

Maybe it's a trap.

UNIT 8 We might go out

You learn
- how to use *might / might not*
- how to use *not going to*
- how to talk about freetime activities

You can
- talk about things that might happen
- talk about what you are (not) planning to do
- write an invitation

Get talking Intentions

 1 What are these people's plans? Talk about them with your partner. Use the words in the box to help you.

watch a DVD	do the shopping	tidy (your) room	play basketball
do (your) homework	stay at a friend's house	have a party	do nothing

A What's she going to do?

B She's going to do her homework.

CD2 16

SbX

 2 Listen to the dialogues and tick (✓) the correct box.

	Sharon	Nick	Chloe	Bill
have a party				
do nothing				
do homework				
stay at a friend's place				

56 UNIT **8**

 WB p. 55, 56

 CYBER Homework 21 Revision

③ CHOICES

CD2 17

A Read the dialogue and complete it with the phrases from the box. There is one phrase you don't need. Then listen and check. Act out the dialogue.

> I'm going to watch TV.   I'm going to do nothing.   And your school project?

Steve	What are your plans for the weekend?
Luke	¹..
Steve	What about TV?
Luke	I'm not going to watch TV. There's nothing good on.
Steve	²..
Luke	I'm not going to do any work this weekend.

B Work with a partner and complete the dialogue with your own ideas. Then act out the scene.

Kevin	Have you got any special plans for the weekend?
Dawn	Well, I'm going to watch DVDs tomorrow night. Do you want to watch them with me?
Kevin	I'd love to*, ...
Dawn	Oh, why not?
Kevin	I'm going to Jenny's party.
Dawn	.... !

VOCABULARY: *I'd love to … – Ich würde gerne …

Grammar chant *not going to*

④ **A chant. Listen and repeat.**

Hey, Dad, listen. I'm sorry.
But I'm not going to tidy my room.
I'm not going to make my bed.
I'm not going to work for school.
I'm going to take it easy instead.

Listen, Sam. That's fine, but …
I'm not going to cook for you.
I'm not going to drive you around.
I'm not going to buy you sweets.
I'm not going to give you a pound.

Hey, listen Dad. That was only a joke. Honestly …
I am going to tidy my room.
I am going to make my bed.
I am going to do my work,
I am now going to go ahead.
Really! Believe me, Dad!

Sounds right *going to*

⑤ **When we say *going to*, it often sounds like *gonna*. Listen and repeat.**

I'm **going to** write a letter,
I'm **going to** put it in the post.

And the letter's **going to** tell you
that I love you the most.

6 Find out about your partner's plans for this weekend.

> **A** Are you going to watch TV?

> **B** No, I'm not. I'm going to watch DVDs. What about you?

7 Look at the mixed-up messages. Match them with the types of communication in the box. Write letters A–I.

☐ ☐ text messages   ☐ ☐ ☐ emails   ☐ ☐ notes
☐ invitation   ☐ Facebook post

A

I've just come home.
We had a great Sunday out.
We, that's Mum, Dad, me and my sister Mia. We went to Brighton to see Grandma. Mia and I climbed a tree – see the photo! She's cool.
I really like my sister.

👍 Like   💬 Comment

B Mia, I saw your note about Sunday this morning. No way! We're all going to visit Grandma, and you're coming with us. You've got another 5 days to do your work for school. No excuse, please.

C Hi, Zoe. There was a phone call from Mia. She's not feeling well. She's not going to come over today. Dad

D Hey, Mum.
I'm really sorry.
I've got a lot of work for school this week. So I'm not going to come along to see Grandma on Sunday.

E
From: zoe_f@likeit.com
Subject: photos on FB
REPLY

Hi Mia, I saw the photos your brother posted on FB. I can see you had a lot of fun. But why did you tell me you're ill? Zoe

F
From: mia_hd@hello.uk
Subject: party
REPLY

Hello Zoe, thanks for your invitation for Sunday. Great! My parents and my little brother Lucas are going to visit Grandma. I'm not going with them. I'll tell them I've got a lot of work for school. LOL! Mia

G OK, I understand. I'm going to join you all, of course. Mia

H
From: mia_hd@hello.uk
Subject: Sorry!!!
REPLY

Hi there, I really, really, really wanted to see you today, Zoe. Then my mum said no. I felt ashamed and didn't want to tell you I had to go with them. It was a big mistake! Sorry for telling you a lie. Can we meet up tomorrow after school? Mia

I
Dear Mia,
Come to my birthday party next Sunday.

Time:
10 a.m. – 6 p.m.

Place:
7, Station Road

Love, Zoe

WB p. 58

CYBER Homework 22

8 Read the messages in **7** again. Tick the correct answer.

1 What does Mia say in her email to Zoe about Sunday?

- [ ] She's going to visit her grandma with her family.
- [ ] She's going to climb a tree with her brother.
- [ ] She's not going to visit her grandma with her family.

2 What message does Mia give Zoe's dad?

- [ ] She's going to come over to Zoe's place two hours later.
- [ ] She's not feeling well and isn't going to come over to Zoe's place.
- [ ] She's not feeling well, but she's going to come over anyway.

3 What does Zoe see on Mia's brother's Facebook page?

- [ ] A photo of Mia's family and their grandma.
- [ ] A photo of Lucas and his grandma.
- [ ] A photo of Lucas and Mia.

4 How does Mia feel when Zoe finds out what she did?

- [ ] She feels sorry she didn't tell Zoe the truth.
- [ ] She's very angry with herself.
- [ ] She's angry with Lucas because he posted the photo.

9 Read the messages again. In what order do they come? Write the letters A–I in the correct order.

1 [I] 2 [ ] 3 [ ] 4 [ ] 5 [ ] 6 [ ] 7 [ ] 8 [ ] 9 [ ]

Story time

SbX **10** Read the story.

William, the worrier

William has got a driving test in the morning, and he's worried. William is always worried!

We're going to the cinema. Do you want to come?

No, thanks. We might miss the last bus home and I have to get to bed early tonight.

Do you want to go for a practice drive?

No, thanks. I might crash the car. I need the car for my test tomorrow.

The next morning.

I'm sorry, William. Your test was yesterday!

11 Here are some more of William's worries. Match the sentence halves.

1 I don't want to go to the beach –
2 I don't want to go skiing –
3 I'm going to study tonight –
4 I don't want to go near that dog –
5 I don't want to answer the teacher's question –
6 I don't want to ride your bike –
7 I'm not going to eat that –
8 I'm not going to go trick-or-treating –

☐ I might break my leg.
☐ I might not get it right.
☐ I might fall off.
☐ it might be poisonous.
☐ the sun might be too hot.
☐ I might get into trouble.
☐ we might have a test tomorrow.
☐ it might bite.

12 Work in pairs. Take turns to test your partner.

A Why doesn't William want to go to the beach?

B Because the sun might be too hot.

A That's right.

13 CHOICES

Writing for your Portfolio

A Read Jill's invitation to her birthday party. Imagine it's your birthday next week. Invite a friend (30–40 words). Write about:

• why there is a party
• when and where it is
• what there is going to be at the party

B Imagine there is going to be a fancy dress party at your school. Draw a mind map first – see the example below. Then use your ideas to write an invitation to a friend (60–70 words).

Party invitation

It's my birthday on Friday and I'm going to have a party on Saturday at my place. There's going to be lots of food and drink and there's going to be a DJ, too. It's going to be great. The party starts at 6 p.m. Don't be late.

See you on Saturday,

Jill

lots of food

me: pirate   you: catwoman?

DJ   costume   18:00 – 21:00

what?

fancy dress party   Friday evening

midnight surprise   at school

GRAMMAR

 going to (negative)

Du verwendest *going to*, wenn du etwas planst oder beabsichtigst, etwas zu tun.
Beim Verb *go* verwendest du normalerweise kein *going to*. Also: *I'm going to a party.*

So bildest du die Verneinung mit *going to*:
negative of *be* + *going to* + *base form* of the verb.

I'm not going to play tennis any more.

I'm not going to play tennis tomorrow.
You **aren't going to like** the film.
He/She **isn't going to do** the shopping.
It **isn't going to rain** this afternoon.
We **aren't going to do** our homework.
They **aren't going to play** volleyball on Sunday.

 might – might not

Wenn du sagen willst, dass etwas möglicherweise
(nicht) eintreten wird, verwendest du:
might (not) + *base form* of the verb.

He might not like chocolate!

I **might go** to the party. I'm not sure.
It **might rain**, so take a coat.
I **might not sleep** well.

MORE fun with Fido!

What am I going to do today?

I know!

Sleep!

 WB p. 60

 CYBER Homework 23

UNIT 9 Strange things from space!

You learn
- space vocabulary
- about the past simple (revision)
- how to use past time markers

You can
- talk about science fiction / UFOs / space
- write an ending to a story

Story time

1 Read the story.

SbX

A new home

The president of the planet Trojan spoke to all the people.

"People of Trojan!" she said. "I'm sorry, but I have bad news for you. Two months ago, we found out that a planet is coming towards us. A hundred years from now, the other planet is going to hit us, and the planet Trojan is going to explode. We can't stop this – it's going to happen."

The Trojan people were very scared. The president said more. "People of Trojan, we have only got one hundred years. But we've got a plan. We're going to build spaceships – huge spaceships, the biggest spaceships in the history of the universe. Each spaceship is going to be big enough to carry 10,000 people – and we are going to build 20,000 spaceships! In this way, we can take every Trojan man, woman and child to another place – a safe place – before the other planet hits us."

The people asked: "Where? Where is this place that we can all go to?"

The president said: "There is another planet, very far from here. It is a planet where Trojan people can live. The air is like our air; the water is like our water; and there is room for us. The name of this planet is: Earth! Earth is going to be our new home. Now, we have to get ready!"

The next day, the people of Trojan started to build the spaceships. It took them a very long time – more than fifteen years – to build the first 1,000 spaceships. And after fifty years, 5,000 spaceships were ready. And finally, all the 20,000 spaceships were ready. The spaceships were round, like huge yellow footballs – so big that 10,000 Trojans could go inside.

Then, one day, the people of Trojan said goodbye to their home. They went into the spaceships. And, one by one, the spaceships took off. And the Trojans began the journey to their new home. Twenty years later, the spaceships arrived at the planet Earth.

WB p. 62, 63, 64

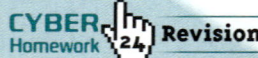
CYBER Homework 24 Revision

One day, Jenny was in her garden. It was a nice, sunny morning. Her dog, Josh, was with her – and suddenly he started to bark very loudly.

"What's the matter, Josh?" she said, and she walked over to him. In the air, there were lots of strange, round, yellow seeds. The seeds fell from the sky, and one by one they landed on the grass. Jenny looked around – there were thousands of the seeds on the ground. Just then, her father came out of the house.

"What are you looking at, Jenny?" he asked. "Come here, Dad," she said. "Look at this!" Her

father came over and looked at the yellow seeds. "How strange!" he said. "But I haven't got time to look at them now. I've got to go to work. Jenny, tidy up here, please!" And her father walked to his car. He walked on some of the seeds and they went "Crack!!" Jenny's father got into his car and went to work. Jenny went into the house. She got a broom and came back to the garden. Then she started to sweep up the little yellow seeds. She put them into the dustbin.

2 How many of these tasks can you do?

1 The planet Trojan is going to explode in 10 years.   T / F
2 Each spaceship can take 10,000 Trojans.   T / F
3 Trojan is very similar to Earth.   T / F

4 The spaceships were like ....
5 The journey to Earth took ....
6 Jenny was .... with her dog.
7 Why was Josh barking? ....
8 Why was Jenny's dad in a hurry? ....
9 Jenny's dad asked her to ....

3 Check your answers with a partner. Then listen to the story.

Vocabulary Science fiction

4 Match the words and the pictures.

☐ spaceship ☐ galaxy ☐ alien ☐ time machine ☐ astronaut ☐ space station

❶  ❷  ❸  ❹  ❺  ❻

Sounds right /ɪd/ /d/ /t/

5 Which is the odd one out? Listen and check.

1 arriv**ed** / land**ed** / plann**ed**   2 look**ed** / start**ed** / bark**ed**   3 ask**ed** / walk**ed** / visit**ed**

  WB p. 62, 63, 64 CYBER Homework 25

 UNIT **9** 63

Complete the sentences. Use the verbs in the box in the past simple.

see	pick	go	be	hear	put	see	turn

They never saw him again!

James ..was.. alone in a town.

He .... a strange noise.

He .... round.

He .... a gold key on the ground.

He .... it up.

He .... a green light in a window.

He .... the key in the door of the house.

He .... into the house.

 Look at the pictures again. Then write the story.

Sentence 1: *One day ...*
Sentence 2: *Suddenly ...*

Sentences 3–5: *He ...*
Sentence 6: *At that moment ...*

Sentence 7: *Then ...*
Sentence 8: *Finally, ...*

A Song 4 U

 CD2 23/24

 Listen and sing.

 **Song of the Trojans**

*Trojans, Trojans,
let's leave this place.
Trojans, Trojans,
off into space.*

*Goodbye sweet, sweet Trojan.
Goodbye sweet, sweet home.
Let's board all our spaceships.
Into space we will roam.*

*Goodbye sweet, sweet Trojan.
The ships they all wait.
We're leaving our Trojan.
We hope it's not too late.*

Trojans, Trojans, ...

*Goodbye sweet, sweet Trojan.
Sleep well, all my friends.
And dream of our planet.
Our Trojan time ends.*

*Goodbye sweet, sweet Trojan.
To Earth we now go.
And a new planet Trojan
out there we will grow.*

Trojans, Trojans, ...

WB p. 65

9 **Read the text and match the sentence halves.**

UFOs – are they really out there?

There are people who believe in UFOs, ufologists, and there are people who don't. There are thousands of photos of unidentified flying objects (UFOs). Many of them are nothing but clouds or balloons and airplanes. And some of them are fakes. Here is one of the most famous UFO photographs and the story behind it:

On May 11th, 1950 Evelyn Trent was in the garden of her farm in McMinnville, Oregon. On her way back to the house, she saw a metallic disk flying in her direction.

She called out to her husband. He quickly got a camera and took pictures of the disk.

Even today ufologists believe that this photo shows a UFO; other people say it is a hoax, a trick to fool people. The Trents died many years ago, so we will never know the truth from them. In 2013, there was a big investigation into the photograph. Scientists used the most modern technology to study the photo, but the experts still couldn't decide if it was real or not.

1	A ufologist	☐ thought she saw a UFO in the back garden.
2	Evelyn Trent	☐ are no longer alive.
3	Mr Trent	☐ studied the photo in 2013.
4	The Trents	☐ believes in UFOs.
5	Scientists	☐ took a photo of the "UFO".

10 **Listen to an interview with ufologist Paul Brady and George Brendel, who does not believe in UFOs. Take notes to answer the questions below.**

1 What does Paul believe aliens are doing?

....

2 Why are they doing this?

....

3 What does George think about his ideas?

....

Writing for your Portfolio

 11 Here are two endings for the story in **6** . Choose the one you like best and say why.

Ending 1

James went into the house. He saw a chair and he sat down. It was very comfortable! Then he found a button on the floor, near the chair. "What's this?" he said, and he pushed the button. The chair started to go round and round very quickly, but after a minute, it stopped. James went out of the house. He was in the year 2090!

Ending 2

James went into the house. He saw a chair and he sat down. It was very comfortable! He went to sleep. Five hours later, James woke up. In front of him were two strange people with pink eyes. "Why are you here?" said one of the strange people. "You shouldn't be here! Now we have to take you to our planet!"

12 Write another ending.

SbX GRAMMAR

 ### Past simple (revision)

Bei regelmäßigen Verben bildest du das Past simple, indem du *-ed* anhängst:

open – open**ed**   laugh – laugh**ed**
look – look**ed**

Es gibt auch viele unregelmäßige Verben:

be – **was/were**   go – **went**
take – **took**   run – **ran**
come – **came**   see – **saw**

Die Verneinung bildest du mit *didn't* + Verb:

They **didn't believe** her.
She **didn't take** another photograph.

Was/were verneinst du mit *wasn't/weren't*.

Mr Brown didn't look before he opened the door.

Past time markers

So kannst du ausdrücken, <u>wann</u> sich etwas in der Vergangenheit ereignet hat:

Two months ago, we found out that a planet is coming towards us.
One day, Jenny was in her garden.
Then she started to sweep up the seeds.
The next day, they started building the spaceships.
After fifty years, five thousand spaceships were ready.
Twenty years later, the spaceships arrived at the planet Earth.
Finally, all the spaceships were ready.

The Story of the Stones 4

DVD

You can run, but you can't hide

1 **Answer the questions about Episode 3. Tick the right answers.**

1	Where were the children?	☐ on the beach	☐ by a river	☐ by a lake
2	Who jumped in the water?	☐ the eagle	☐ the rat	☐ the tiger
3	What is the new girl's name?	☐ Lillian	☐ Gillian	☐ Debbie
4	Why was she in the water?	☐ to save a dog	☐ to save a cat	☐ to save a rabbit

2 **Complete the summary of Episode 3 with *Gillian, Emma, Sarah* or *Darkman*.**

¹................................ goes to Emma's house and gives the children a box of chocolates. Gillian tells them that she met a strange man. The children are worried it was probably ²................................ . He wanted to know about the kids.

Before she leaves, Gillian gives them a box that ³................................ gave to her. ⁴................................ opens the box. A gas escapes. She and ⁵................................ are unconscious*.

⁶................................ returns and saves them. ⁷................................ tells her about the morphing.

VOCABULARY: *unconscious – bewusstlos

DVD **3** **Watch Episode 4 and match the questions with the answers.**

1 Why did Emma tell Gillian about the morphing?

2 Why does Sunborn want to give Gillian morphing powers?

3 Why does Gillian want them to close the door quickly?

4 Why doesn't Gillian want to join the team?

5 Why does Darkman break into the house?

☐ Because he wants the stones.

☐ Because she can help them make a stronger team.

☐ Because she doesn't like fighting.

☐ Because Darkman is after her.

☐ Because she saw the eagle on the floor.

Everyday English

DVD **4** **Watch Episode 4 again. Complete the sentences.**

In that case	Calm down	One thing at a time	Look

Gillian He was behind me. I know it.

Emma ¹................................ , Gillian. You're safe here with us.

Sarah ²................................ – we know who this man is. His name's Darkman and he's after us.

Sunborn Sometimes I feel that Darkman is very close indeed.

Daniel ³................................ , I think we should give Gillian morphing powers.

Sunborn ⁴................................ , Daniel. First I have to meet her.

THE STORY OF THE STONES 4   67

The Twins 3

DEVELOPING SPEAKING COMPETENCIES

Language function
- buying a cinema ticket (*Kinokarten kaufen*)

Speaking strategy
- expressing disappointment (*Enttäuschung ausdrücken*)

At the cinema

Vocabulary Problems

 1 Read what these signs say. How would you say them in German?

CD2 26

 2 Watch or listen to the dialogue. Then read it. What's the problem for Lucy and Leo?

Leo	Two tickets for the 5 o'clock showing of *They Came From Mars*, please.
Assistant	I'm sorry. It's sold out.
Leo	What a shame.
Lucy	What time is the next showing, please?
Assistant	It's not until 7.30. However, there's a showing at 5.30, but it's in 3D.
Lucy	What film is that?
Assistant	It's the same film: *They Came From Mars*.
Leo	That's great.
Assistant	But it's in 3D, so it's more expensive.
Lucy	That's a pity.
Leo	Lucy? Are you crazy? It's in 3D! Let's go.

Lucy	Oh, OK. Two tickets, please.
Assistant	Where would you like to sit?
Lucy	Just a moment. Er … row 12, please.

 **3** Read the sentences and correct them.

1 There is only one ticket for the 5 o'clock showing of *They Came From Mars*.
2 The showing at 7.30 is more expensive than the showing at 5 o'clock.
3 Leo does not like 3D films very much.
4 Lucy doesn't think it's a problem that the 3D showing is more expensive.
5 The twins don't buy tickets for the 3D showing.

 WB p. 67

Useful phrases Buying a cinema ticket

4 Who says what? Write C (*Customer*) or A (*Assistant*).

1 I'm sorry. It's sold out. ☐
2 Two tickets for the … o'clock showing of …, please. ☐
3 What time is the next showing, please? ☐
4 It's not until 7.30. ☐
5 There's a showing at 5.30, but it's in 3D, so it's more expensive. ☐
6 Where would you like to sit? ☐
7 Row 12, please. ☐

? What do you think? Answer the questions.

• What do they do until the film begins?   • Does the film begin on time?

Mobile homework

Watch part 2 of the video. Use the verbs from the box in the correct form and information from part 2 to complete the sentences.

have got	buy	begin	win	notice	want

1 Lucy and Leo .... until the film ....
2 First they .... a hot dog.
3 Leo .... play .... on the mobile.
4 Leo .... the game and he is very ....
5 Lucy suddenly .... started 15 minutes before.

Speaking strategy Expressing disappointment

5 Complete. Then check with the dialogue in **2**.

1 **Assistant** I'm sorry. It's sold out.
   Leo .... shame.

2 **Assistant** It's in 3D, so it's more expensive.
   Lucy .... pity.

6 CHOICES

A Work in pairs. A mentions a problem (from **1**). B reacts and shows disappointment.

> **A** The shop's closed.

> **B** What a pity.

B ROLE PLAY: Look at the situations from **1**. Choose one. Work in pairs and extend it into a longer dialogue. Take 2 or 3 minutes to practise it. Don't write it down. Act it out in class.

UNIT 10 Are you ready to order?

You learn
- how to use *some* and *any*
- some food words
- about ordering food in a restaurant

You can
- talk about food
- order food in a restaurant
- write a story

Vocabulary Food

CD3 1

SbX

1 Listen and look at the pictures. Then write the numbers next to the words.

- ☐ pears
- ☐ pork
- ☐ beef
- ☐ chicken
- ☐ plums
- ☐ lamb
- ☐ rice pudding
- ☐ pumpkin pie
- ☐ peppers
- ☐ onions
- ☐ tomatoes
- ☐ chocolate ice cream
- ☐ cabbage
- ☐ cheesecake
- ☐ strawberries
- ☐ turkey
- ☐ pancakes
- ☐ peaches
- ☐ grapes
- ☐ potatoes

2 Write the food words from **1** in the table below.

fruit	vegetables	meat	desserts
....	....	....	....
....	....	....	....
....	....	....	....
....	....	....	....
....	....	....	....

WB p. 69, 70

CYBER Homework 27 Revision

3 Listen and write the names of the people under the shopping baskets.

Henry   Ella   Jacob   Laura

....

4 Write the words under the pictures.

sausages
cheese
ham
mushrooms
olives

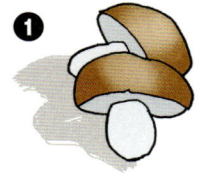 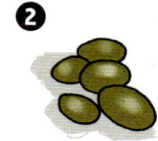 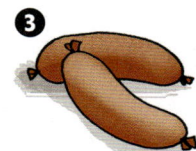  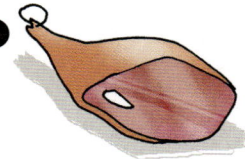

....

SbX **5** Read the dialogue. Then write the names under the pizzas.

Waiter	Are you ready to order?
Mr Hutton	Yes, we are.
Mrs Hutton	I'd like a pizza with ham, cheese and tomatoes.
Waiter	And to drink?
Mrs Hutton	Mineral water, please.
Mr Hutton	I'd like a pizza too – with ham, mushrooms and green peppers. And an orange juice, please.
Ben	For me a pizza with ham, sausage and cheese.
Waiter	And to drink?
Ben	A cola, please.
Vicky	And for me a pizza with mushrooms, tomatoes and sausages.
Waiter	And to drink?
Vicky	An apple juice, please.

....

6 Listen to the dialogue and act it out.

WB p. 69, 70, 71 CYBER Homework 28

UNIT **10**   71

Time for a sketch

  7 **Read the sketch.**

The best restaurant in town

Menu

Starters:
Onion soup • Tomato soup

Main courses:
Lamb chops with potatoes and cabbage
Chicken with rice and peas
Beef with chips and carrots
Turkey with potatoes and cabbage
Pork chops with chips and peas
Vegetable curry
Fish of the day

Desserts:
Chocolate ice cream
Cheesecake
Rice pudding
Pancakes
Pumpkin pie

SCENE 1

In the restaurant.

Man	A table for two, please.
Waiter	Next to the window, sir?
Man	That's fine.
Woman	Can we have the menu, please?
Waiter	Certainly, madam. Straightaway. Can I get you something to drink?
Woman	Mineral water, please.
Man	The same for me.

(Two minutes later.)

Waiter	Here you are. Are you ready to order?
Woman	Onion soup.
Man	And the onion soup for me, too.
Waiter	Thank you.

SCENE 2

In the kitchen.

Waiter	Two onion soups and …
Chef	Onion soup? We haven't got any onions.
Waitress	I can run over to the supermarket and buy some.
Chef	Too late. Let me think. Run over to Johnny's Restaurant and get two bowls of onion soup.
Waitress	OK.

(Five minutes later.)

Chef	But that's tomato soup.
Waitress	They didn't have any onion soup.

SCENE 3

In the restaurant.

Waiter	I'm sorry. There isn't any onion soup. But we've got some tomato soup. It's a special recipe of the chef's grandma.
Woman	OK. Bring us the tomato soup.

SCENE 4

In the restaurant.

Waiter	How did you like our chef's tomato soup?
Man	It was fine. Now I'd like the beef with chips and carrots.
Woman	And for me, the lamb with potatoes and cabbage.
Waiter	Certainly.

❯ WB p. 69, 71, 72

Liebe Schülerin, lieber Schüler,

wir sind überzeugt davon, dass du den Englischunterricht mit MORE! cool findest.
Wichtig ist aber auch, dass du bei allem Spaß am Englischlernen nicht aufs Üben vergisst, damit du in der Fremdsprache mit Sicherheit immer fit bist!

Wer Englisch zu Hause intensiv üben möchte, kann dies am besten mit dem **MORE! Test-Training** oder dem ansprechenden Grammatiktraining **MORE! Grammar Practice** tun.
Mit der **MORE! Media App** hast du außerdem die Möglichkeit, die Videos, Audios und Stories aus dem Unterricht zu Hause zu wiederholen. Für das Wiederholen des Lernstoffes in den Ferien ist das **MORE! Holiday Book** erhältlich. Darüber hinaus bieten wir jede Menge **Readers** zu den unterschiedlichsten Themen und Interessen an. Da ist sicher auch für dich die passende Lektüre dabei!

Auf der **MORE! Homepage www.helbling-ezone.com** findest du zusätzliche **kostenlose Angebote**:

- MP3-Downloads der Stories, Songs, Chants und Poems aus dem Student's Book. So kannst du sie dir zu Hause nochmals in Ruhe anhören!
- Online Progress Checks

Schau doch mal (am besten mit deinen Eltern) rein!

Viel Spaß beim Lernen – mit MORE!
wünscht dir das MORE!-Team

MORE! ② Test-Training
Schularbeiten optimal vorbereiten

Englischlernen macht Spaß! Mit dem **MORE! Test-Training** kann der Lernstoff zu Hause effizient geübt und gefestigt werden. Dank der zahlreichen Übungen zu Grammatik und Wortschatz, Diktaten, Schreibtraining, Leseverständnis- und Hörverständnisübungen bist du optimal auf Schularbeiten und Tests vorbereitet. Zusätzlich zum Buch stehen dir online eine Vielzahl abwechslungsreicher Übungen zur Verfügung, die automatisch ausgewertet werden. Somit siehst du gleich deine Ergebnisse und kannst gezielt weiter trainieren.

MORE! ② Grammar Practice mit Lernsoftware

Dieses Übungsheft mit Lernsoftware bietet auf 84 Seiten zusätzliche Übungen zu allen wesentlichen Grammatikinhalten von MORE!②. An den Themen und damit an der Wortschatzprogression von MORE! orientiert, kannst du dich speziell auf die grammatikalischen Aufgabenstellungen konzentrieren, ohne vorher neue Inhalte erarbeiten zu müssen.

Die Lernsoftware bietet zusätzliche Übungen mit innovativen Features. Diese helfen dir komplexe grammatikalische Strukturen, deren alltägliche Verwendung und vor allem den Unterschied zur Grammatik der Muttersprache besser zu verstehen.

MORE! ② Media App

Mit der **MORE! Media App** kannst du Audios, Videos und *Graphic stories* aus deinem Buch direkt starten. Du musst dazu nur die kostenlose App aus dem Apple App Store oder dem Google Play Store herunterladen. Symbole im Student's Book zeigen dir an, welche Inhalte über die App verfügbar sind.

MORE! ② Holiday Book inklusive Audios

Das MORE! Holiday Book ist zur Wiederholung des Jahresstoffes in den Sommerferien gedacht.
Es ist in *10 Days* unterteilt, die die Themen der *20 Units* aus dem *MORE! Student's Book* aufgreifen und Grammatik- bzw. Sprachschwerpunkte üben.

Eine Seite pro *Day* ist der *Story Time* mit den *International Crime Busters* gewidmet.
Die letzte Seite jedes *Days* ist eine Projekt-Seite mit *Brain-Workout* und *Fido-Cartoon*.

Am Ende des Buches findest du die Lösungen zur Selbstkontrolle.

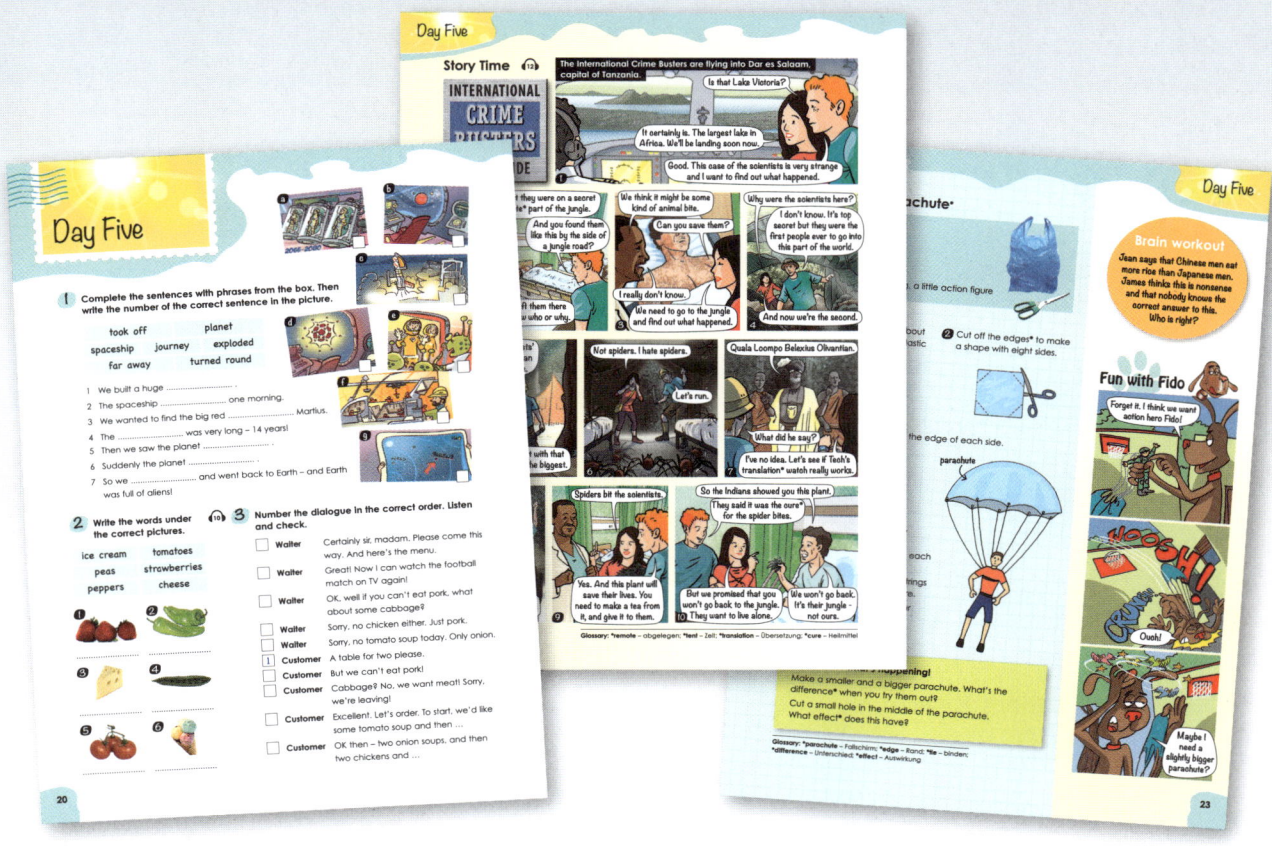

Liebe Eltern!

Auch fürs Englischlernen gilt: Übung macht den Meister/die Meisterin! Wer zu Hause regelmäßig übt, erzielt mit Sicherheit die besseren Leistungen.

MORE! bietet für das Üben zu Hause attraktive Materialien: das MORE! Test-Training, MORE! Grammar Practice, das MORE! Holiday Book und die MORE! Media App. Die Helbling Readers runden das Angebot mit interessantem Lesestoff ab.

Sie können das MORE! Test-Training, das Grammatikheft, das Holiday Book oder die Readers ganz bequem im Webshop oder per E-Mail bestellen. Zudem stehen Ihnen auf **www.helblinglanguages.at** umfangreiche Produktinformationen zur Verfügung.

Ihrem Kind viel Spaß beim Lernen – mit MORE!
wünscht das MORE!-Team

→ **Bestellinformation**

Einfach zu bestellen!
- im Webshop: **www.helblinglanguages.at**
- per E-Mail: **office@helbling.com**

Einfach zu bestellen!

HELBLING READERS – RED SERIES

Wer viel liest, kann bald besser Englisch!
Hast du Lust darauf, englischen Lesestoff zu Hause zu genießen?
Die HELBLING READERS bieten dir Gelegenheit dazu!

The Surprise by Günter Gerngross
Als Tante Elizabeth aus Grönland zurückkommt, hat sie für Roger und Helen ein seltsames Geschenk im Gepäck – ein großes Ei. Eines Tages beginnt sich das Ei zu öffnen …

Holly the Eco Warrior by Martyn Hobbs
Hollys Lieblingsplatz ist das Baumhaus in der alten Eiche im Garten. Als ihr Vater beschließt, den Baum zu fällen um ein Büro zu bauen, greift sie zu einer ungewöhnlichen Maßnahme und zieht in das Baumhaus. Wer wird den Kampf um den Baum gewinnen?

The African Mask by Günter Gerngross
Janet bekommt völlig überraschend einen Brief von ihrem alten Freund Donald McKinnon. Er lädt sie zu sich nach Schottland ein. Dort angekommen passieren seltsame Dinge. Warum ergreifen die Menschen die Flucht, sobald sie Donalds Namen hören? Warum ist Donald so traurig und was hat seine afrikanische Maske mit all den seltsamen Vorgängen zu tun?

Weitere Helbling Readers findest du unter: → **www.helblinglanguages.at**

www.helbling.com

Helbling Verlagsgesellschaft m.b.H.
6063 Rum · Kaplanstr. 9
Tel.: +43 512 262333-0
Fax: +43 512 262333-111
E-Mail: office@helbling.co.at

HELBLING

SCENE 5
In the kitchen.

Waiter One beef and one lamb.

Chef Is there any lamb in the fridge?

Waitress No, there isn't.

Chef What about beef? Have we got any beef?

Waitress No, sorry, there isn't any beef.

Chef What can we do?

Waitress Johnny's Restaurant does a good chicken.

Chef Run over and get two chickens.

SCENE 6
In the restaurant.

Waiter Here you are.

Woman But we ordered lamb and beef.

Waiter Madam, the chicken is the best in town. It's the chef's special recipe. Chicken Volcano.

Woman OK. The chicken then.

SCENE 7
In the kitchen.

Waiter Run over to Johnny's again and get some rice pudding and chocolate ice cream.

Waitress OK.

SCENE 8
In the restaurant.

Waiter For dessert we have rice pudding and chocolate ice cream.

Woman That's fine.

Waiter Here you are.

Man Look. There's a flag on my ice cream. It says: "Johnny's Restaurant".

Woman I don't think we're in the best restaurant in town. Next time we're going to Johnny's.

8 **How many of these tasks can you do?**

1 The man and woman sit next to the window. T / F

2 For a starter they order tomato soup. T / F

3 The waiter brings them nothing for a starter. T / F

4 The man orders .... for his main course.

5 The woman wants .... with her lamb.

6 .... is missing from the fridge.

7 How many times does the waitress go over to Johnny's? ....

8 What does the waiter offer the couple for dessert? ....

9 What do the couple decide to do after dessert? ....

   9 **Check your answers with a partner. Then listen to the sketch.**

A Song 4 U

 10 Listen and sing.

My dream

Last night I dreamed of chicken,
of rice and cabbage stew.
Last night I dreamed of pancakes,
and then I dreamed of you.

You served me cakes.
You served me grapes.
You served me pumpkin pie.
You said to me,
you said to me,
you said to me: Please try.

Last night I dreamed of strawberries,
of grapes both green and blue.
Last night I dreamed of ice cream,
and then I dreamed of you.

You served me cakes …

I tried and tried. I tried and tried.
I felt like a balloon.
Then I woke up. You said to me:
Come on, it's breakfast soon!

11 CHOICES

Writing for your Portfolio

Read these two stories about a visit to a pizza place. Underline the differences in the second text. Which text is more interesting to read, and why is it better?

Last Sunday my dad and I went to a restaurant. We had tomato soup and a pizza. Suddenly Dad stopped eating. There was something under the cheese. It was a coin. Dad called the waiter. The waiter was very sorry and Dad got another pizza.

Last Sunday my dad and I went to a restaurant. We had tomato soup and a pizza. Suddenly Dad stopped eating. "What's the matter?" I asked. "I don't know," Dad said. "There's something under the cheese." "Yes," I said, "your pizza." "Very funny," Dad said. Then he lifted the cheese. There was a coin under it! Dad called the waiter. "I'm so sorry," the waiter said. Dad got another pizza.

A **Look at the picture. Write a story about it (50–60 words). Use these words and phrases to help you.**

On Saturday Mrs Green went to a … with her … .
Mrs Green had …, Sue had … and James had … .
Suddenly Sue said, "Don't eat your …, Mum! There's a … ."
Mum called the … . She … .

B **Look at the picture. Write a story about it (80–100 words). Use dialogue to make it more interesting.**

Complete the sentences with *some* or *any*. Then listen and check.

Dad Sue, are there ¹....................... plums and peaches in the fridge?

Sue There are ²....................... plums, but there aren't ³....................... peaches. Are you making fruit salad?

Dad Yes. What have we got?

Sue There are ⁴....................... grapes and ⁵....................... pears.

Dad OK. Are there ⁶.................... strawberries?

Sue No, sorry, Dad. There aren't ⁷....................... .

SbX # GRAMMAR   *some – any*

*Run over to the supermarket and buy **some** tomatoes.* (= einige Tomaten)
Du verwendest in diesem Satz *some*, weil nicht angegeben wird, wie viele Tomaten es sind.

*Get **some** rice pudding and chocolate ice cream.* (= etwas Reispudding)
In diesem Satz sagst du *some*, weil du von etwas sprichst, das man nicht zählen kann.

*We haven't got **any** onions.* (= keine Zwiebeln)
Hier verwendest du *any*, weil du ausdrücken willst, dass etwas *nicht vorhanden* ist.

*There isn't **any** onion soup. But we've got **some** tomato soup.*
Hier sagst du, dass etwas *nicht vorhanden* ist (die Zwiebelsuppe), aber etwas anderes *vorhanden* ist (die Tomatensuppe).

> Sorry. There isn't any ice cream.

Read the questions. Write *some* or *any*.
*Have we got **any** beef?*
*Can I have **some** ice cream?*
Mit ¹.......................... fragst du nach etwas, von dem du weißt, dass es vorhanden ist.
Mit ².......................... fragst du, ob etwas vorhanden ist.

> POP!

> My compliments to the chef.

MORE fun with Fido!

Kids in NYC 2

The baseball star

Before you watch

1 Write the words under the pictures.

team
pitch
bat
hit

1 .... 2 .... 3 .... 4 ....

2 In what order do you think the pictures come in the DVD? Write 1–4.

Watch the story

3 Check your answers to **2**.

4 Circle the correct answer.

1 Emma *likes / doesn't like* baseball.
2 Gerry is *tall / short* with blue eyes.
3 The boys have got a big game on *Thursday / Friday*.
4 Emma wants to *pitch / hit* a few balls.

5 **Circle T (*True*) or F (*False*).**

1 Emma is a new student at East Central High.   T / F
2 Gerry Wood has blonde hair and blue eyes.   T / F
3 Steve doesn't want Emma to play baseball.   T / F
4 Emma plays baseball on the school team.   T / F
5 The ball hits Gerry on the arm.   T / F

6 **Complete the dialogue.**

reddish
new
interesting
tall
great
fair

Emma I love watching baseball.
Jenny You love watching baseball or you love watching Gerry Wood play baseball?
Emma Which one's Gerry Wood? Remember, I'm ¹... at the school.
Jenny He's pitching now. He's ²... with ³... hair and blue eyes.
Emma He seems ⁴... . But I'm more interested in the baseball.
Jenny Really?
Emma Yeah, what a ⁵... game. Why can't girls play? It isn't ⁶... .
Jenny Do girls want to play baseball?
Emma Well, I do.

Everyday English

7 **Complete the dialogues.**

By the way,
it's no trouble at all.
It isn't fair.

1 Why can't girls play?
....

Do girls want to play baseball?

2 Hi, Emma, I'm Gerry.

.... I'm Emma. I'm new at the school.

3 Listen, if it's any trouble …

No, ...

UNIT 11 The curse of the pharaoh

You learn
- about irregular plurals
- how to form questions with *who*
- about ancient Egypt

You can
- talk about ancient Egypt
- complete a story
- write about the best place in your home

Vocabulary Ancient Egypt

CD3 9

1 Listen and look at the picture. Then number the words.

SbX

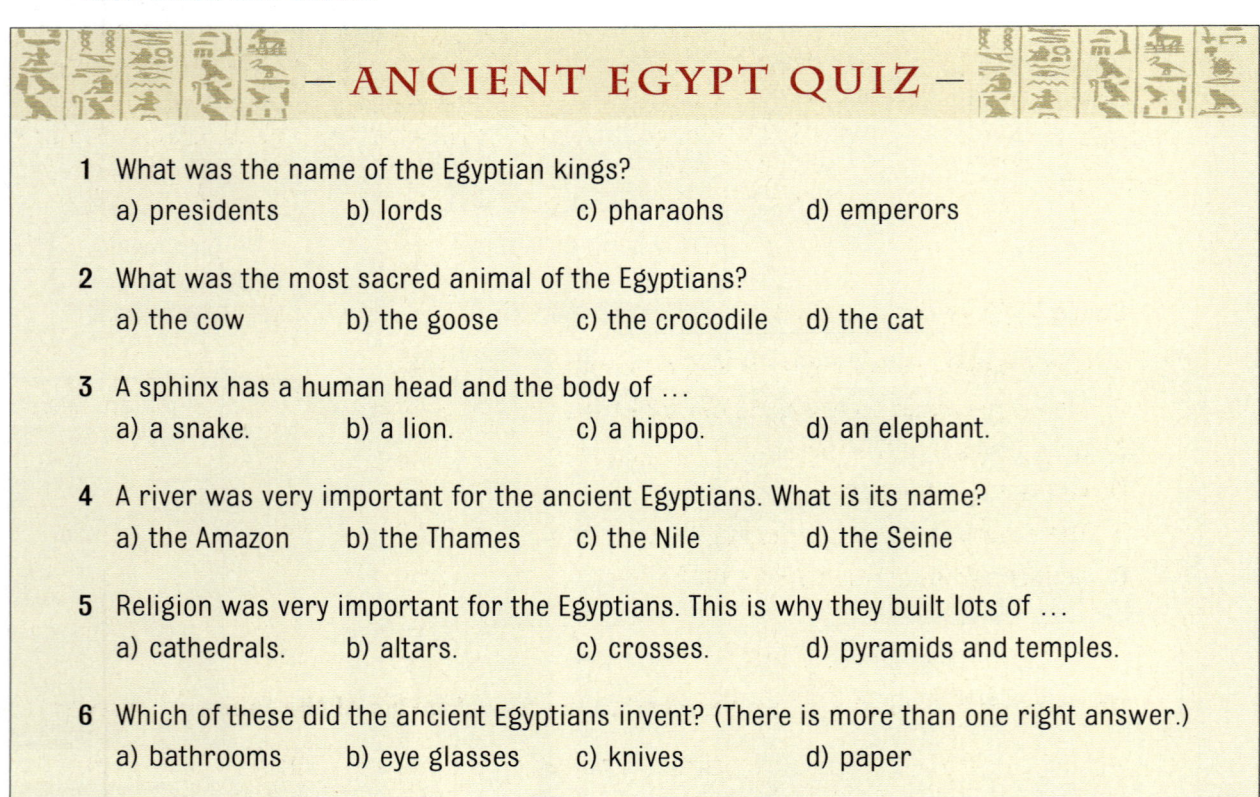

- [ ] a pyramid
- [ ] hieroglyphics
- [ ] a sphinx
- [ ] a mummy
- [ ] a temple
- [ ] a tomb
- [ ] a papyrus

CD3 10

2 Are you good at history? Do the quiz about ancient Egypt and find out. Then listen and check.

— ANCIENT EGYPT QUIZ —

1 What was the name of the Egyptian kings?
   a) presidents   b) lords   c) pharaohs   d) emperors

2 What was the most sacred animal of the Egyptians?
   a) the cow   b) the goose   c) the crocodile   d) the cat

3 A sphinx has a human head and the body of …
   a) a snake.   b) a lion.   c) a hippo.   d) an elephant.

4 A river was very important for the ancient Egyptians. What is its name?
   a) the Amazon   b) the Thames   c) the Nile   d) the Seine

5 Religion was very important for the Egyptians. This is why they built lots of …
   a) cathedrals.   b) altars.   c) crosses.   d) pyramids and temples.

6 Which of these did the ancient Egyptians invent? (There is more than one right answer.)
   a) bathrooms   b) eye glasses   c) knives   d) paper

WB p. 76, 77

CYBER Homework 30 Revision

3 Read the text. Then listen to it.

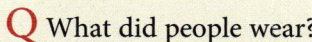

LIFE IN ANCIENT EGYPT

Q How do we know what life in ancient Egypt was like?

A From documents written on papyrus, from hieroglyphics on stones, and from wall paintings and objects found in tombs.

Q What did people wear?

A People only wore light clothes because it was very hot. They wore sandals on their feet or they went barefoot. The sandals were made of palm leaves. Slaves, workers and children were often naked. People cared a lot about their looks. Men and women wore eye make-up and jewellery. They also used perfumes.

Q What work did the Egyptians do?

A Many Egyptians worked as farmers. They worked on the fields, but they also helped to build the pyramids and temples.

There were also other jobs. Weavers, for example, made beautiful clothes. They sold the clothes to other people. People paid for the clothes with food, salt and other things.

Q What did people eat?

A The Egyptians had lots of different food. They hunted fish, ducks and geese. Many people were farmers and had sheep, cattle, goats, pigs, and later also horses. These animals gave them milk, wool, meat and eggs. But they also used the leather, the horns and the fat. The Egyptians even had farms where they kept oxen. They also had lots of vegetables and fruit.

Q What did people do in their free time?

A Hunting and fishing were the most popular sports for the men. Children played with balls and animals made from wood. Rich Egyptians often gave big parties with lots of food and drink. There were

musicians, singers, dancers, jugglers and acrobats. Servants put big pieces of perfumed fat on people's heads. When the fat melted, it ran down their faces. This made them smell nice.

4 Circle T (*True*) or F (*False*).

1 Some people in Egypt did not wear clothes. T / F
2 Men wore make-up and used perfumes too. T / F
3 Only slaves built the pyramids. T / F
4 Weavers got a lot of money for their work. T / F
5 The Egyptians ate meat, vegetables and fruit. T / F
6 Children went hunting and fishing. T / F

5 Go through **2** and **3** and underline the plural forms of the following words:

| man | child | woman | person | foot | goose | fish | knife | leaf | ox |

  CYBER Homework 31

6 Read about the pyramids at Giza. Put the numbers where you think they go.

100,000	230	20	143	2 million	2,000

The pyramids in Egypt are the tombs of the pharaohs. The biggest pyramid is the one for the Pharaoh Khufu. Did you know?

1 It is .... metres high, and each side is more than .... metres long.

2 There are more than .... stone blocks in the pyramid.

3 Each stone is about .... kilograms.

4 More than .... men worked to build it.

5 It took more than .... years to build it.

7 Listen to the interview and check your answers.

8 CHOICES

A Read more about the pyramids and answer the questions below.

When a pharaoh died, the priests put the mummy inside a pyramid. The Egyptian people believed that after a long time, the pharaoh's spirit woke up. Then it climbed up the steps of the pyramid to meet Ra, the sun god. They also believed that when the pharaoh woke up, he needed many things – for example food, clothes and jewellery. The people put these things in the pyramid with the mummy.

Of course, everyone knew there were wonderful things inside the pyramid. Soldiers guarded the tombs day and night to stop thieves.

But hundreds of years later, robbers found many of the tombs and stole everything inside.

One of the most famous pharaohs was Tutankhamun. He became pharaoh when he was nine, but he died when he was only nineteen. He is famous because the robbers did not find his tomb. When an Englishman called Howard Carter found the tomb of Tutankhamun in 1922, it was still full of wonderful clothes and jewellery.

1 Who put the mummy in the pyramids? ....

2 Who met the pharaoh's spirit at the top of the pyramid? ....

3 Who was Ra? ....

4 Who guarded the tombs? ....

5 Who died when he was only 19? ....

6 Who found Tutankhamun's tomb? ....

B **Read the text. Then put the sentences in the correct order. Write numbers.**

THE STORY OF HOWARD CARTER

Howard Carter was born in England in 1874. He was very interested in history. When he was 17, he went to Egypt. He had one wish – he wanted to find the tomb of Tutankhamun. Another Englishman, Lord Carnarvon, had the same dream. He gave Howard some money to find the tomb. For five years Carter tried to find it, but he didn't find anything.

Then he went back to England. When he returned to Egypt, he brought a yellow canary with him. "A golden bird!" shouted one of the Egyptian workers. "The bird will show us the tomb!"

On November 4ᵗʰ, 1922, Carter's workmen discovered the tomb of a pharaoh. Carter wanted to open it the next day. When he came back to his house that night, his servant came up to him and said: "A snake killed your yellow bird. I'm sure it was the pharaoh's snake. Don't open the tomb! There is a curse on the tomb – the curse of the pharaoh! It can kill hundreds of people and animals." But Carter didn't listen to him.

He sent a telegram to Lord Carnarvon in England. Carnarvon arrived in Egypt on November 26ᵗʰ. Carter made a hole in the door of the tomb. He took a candle and looked inside. Behind him, Lord Carnarvon asked: "Can you see anything?" Carter answered: "Yes, wonderful things!" In the tomb there were lots of treasures. There was also the mummy of the boy-king, Pharaoh Tutankhamun!

A few days later, an insect bit Lord Carnarvon on the left cheek. He became ill and died. Back in England, his dog died on the same day.

When workmen took off the bandages from the mummy of Tutankhamun, they saw that there was also a wound on the pharaoh's left cheek. Was there really a curse of the pharaoh?

- [ ] But Howard Carter didn't listen. He sent a telegram to Lord Carnarvon.
- [ ] But when Lord Carnarvon was back in England, he and his dog died on the same day.
- [1] When Howard Carter was seventeen, he went to Egypt.
- [ ] His servant was scared and said: "Don't open it! There's a curse!"
- [ ] One day, his workmen discovered a tomb.
- [ ] He wanted to find the tomb of Tutankhamun.
- [ ] They found lots of treasures inside, and the mummy of Tutankhamun.
- [ ] When Lord Carnarvon arrived, they opened the tomb.

Sounds right /dʒ/ /tʃ/

9 **Listen and repeat the tongue-twister. How quickly can you say it?**

Jim juggles jam
and Chuck chooses chickens.

Story time

CD3 14/16

SbX

10 **Read the story. Then listen to it.**

The curse of the pharaoh

First Hannah, Luke and their parents looked at the pictures on the walls in the tourist centre. They showed scenes from ancient Egypt. There were hundreds of farmers and slaves building a pyramid. Then they took a tour to one of the pyramids. Inside the pyramid it was so much cooler than in the hot sun.

"Stay with me all the time!" the guide said. "It's dangerous in here. There's a curse of the pharaoh!"

"The curse of the pharaoh?" asked another tourist in the group. "What's that?"

"There's one more tomb in this pyramid. But nobody knows where it is," said the guide. "A few years ago, some scientists wanted to find it. They went into the pyramid, but they never came back. People say the curse of the pharaoh killed them!"

"The curse of the pharaoh!" Hannah laughed out loud. "But I'd love to find that tomb!" she whispered to Luke.

Luke didn't say anything. He was in front of a hole in the wall. "That's funny. The guide didn't say anything about this hole!" he said. "Let's go through here! I've got a torch so we can find our way back."

"Shh!!" said Hannah. "Mum and Dad mustn't see us!"

The two children climbed through the hole. Suddenly, there was a loud noise and a second later a big stone filled the hole! Hannah and Luke tried to move the big stone. But they couldn't get out. "The curse of the pharaoh!" whispered Luke.

Get talking Completing a story

 CD3 15

11 **Work in pairs. Say what you think happened next. Then listen and find out.**

12 **How many of these tasks can you do?**

1 First the family go to the visitor centre. T / F
2 Inside the pyramid it is not as hot as outside. T / F
3 The guide tells everyone to stay close. T / F

4 The guide says there is one .... in the pyramid.
5 The scientists who looked for the tomb ....
6 Hannah really wants to ....

7 What do the children decide to explore? ....
8 What happened when the children climbed through the hole? ....
9 What does Luke try to understand at the end? ....

13 **Check your answers with a partner.**

WB p. 79

(14) CHOICES

Writing for your Portfolio

A Write an ending to the story about Luke and Hannah (50–60 words).
Use these words and phrases to help you.

heard voices	walked on	came to a door	some men
gold and diamonds	pharaoh	invited them	dream

B Read the questions below. Think of an ending to the story about Luke and Hannah.
Then write the story (100–120 words). Write about:

- what they did
- what the people told them
- the people they met
- how they got out of the pyramid

SbX GRAMMAR

Irregular plurals

Complete. Write *people / children / leaves / women / feet / teeth.*

Einige Nomen (*nouns*) sind unregelmäßig. Sie bekommen im Plural kein *-s*.

man	**men**	woman	3...
goose	**geese**	person	4...
child	1...	tooth	5...
foot	2...		

Einige Nomen (*nouns*) haben im Singular und im Plural die gleiche Form:

one fish – two **fish** one sheep – two **sheep**

Nomen, die auf *-f* oder *-fe* enden, bekommen im Plural meist ein *-ves*.

knife – **knives**   thief – **thieves**   leaf – 6...

> Who took the mummy?

Questions with "*Who …?*"

Wenn du mit *Who …?* nach dem Subjekt fragst, verwendest du
kein *do/does* oder *did*:

Who put the mummy in the pyramids? (**Not:** Who ~~did~~ put … ?)
Who found Tutankhamun's tomb? (**Not:** Who ~~did~~ find … ?)

The Story of the Stones 5

DVD

It's you!

1 **How well do you remember Episode 4? Circle T (*True*) or F (*False*).**

1 Daniel thinks Darkman is trying to kill them.   T / F
2 Darkman attacked Gillian on the beach.   T / F
3 Gillian hit Darkman with her bag.   T / F
4 Gillian doesn't want to join the team.   T / F
5 Gillian is going to meet Sunborn.   T / F

2 **Look at the picture. Who do you think says:**

1 Hello, Gillian. And welcome to the team.
2 Do you know where he is?
3 How about a wolf?
4 Isn't there a stone for me?
5 Darkman is very close.

DVD **3** **Watch Episode 5. Complete the sentences with the words in the box. There are some words you don't need.**

wolf	snake	Darkman	kill	Gillian
Sunborn	an alien	Emma	Daniel	Darkman

1 Darkman is trying to .... the children.
2 Gillian wants to be a ....
3 Gillian is really ....
4 .... kills ....

Everyday English

DVD **4** **Watch Episode 5 again. Complete the sentences.**

Sunborn Yes. Hello, Gillian. And welcome to the team. We're happy to have you, [1]..................... .

Daniel Do you know where he is?
Sunborn [2]..................... , but he's close.

Emma ... but you didn't know that we had brought him here.
Sunborn No, I didn't. But [3]..................... — and you've helped me again.
Sarah And [4]..................... for the last time!

| hopefully | it wasn't your fault | that's for sure | Not exactly |

UNIT 12 Families

Vocabulary Family

1 Listen and write the first names.

| William | Natasha | Anthony |
| Susan | Fred | Jo | Lisa |

grandmother   grandfather

aunt   uncle   mother   father

cousin   Ben

Get talking Who's who?

2 Work in pairs. Write down the first names of people in your family (uncles, cousins, parents, etc.). Give the list to your partner. Your partner asks you who is who.

A Who's Vera? – **B** She's my aunt.
A Who are Charlotte and Tina?
B They're my cousins.

3 Read the text about Angelina Jolie and her family.

A FAMOUS MOTHER

Angelina Jolie is an American superstar. In 2001, when she was 26, she became famous all over the world with the film *Lara Croft: Tomb Raider*. But Angelina Jolie is not only a superstar. She also visits refugee* camps in Asia and Africa and in 2001 she gave a million dollars to help refugees. She also built schools in Cambodia and gives money to hospitals for children. In 2002, Jolie adopted her first child, the seven-month-old Maddox Chivan. The boy was born in a small village in Cambodia and had no Mum or Dad. In 2005, Jolie and her third husband Brad Pitt adopted Zahara, a baby from Ethiopia. And a year later their first child, a daughter, was born. Her name is Shiloh Nouvel. In 2007, Jolie adopted a three-year-old boy from Vietnam. His name is Pax Thien. Like Maddox, the boy didn't have a Mum or Dad. In 2008, Jolie had twins, a boy, Knox Léon and a girl, Vivienne Marcheline. American magazines bought the first pictures of the babies for 14 million dollars. The money went to the Jolie-Pitt foundation* that helps children all over the world.

VOCABULARY: *refugee – Flüchtling; **foundation** – Stiftung

4 Circle T (*True*) or F (*False*).

1 Angelina Jolie gives a lot of money to poor people. T / F
2 Angelina Jolie adopted her first child before she became famous. T / F
3 Angelina Jolie has six children. T / F
4 Angelina Jolie sold the picture of her baby twins for a lot of money. T / F

5 Read the magazine article. How did each of these kids learn the things they talk about?

The COOLEST THINGS kids learn

For most parents, what is important is that their child is good at school. Maths, reading, writing, foreign languages … well, yes, of course! But what other things are there that kids have learnt and are proud of? Read our interviews and find out.

Joanna, 12

Make a fire

Two years ago during a summer holiday my mum taught me how to make a fire without burning myself. I loved that. Now, we live in the city, so I can't often make fires. But sometimes we go to the countryside for short holidays, and that's my big chance. There is nothing better than cooking some sausages on a fire you have made yourself. And it's great to sit around a fire with friends in the evening and have a chat.

Jonathan, 13

Drive a tractor

Last summer, my family and I spent two weeks on a farm. First I was a bit bored – I missed my friends. One day, the farmer saw me hanging around, doing nothing. So he asked me if I wanted to help him. I wanted to say no, but said yes of course. We got on the tractor and drove out to the fields. There, he asked me if I could drive the tractor for him. Of course I couldn't. So he showed me and it wasn't that difficult. I so loved it. The coolest holiday ever!

Vicky, 12

Stay calm*

When things went wrong, I often panicked and started to shout or to cry. In my last holiday, my best friend Elisabeth invited me to go on a course with her, *What teens should learn for life*. The first thing I learnt was not to panic. I learnt that when we are in panic, we make big mistakes, we get confused, or get scared and then make bad decisions*. So you know what I learnt? When something goes wrong, breathe, and count to ten. Keep calm.

VOCABULARY: *stay/keep calm – ruhig bleiben; **decision** – Entscheidung

6 Read the article again. Then answer the questions.

1 What does Joanna like about making a fire? ....
2 What did Jonathan think of their farm holidays first? ....
3 Why do you think he said yes when the farmer asked him to help him?
....
4 Why does Vicky think it's important to keep cool? ....
5 How does Vicky keep calm? ....
6 What is the coolest thing you can do? ....

Vocabulary Activities

7 Listen and find out what things Natalie and Dylan like doing. Write N or D.

- ☐ making fires
- ☐ building things
- ☐ reading
- ☐ playing football
- ☐ using tools
- ☐ climbing trees
- ☐ going shopping
- ☐ dancing

Get talking Favourite activities

8 Work in pairs. Tell your partner what you like doing. Look at **5** and **7** for words.

WB p. 86, 88

9 Read the texts about the families.

What's in a family?

I'm **Lisa,** and I'm from Galway in Ireland. My mum, my mum's boyfriend Mike, my sister Hannah and I live in a large flat. Mike moved in with us three years ago. My real dad also lives in Galway, but he and Mum aren't married any more. He moved out five years ago, and now he lives in a little house with his new wife, Dorothy. Hannah and I go to see them every weekend. Mum says we are a single parent family, but I don't think so. We still see our father, and there are Mike and Dorothy. They're both very nice, and we have a lot of fun with them.

I'm **Amar** and I'm from Birmingham in England. I live with my mum and dad and my brother Vikas and my sister Karisma in a nice house in Selly Oak. My grandmother Jaya also lives with us, and for two years my cousin Kunal also lived in our house. He was here from Allahabad in India. He studied at the university in Birmingham. I like him, and next summer I'm going to visit him in Allahabad.

I'm **Les**. I'm from Sydney in Australia. My mum's a single parent and I live with her. My dad lives in Darwin and I don't see him very often. I haven't got any brothers or sisters. My mum works in a restaurant, and I often stay with my grandparents. They live down the road. Sometimes I go and see my mum at the restaurant.

I'm **Denise**, and I'm from Angola, but I live in the Dukwi refugee camp in Botswana. We had to leave Angola eight years ago because of the war. Now my mum, my dad, my three brothers and my uncle João live in Dukwi camp. I go to school here. My brothers have to help my dad with farming. It's very hard work and we don't have much food. My uncle João works for the Red Cross and translates from Portuguese into English. He likes his job.

10 How many of these tasks can you do?

1 Lisa lives with her *mum / dad* in Galway in Ireland.
2 Her dad *doesn't live / lives* with his new wife, Dorothy.
3 Lisa *likes / doesn't like* her mum's new partner, Mike.

4 Les sees his .... more often than his ....
5 When Les' .... is working, he .... with his grandparents.
6 Amar lives in .... , but his cousin is from ....

7 Who lives with both of their parents? ....
8 Who of the four children do you think has the most difficult life? Why?
....
9 Compare Lisa and Les. What is the same about them?
....

11 Check your answers with a partner.

12 Put the dialogue into the correct order. Then check with a partner. Act it out.

☐	**Dad**	Yes, but you must be home by eight. You mustn't be late, Rory!
☐	**Dad**	No, you mustn't stay out so late. Let's say you must be home by 9.30.
☐	**Dad**	I don't care about the others.
☐	**Rory**	Dad, please. I just want to stay till ten.
☐ 3	**Rory**	But Dad. That's not fair. All the others stay till ten.
☐	**Rory**	Great. Thanks, Dad.
☐ 1	**Rory**	Dad, can I go?

CD3 19
13 Listen to the dialogue between Fred and his mum. Tick the things he mustn't do.

☐ go into private files ☐ delete a file ☐ print out everything ☐ chat ☐ surf around

Get talking Rules at home

14 Work in pairs. Tell your partner three things you must (mustn't) do at home.

15 Read the anecdote.

Today's anecdote is about Norbert Wiener (1894–1964). He was a famous mathematician who lived in America. Professor Wiener was a real genius, but he was also a bit absent-minded*. This is why there are a few funny anecdotes about him. Here is our favourite:
One day the Wieners moved to another house. His wife gave him a little piece of paper and said: "Norbert, we're moving today. I wrote the new address on this piece of paper." "Thank you," said Wiener and put the piece of paper into his jacket. At the university, he needed a piece of paper to make some notes. He took the paper out of his jacket. He wrote something on it. Later, he left it in his office. Then he walked home – but to the old address. Suddenly he remembered. "Ah yes, a new house, a new address. Damn, where's that piece of paper?" But of course he couldn't find it. Then he looked around and saw a little girl. "Little girl," he said, "do you know where the Wieners live?" "Yes, Dad. Mum sent me to find you. I'll take you home now," the girl answered.

VOCABULARY: *absent-minded – zerstreut

16 How many of these tasks can you do?

1	Norbert Wiener was good at maths.	T / F
2	He often forgot things.	T / F
3	Mrs Wiener wrote the new address on some paper.	T / F
4	Mr Wiener worked at	
5	Mr Wiener wrote .... on the piece of paper.	
6	Mr Wiener left his address	
7	Where did Mr Wiener go after work?	
8	Who was the little girl?	
9	Why was she at the house?	

17 Check your answers with a partner.

 WB p. 87, 89

(18) The owner of the Horrible Hotel doesn't want young people in his hotel. Think of more rules: *Young people must / mustn't …* . Then write a leaflet "What people must know about our hotel" (70–90 words).

young people must	young people mustn't
· be in bed before 7 p.m.	· eat any sweets between 6 a.m. and 11 p.m.

SbX GRAMMAR

 ## like (doing)

So sagst du, dass jemand etwas gerne macht:

I **like** juggl**ing**. She **likes** roller-skat**ing**.
She **doesn't like** work**ing** out.

I don't like roller-skating.

Complete. Write in the right order -ing / like / person.

Bildung: ¹............................ + ²............................ + ³............................

 ## must – mustn't

Du verwendest *must*, um zu sagen, dass jemand etwas tun muss.
I **must** get a birthday present for Joanne.

So sagst du, dass jemand etwas nicht tun darf oder etwas nicht geschehen darf:

Bildung: person + *mustn't (must not)* + *base form* of the verb

You mustn't be home later than 8 o'clock. **We mustn't forget** Mum's birthday.

You mustn't use all the paper!

MORE fun with Fido!

Fido, you mustn't come in here.

Stop it, Fido. You mustn't do that.

YOU MUSTN'T SHOUT AT FIDO!

Language function	Speaking strategy
• ordering food (*Essen bestellen*)	• changing your mind (*seine Meinung ändern*)

The pizza

Vocabulary Pizza toppings

CD3 20

1 Match the food and the pictures. Listen and check.

pepperoni	mushroom
tomato	cheese
pineapple	ham

1 ....

2 ....

3 ....

4 ....

5 ....

6 ....

CD3 21

2 Watch or listen to the dialogue. Then read it. What toppings from **1** do the family choose on their pizzas?

Assistant	Hello, can I take your order?
Dad	Pizzas for everyone?
Leo	Yes, I'd like the ham and pineapple pizza.
Lucy	Can I have a cheese and tomato one?
Mum	And I'll have a pepperoni one.
Dad	So that's one ham and pineapple, one cheese and tomato … two pepperoni. Hang on. Er … Make that one pepperoni and two cheese and tomato.
Assistant	What would you like to drink?
Dad	Four cokes, please. No, wait a second. Make that three cokes and a bottle of water.

Assistant	Eat in or take away?
Dad	Eat in.
Assistant	OK, that's £24, please. If you'd like to take a seat, your food will be ready in ten minutes. Your order is 21.
Dad	Thanks.

WB p. 90

3 Complete the waiter's order.

Order number [1]..................................
Pizzas: 1 x [2].............................. and [3].............................. , 1 x [4]..............................
                2 x [5].............................. and [6]..............................
Drinks: 3 x [7].............................. , 1 x [8].............................. Total £ [9]..............................

Useful phrases Ordering food

4 Read the sentences. Write C (*Customer*) or A (*Assistant*).

1 Can I take your order? ☐
2 I'd like a ham and pineapple pizza. ☐
3 Can I have a cheese and tomato one? ☐
4 Eat in or take away? ☐

? What do you think? Answer the question.

• Does everyone get what they ordered?

Mobile homework

Watch part 2 of the video and circle T (*True*) or F (*False*).

1 Mum falls in the pond.   T / F
2 Dad misses the bus.   T / F
3 Leo is scared on the London Eye.   T / F
4 Dad wants his pizza in six slices.   T / F

Speaking strategy Changing your mind

5 Complete. Then check with the dialogue in **2**.

Dad   So that's one ham and pineapple, one cheese and tomato … two pepperoni.
              [1]H...................... o...................... . Erm … Make that one pepperoni and two cheese and tomato.
Assistant What would you like to drink?
Dad   Four cokes, please. No, [2]w...................... a s...................... . Make that three cokes and
              a bottle of water.

6 CHOICES

A Work in pairs. Use the prompts.

[**A** Order a pizza.] → [**B** Repeat the order.] → [**A** Change your mind.]

(**A** Can I have a pepperoni pizza, please?) (**B** A pepperoni pizza.) (**A** Hang on. I'd like a ham one.)

B ROLE PLAY: Work in fours.

Student A, B and C	**Student D**
You are customers in a pizza restaurant. Order pizzas and drinks.	• Take the other students' order. • Ask if it's eat in or take away.

UNIT 13 Magic

A song 4 U

1 Listen and sing. Then put the pictures in the correct order.

Welcome

Welcome, welcome to our school.
A place for ghosts and that's so cool.

Here you learn to pass through doors.
Here you learn to float above floors.
Here you learn to rattle chains.
Here you learn to make big stains.

Welcome, welcome …

Here you learn to take off heads.
Here you learn to float above beds.
Here you learn to scream at night and how you can win a fight.

Welcome, welcome …

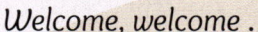

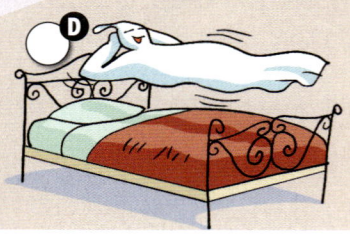

Time for a sketch

 2 Read the sketch.

The school for young ghosts

It's the first night at school for the young ghosts.

Teacher	Good evening.
Ghosts	Ooooooooooooooooooooooh.
Teacher	Welcome to our school. On your first night I'm going to teach you …
Ghost 1	About castles in Britain?
Teacher	No, that's next week. Tonight you're going to learn how to pass through walls.
Ghost 2	And doors?
Teacher	Yes, of course.

 WB p. 92, 93, 94

 CYBER Homework 36 Revision

Ghost 3	But we can open doors easily.
Teacher	Be quiet, you silly ghost! Passing through locked doors, of course.
Ghost 3	Sorry, sir.
Ghost 4	Do we learn how to scream loudly too?
Teacher	Not this year. That's in year three.
Ghost 5	What about scaring people?
Teacher	That's next month.
Ghost 6	I want to learn how to take my head off.
Teacher	That's in year two. Tonight you're going to learn how to pass through walls. OK?
Ghost 6	Is it difficult to learn?
Teacher	Passing through a wall can be difficult. Sometimes ghosts get stuck.
Ghost 7	I know, sir. My aunt got stuck in a wall when I was a baby. She's still there.
Teacher	The poor woman!
Ghosts	Oooooooooooooooooh!
Teacher	Be quiet! Now, you have to walk quietly. You mustn't say a word.
Ghost 8	Can I rattle my chains?
Teacher	Aren't you listening? You have to walk quietly. No rattling.
Ghost 7	Fast or slowly?
Teacher	Don't walk too fast and don't walk too slowly. I'll show you.
Ghosts	Yes, please.
Teacher	OK, watch me ...
Ghost 6	Where's the teacher now?
Ghost 5	In the wall. He got stuck.
Ghosts	Hurray! What a great first lesson!

3 **How many of these tasks can you do?**

1 It's the first *day* / *night* at the school for the young ghosts.
2 They are going to learn about castles in Britain *this* / *next* week.
3 The ghosts are going to learn how to pass through *locked doors* / *walls*.

4 When do they learn how to scream loudly? ....
5 What do the young ghosts want to know about passing through walls? ....
6 Where is the aunt of ghost 7? ....

7 The teacher says to the ghosts that they mustn't walk too fast or ....
8 The teacher gets .... at the end of the lesson.
9 The ghosts think that the first lesson ....

   4 **Check your answers with a partner. Then listen to the sketch.**

  5 **Listen to the sketch again and act it out.**

 WB p. 92, 93, 94

Vocabulary

6 Listen and look at the pictures. Then number the words.

- ☐ car boot
- ☐ nail
- ☐ put a spell on someone
- ☐ feather
- ☐ roast potatoes
- ☐ fence
- ☐ cooker
- ☐ deckchair
- ☐ sprinkle
- ☐ prison

Story time

7 Read the story.

Abracadabra, one, two, three

Debbie and her brother Robert were playing ball behind the house. Suddenly the ball landed in their neighbour's garden. "I'll get it," said Robert.

"Be careful," Debbie said, "Mr Blogg loves to eat children for lunch." Robert didn't laugh. Mr Blogg was very unfriendly and Robert was scared of him.

Slowly and quietly, Robert climbed over the fence. He looked through the bushes. The ball was right behind Mr Blogg's deckchair. Then everything happened very fast. Mr Blogg got up and shouted: "This time I'll get you!" Robert quickly climbed back over the fence. After a

minute, something came flying through the air. Robert and Debbie looked at it. "That was our ball," Robert said quietly. There was a big nail in the ball.

The following Saturday was Debbie's thirteenth birthday. They had a party in the garden with lots of friends. The young people were having a lot of fun. Suddenly Robert and Debbie's dad came into the garden. "Mr Blogg was here," he said. "You're making too much noise. Come into the house." The young people walked angrily into the house.

"Can we go out later and roast some potatoes over a fire?" Debbie asked.

"Of course," said her dad, "but don't make any noise."

An hour later they went out to roast the potatoes. They were very quiet, but after ten minutes they heard the doorbell. It was Mr Blogg. Then Dad came into the garden and told them to put out the fire. "Mr Blogg says there is too much smoke," he said. "I really don't like Mr Blogg," said Debbie.

Three days later Debbie and Robert were looking for Snowy, their cat. They found her under the bushes near the fence.

Snowy was very ill. Robert also found a rotten fish. "We didn't have fish this week," said Debbie. "I'm sure Mr Blogg threw the fish over the fence." They carried the cat into the house. "Poor Snowy," said Debbie, "I really don't like Mr Blogg."

The next day Debbie was in the garden with a book. "What are you reading?" Robert asked. "It's a book on magic," said Debbie. "Sally gave it to me."

"Why are you reading that?" asked Robert.

"I want to put a spell on Mr Blogg."

"Spells don't work," said Robert.

"Do you want to help me or not?" asked Debbie.

"OK," said Robert. "What do I have to do?"

"The book says that we have to get five things from Mr Blogg," answered Debbie.

"We can do that easily," said Robert.

At ten o'clock that night, Debbie and Robert climbed the fence into Mr Blogg's garden. They found a feather, the rest of a cigar, a piece of bread, half a hot dog and a bottle of beer that was half full. They climbed back into their garden, put all the things in a pot and hid it in the garden shed. The next day they put the pot on the cooker and filled it with water. They cut up the feather, the rest of the cigar, the piece of bread, the rest of the hot dog and threw it in the water together with the beer. Then they filled an empty bottle of orange juice with the brown stuff.

"What do you want to do now?" Robert asked. "We have to go into Mr Blogg's garden and sprinkle this stuff round his house."

They went over to the fence and listened carefully. Nothing. They climbed over and started to sprinkle the brown stuff. When Robert and Debbie got to the garage they stopped. The door of the garage was open and they could see Mr Blogg by his car. He was putting boxes into the boot. When he saw Debbie and Robert, he shouted: "Now I've got you." Debbie and Robert ran as fast as they could.

When they climbed the fence Robert lost one of his trainers. Mr Blogg picked it up.

"I'll show it to your dad when he comes home," he shouted. Then he got into his car and went away. "What can we do now?" asked Robert. "Dad's going to be very angry." "Let's go into town and see Grandma," said Debbie. "We can have dinner with her. And when we get back, everything will be over."

When they arrived at Grandma's place they phoned their mum. "We'll be back after dinner," Debbie said. After dinner Grandma brought them back in her car. There was a police car in front of Mr Blogg's house. Debbie and Robert went over and talked to a policeman. "Mr Blogg had an accident in town," the police officer said. "Is he in hospital?" asked Debbie. "No, he's in prison because we found lots of stolen computers in the boot of his car. And the house is also full of stolen things." "So your spell worked," said Robert. "Yes, it did," said Debbie. "But I'm glad he isn't in hospital."

8 How many of these tasks can you do?

1 The children live next door to Mr Blogg.   T / F
2 Robert is afraid of Mr Blogg.   T / F
3 Mr Blogg complains about Robert's party.   T / F

4 What did Mr Blogg give to Snowy? ....
5 What do the children decide to do? ....
6 What do they need for the spell? ....

7 One of .... falls off when he climbs over the fence.
8 The children go .... to help them stop worrying.
9 The police find lots of .... in Mr Blogg's house.

 9 Check your answers with a partner. Then listen to the story.

 10 Listen to the interview with Julia and write the information in your exercise book.

1 two reasons why Julia likes *Wizards of Waverly Place*
2 who is her favourite character, and why
3 how she watches the show

11 Read the text and finish the sentences.

"What can we do?" said a ghost. "We must help our teacher," said the smallest ghost. He gave his chains to another ghost. He walked to the wall. "Don't walk too slowly and don't walk too fast," the others shouted. So the smallest ghost began to walk slowly and quietly through the wall. In the wall, he took the teacher's hand and they both went through the wall. "Hurray!" all the young ghosts shouted and they rattled their chains loudly. "Thank you very much," the teacher said to the smallest ghost. "That's alright," said the smallest ghost.

1 The smallest ghost wanted …   3 Then he started to …   5 They both went …
2 He gave his chains …   4 In the wall, he took …   6 The teacher thanked …

12 CHOICES

Writing for your Portfolio

A Look at the pictures. Use the phrases from the box to help you write a story of about 60 words.

Archibald was a young …
One night he wanted to …
He was very …
Suddenly he heard …
He got scared and …
The dog …
Then Archibald …
In the end, the dog …

B **Look at the pictures and write a story of about 120 words. Find a title for your story. Before you write anything, look at each picture carefully. For each picture write down five words you could use. Use at least three adverbs from the box.**

quickly
slowly
carefully
angrily
loudly
easily

Start like this: It was the last lesson of the night …

GRAMMAR   Adverbs of manner

Mit dem Adverb der Art und Weise drückst du aus, *wie* jemand etwas macht oder *wie* etwas geschieht.

*Young ghosts learn how to scream **loudly**.*
*You have to walk **quietly**.*
*You mustn't walk too **slowly**.*
*Robert climbed back **quickly** over the fence.*
*The young people walked **angrily** into the house.*
*They climbed over the fence and listened **carefully**.*
*We can do that **easily**.*

Bildung: Adjektiv + *ly*
quiet – quiet**ly**
quick – quick**ly**
slow – slow**ly**
careful – careful**ly**

Bei den Adjektiven, die auf *y* enden, wird das *y* zu einem *i*:
easy – eas**ily**
happy – happ**ily**
angry – angr**ily**

Ausnahmen:
fast – **fast**   *Don't walk too **fast**.*
good – **well**   *I'm glad that it worked so **well**.*

Complete with *adverb* or *adjective*.

Mit einem [1]...................................... kannst du ein Nomen beschreiben.
Mit einem [2]...................................... kannst du ein Verb beschreiben.

Annabel jumped quickly over the fence.

DVD

Farewell!

1 Use the pictures to tell the story of Episode 5.

2 What do you think happens to these in the final episode?

DVD **3** Watch Episode 6 and answer the questions.

1 Why does Sunborn destroy the belt and stones?
2 What happens when she destroys the belt and stones?
3 What can the children no longer do?

4 Complete the sentences about you.

1 My favourite character in *The Story of the Stones* is ....
because ....

2 My least favourite character in *The Story of the Stones* is ....
because ....

3 My favourite scene was ....

Everyday English

DVD **5** Watch Episode 6 again. Complete the sentences (1–4) with the words in the box. Then
match them to the questions (a–d).

I'm afraid so	believe me	it doesn't matter	I'm afraid not

☐ 1 That's right, Daniel. But ....

☐ 2 .... There's no place for me
here on Earth.

☐ 3 The Lord of the Fire still lives.
He won't give up, ...

☐ 4 .... , Sarah. But I'll never
forget you.

a Will it all start again?

b So we can't morph any longer?

c Does this mean we won't see you again?

d Can't you stay here?

UNIT 14 Where we live

You learn
- about possessive pronouns
- how to use the possessive *'s*
- about houses and words for furniture
- how to form questions with *whose*

You can
- talk about your flat or house
- ask to whom things/animals belong

SbX **Read the text.**

We all know what a house is. It has a roof, walls, rooms, windows and doors. There might be a staircase. There might be a cellar underneath it or a garden around it. But not all houses are like this. Take a look around the world and see how different houses can be.

Houses and Homes

Around twenty million Americans live in trailer homes. They usually keep them in special parks. They are like little villages. In the park the owners connect their trailers to electricity and water. Trailers are a cheap way of living in your own home and, if you get tired of one place, you can always move your home to another park.

The Americans aren't the only people who have moveable houses. The Mongolian people in Central Asia move their houses a lot. Their houses are "yurts". When there isn't enough grass for their sheep any more, they take down their houses. They put the parts on the backs of their camels and horses. They then carry the parts to other places where there is enough food for the animals.

In some parts of the world people live in houses that are not on the ground. For example, some people in South East Asia build their houses on stilts*. They do this because their houses are near water. The stilts keep their homes high above the water and out of danger.

Other people actually live on the water. The Uros people live on Lake Titicaca in Peru. There are about two thousand of them on fifty floating islands of reeds. Reeds are long, strong grasses. They use the reeds to build their houses. When the Uros want to visit a neighbour they move from island to island by boat.

Finally, in the jungle of Costa Rica some people live in tree houses. There is even a tree house hotel. There are wooden bridges between the houses so that people can visit their neighbours easily.

VOCABULARY: *stilt – Pfahl

2 **Read the text again and answer the questions.**

1 How many Americans live in trailer homes?
2 When do the Mongolian people move their homes?
3 Why do people build their houses on stilts?
4 What do the Uros use to build their houses?
5 How do the people in Costa Rican tree houses visit their neighbours?

Vocabulary Inside a room

3 Listen and look at the picture. Then number the words.

☐ wardrobe	☐ fridge	☐ sink	☐ radiator
☐ bed	☐ cooker	☐ cupboard	☐ sofa
☐ table	☐ bedside table	☐ carpet	☐ curtains
☐ chair	☐ armchair	☐ rug	☐ lamp

Get talking Memory game

4 Work in pairs. One of you closes your book. Test each other.

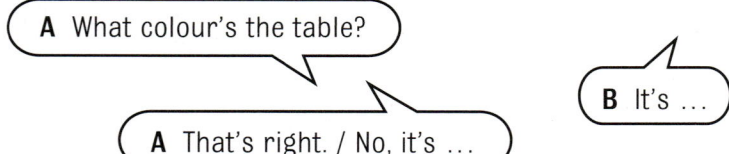

A What colour's the table?

A That's right. / No, it's …

B It's …

Sounds right /juː/ /ʊ/

5 Listen and say the poem.

New curtains for the window,
new cupboards for my books.
A wardrobe for my clothes,
and how nice my bedroom looks!

WB p. 99, 100   CYBER Homework

Get talking Remembering

 6 **Work in pairs. Look at the plan of the house. Close your book. Say what's in each room.**

In the living room, there's a television, and …
In the kitchen, there are …

> living room
> kitchen
> bathroom
> Mike and Nick's
>   room
> Joanna's room

CD3 31 **7** **Listen. Which room are the people in?**

Conversation 1: ....
Conversation 2: ....

Conversation 3: ....
Conversation 4: ....

CD3 31 **8** **Listen again and complete. Use the words in the box.**

> mine
> yours
> hers
> his
> whose
> ours
> theirs
> whose

Mum	[1].. school bag is this?
Mike	It's Joanna's.
Mum	Well, it shouldn't be on the sofa. Take it to her room, please.
Mike	Why me? It's [2].. , not [3].. !

Simon	I like your room.
Nick	Thanks. I share it with my brother. This is my bed, and that's [4].. .
Simon	Right. Is this your computer?
Nick	Yes and no — I mean, it's [5].. !

Mum	[6].. trainers are those? Are they [7].. ?
Joanna	No — they're Mike's! I borrowed them, and they got dirty — so now I'm cleaning them.
Mum	OK — but don't clean them here, in the bathroom! Wash them in the kitchen!

Mike	Mum — why is there a dictionary here on the fridge?
Mum	Oh, that — yes, can you take it to Mr and Mrs Smith next door, please?
Mike	OK. Is it [8].. ?
Mum	No, it's ours, but they want to borrow it.

➤ WB p. 101, 102, 103

9 **Listen to the dialogue. Then act out similar dialogues using the things in the pictures.**

Susan Whose pen is this? Is it yours?
Mark No. It's hers.

  10 **Listen and complete. Then repeat.**

Whose is it? Is it yours?
No, it isn't [1].......................... .
Whose is it? Is it Mike's?
No, it isn't [2].......................... .
Whose is it? Is it Sue's?
No, it isn't [3].......................... .
Whose is it? Jane and Paul's?
No, it isn't [4].......................... .

Whose is it? Whose is it?
Give it to us.
It's ours!
And it's so good!
Mmm!

Writing for your Portfolio

11 **Read Emily's text and answer the questions.**

- Which is her favourite room?
- Why does Emily like this room best?

The best place in my house

The best place in my house is the kitchen. There's a big table and four chairs where we have breakfast and dinner. There's a big window and we can look into the garden. There's a sink and a fridge, but no washing machine (that's in the garage). Our cat's basket is in the kitchen, too, and she sleeps there at night.
I like the kitchen because it's a place for all the family. It's always warm in there, too!

12 **Write a text about the best place in your house or flat. Write 60–80 words.**
Think about:

- where the place is
- what you do there
- what it looks like
- why it is your special place

102   **UNIT 14**

 WB p. 101, 102, 103

Whose ... ?

Wenn du fragen willst, wem etwas gehört, fragst du mit **Whose ... ?**

Whose school bag is this?   *Whose trainers are those?*

 ### Possessive *'s*

Wenn du sagen willst, wem etwas gehört, hängst du an den Namen der Person oder das Nomen *'s* an:

*Whose bag is this? – It's **Joanna's**.*   *They're **Mike's** trainers.*
*This is **my brother's** bed.*

Wenn der Name oder das Nomen im Plural steht oder auf *-s* endet, setzt du ans Ende des Wortes ein ' (Apostroph):

*This is my **parents'** room.*   *It's our **neighbours'** dog.*   *That's **Les'** mum.*

Bei Wörtern mit unregelmäßiger Pluralform setzt du *'s* ans Ende des Wortes:

*That's the **children's** school.*   *Don't take other **people's** things!*

 ### Possessive pronouns

Du verwendest ein *possessive pronoun*, wenn du sagen willst, wem etwas gehört – ohne dass du den Namen der Person verwendest.

Complete with *he / I / they / she*.

(¹...............) It's **mine**.
(²....you.....) Are they **yours**?
(³...............) This is my bed, and that's **his**.
(⁴...............) The bag is **hers**.
(⁵....we.....) The computer is **ours**.
(⁶...............) The dictionary isn't **theirs**.

Is that elephant yours?

MORE fun with Fido!

Look Fido! A new basket. It's yours.

Home, sweet home!

The Twins 5
DEVELOPING SPEAKING COMPETENCIES

Language function
- describing an object (*einen Gegenstand beschreiben*)

Speaking strategy
- checking what someone says (*bei jemandem nochmal nachhaken*)

Leo's watch

Vocabulary Materials and patterns

 1 Match the materials **and** the patterns with the pictures.

Materials:
1 made of leather
2 made of plastic
3 made of cotton

Patterns:
A spotted
B plain
C striped

sunglasses

jacket

watch strap

2 Watch or listen to the dialogue. Then read it. What's Leo's problem?

Leo	Hello. I'm looking for my watch. I think I lost it at school this morning.
Secretary	OK, let's see what we can do. What's it like?
Leo	Well, it's white. It's made of plastic.
Secretary	OK, so it's plain white, is it?
Leo	No, sorry. The watch face is white with some orange on it, but the strap is different.
Secretary	OK. So what's the strap like?
Leo	It's striped. Orange, green, purple and … erm … red.
Secretary	Are you certain?
Leo	Yes, it's orange, green, purple and red.

Secretary	And what's the strap made of?
Leo	It's made of metal. No, sorry. It's made of plastic.
Secretary	Are you sure?
Leo	Yes, yes. It's made of plastic, and it's striped orange, green, purple and red.
Secretary	OK, so let's see what we've got.

3 Cover up the dialogue in **2**. Try to answer the questions. Then check.

1 Where does Leo think he lost his watch? ....
2 What's the watch strap like? ....
3 What's the watch face like? ....

WB p. 104, 105

Useful phrases Describing an object

 4 Write two sentences to describe each object.

 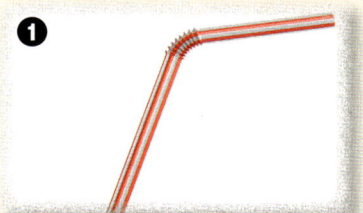  

It's made of plastic. ....
It's ....

 What do you think? Answer the questions.

• Where did Leo lose his watch?   • How does he find it?

Mobile homework

Watch part 2 of the video. Read the sentences and correct them.

1 The secretary hasn't got any lost and found watches. ....
2 The librarian shows Leo a watch, but it's not his. ....
3 Leo goes to the gym to do some exercise there. ....
4 Leo talks to his friends. They don't want to help him. ....
5 In the end Leo finds the watch. He is wearing it. ....

Speaking strategy Checking what someone says

 5 Fill in the correct words. Then check with the dialogue in .

| 1 | **Leo** | It's striped. Orange, green, purple and ... erm ... red. | 2 | **Leo** | It's made of metal. No, sorry. It's made of plastic. |
| | **Secretary** | A........................ you c........................ ? | | **Secretary** | A........................ you s........................ ? |

 CHOICES

A Work in pairs. A says what he/she can't find and describes it. B checks what A says.

> **A** I can't find my T-shirt. It's ... erm ... blue.

> **B** Are you sure?

> **A** Yes, I am. It's blue.

B ROLE PLAY: You are in a lost and found office. One of you is the assistant in the office. The other one lost something a few days ago (a watch, a camera, a pen, etc.). Work in pairs and extend it into a longer dialogue. Take 2 or 3 minutes to practise it. Don't write it down. Act it out in class.

You learn
- about the present perfect and past participles
- words for aches and pains

You can
- ask what has happened to someone
- write a message to someone who has had an accident

1 Listen to the jokes. Then read them and colour 1–5 stars to give a score for each joke.

http://www.jennysjokes.uk

Jenny's Jokes!

Hi! My name's Jenny and welcome to my joke pages. Every week I choose a topic and ask you to send me your favourite jokes. Last week I chose "doctor, doctor" jokes. You sent me hundreds. Here are my favourite six. What do you think? Vote for each joke on the star chart and let's find out which is the greatest "doctor, doctor" joke in the world.

Patient Doctor, doctor, every time I drink a cup of hot chocolate I get a pain in the eye.
Doctor Try taking the spoon out first.

Vote now: ★ ★ ★ ★ ★

Patient Doctor, doctor, I've only got 59 seconds to live.
Doctor OK. Give me a minute and I'll call you back.

Vote now: ★ ★ ★ ★ ★

Patient Doctor, doctor, I've lost my memory.
Doctor When did this happen?
Patient When did what happen?

Vote now: ★ ★ ★ ★ ★

Patient Doctor, doctor, I've broken my arm in two places.
Doctor Don't go back to either of them.

Vote now: ★ ★ ★ ★ ★

Patient Doctor, doctor, I couldn't drink my medicine after my bath like you told me.
Doctor Why not?
Patient Well, after I drank my bath, I didn't have room for the medicine.

Vote now: ★ ★ ★ ★ ★

Patient Doctor, doctor, please come to my house quickly. My son has swallowed* my pen. What should I do?
Doctor Use a pencil until I arrive.

Vote now: ★ ★ ★ ★ ★

VOCABULARY: *swallow – hinunterschlucken

 WB p. 108

 CYBER Homework 42 Revision

Here are three more "doctor, doctor" jokes. In pairs, think of an ending for each one. Then listen and check.

1 **Patient**   Doctor, doctor, I think I need glasses.
   Doctor   You certainly do. ....

2 **Patient**   Doctor, doctor, I think I'm a sheep.
   Doctor   How do you feel?
   Patient   ....

3 **Patient**   Doctor, doctor, what's the quickest way to get to hospital?
   Doctor   ....

SbX **Write the names of the people under the pictures.**

....

Sue has got a pain in her ankle.   Emily has got a pain in her back.
Tim's head hurts.   William's throat hurts.
Jacob's knee hurts.   Jessica has got stomach ache.

> **Note:**
> I've got stomach ache.
> (or stomachache).
> I've got earache.
> I've got toothache.
> I've got backache.
> But we usually say
> "I've got **a** headache."

Sounds right /p/ /b/ /æ/ /e/

   Listen and repeat.

A **pa**in in your h**a**nd?   A **pa**in in your l**e**g?
A **pa**in in your b**a**ck?   A **pa**in in your h**ea**d?
That's too **ba**d!   Then st**ay** in **be**d!

Get talking Aches and pains

 Work in groups of three. Act out a problem and talk about it.

A What's the matter with Jane?

B She has got stomach ache.

6 Listen and number the pictures in the order you hear them.

7 Complete the dialogues with the words in the box. Practise the dialogues in pairs.

dropped
cut
broken
walked
fallen
hurt

1 Does your head hurt?
Yes, I've just .... into a lamp post.

2 What's the matter?
I think I've .... my toe.

3 Come quickly!
Why? What's the matter?
Kevin has .... out of the tree!

4 Why is he walking like that?
He has .... his ankle.

5 Why is she crying?
She has just .... a heavy box on her foot.

6 There's blood on your shirt.
Yes, I've just .... my hand.

8 Look at the conversations again and find the past participles of these verbs. Write them.

walk	break	cut	hurt	fall	drop
....	....	....	....	....	....

9 Here are some more past participles. What do you think the base forms of the verbs are?
Write them.

eaten	loved	thought	hit	told	played
....	....	....	....	....	....
put	met	known	wanted	rung	read
....	....	....	....	....	....

 WB p. 110

 CYBER Homework 43

10 **Read the text about the Amazon Rainforest.**

The world's new gold

The Amazon Rainforest is very important for our planet. It's the largest rainforest in the world and it produces more than 20% of our oxygen*. But the Amazon is in danger. People are cutting down the trees to sell the wood and make money quickly. Big companies are clearing away the trees so they can have more land for their huge farms.

The Amazon is also home to a lot of wildlife and many of the world's animals, birds, insects and fish live there. There are also more than 430,000 different types of plants in the forest and some of them are very special. These plants can help sick people. Scientists have found more than 2,000 plants in the Amazon Rainforest that can help the fight against cancer. There are also many other plants there that can help the fight against different illnesses. These plants are really valuable* for medical science. They are the world's new gold.

Five hundred years ago, more than 10,000,000 Indians* lived in the Amazon Rainforest. Now there are less than 200,000. The Indian medicine men know a lot about these special plants. They know what illnesses the plants can fight against and they know how to use them. But many of the medicine men are now very old. We must listen to what they can tell us. It is important for the world that we learn what they know!

VOCABULARY: *oxygen – Sauerstoff; **valuable** – wertvoll; **Indians** – Indios (Ureinwohner Südamerikas)

11 **How many of these tasks can you do?**

1 The Amazon Rainforest produces *20%* / *100%* of our oxygen.
2 People cut down lots of trees to make *big fires* / *big money*.
3 You can find lots of animals, birds, fish and plants in the Amazon *River* / *Rainforest*.

4 There are more than 430,000 types of plants – they can all help sick people.   T / F
5 Scientists are interested in plants that can help people with cancer.   T / F
6 The Indians don't know much about the special plants in the rainforest.   T / F

7 There are fewer Indians living in the rainforest than in the past. Why is this, do you think?
....

8 If more and more of the rainforests are cut down, what will the consequences be?
....

9 Why is it important to listen to the medicine men?
....

12 **Check your answers with a partner.**

Grammar chant Present perfect

13 A chant. Listen and repeat.

I've hurt my head.
I've hurt my back.
I've hurt both of my knees.
I've hurt my arm.
I've hurt my leg.
Please, call a doctor, please.

She's hurt her head.
She's hurt her back.
She's hurt both of her knees.
She's hurt her arm.
She's hurt her leg.
Please, call a doctor, please.

14 CHOICES

Writing for your Portfolio

Read this text message and answer the questions.

* Where is the writer?
* What's the problem?
* Who gets the message?

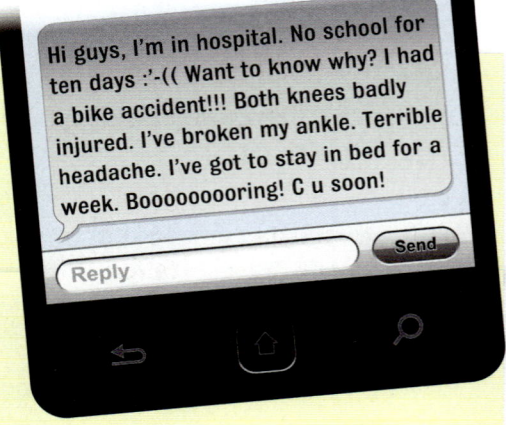

Hi guys, I'm in hospital. No school for ten days :'-((Want to know why? I had a bike accident!!! Both knees badly injured. I've broken my ankle. Terrible headache. I've got to stay in bed for a week. Booooooooring! C u soon!

Reply   Send

A Imagine the writer of the text message is your friend. Write a text message (30–40 words) to make him/her feel better. Think of the following points:

* say how you feel about the fact that he/she can't come to school
* make suggestions what he/she could do to make the time in hospital less boring
* say you are going to phone him/her soon

B Imagine the writer of the text message above is your friend. Write an email (about 150 words).

* try to make him/her feel better
* tell him/her about something funny/interesting that happened in school since he/she has been in hospital
* make suggestions what he/she could do while in hospital so it's less boring

Present perfect

Du verwendest das Present perfect, um jemandem eine Neuigkeit zu erzählen.
Dabei wird nicht erwähnt, wann dies geschehen ist.

I've lost my cat.   *We've bought* a new car.   *She has cut* her finger.
David has broken his leg.   *They've gone* on holiday.

Wenn du betonen willst, dass etwas gerade geschehen ist,
verwendest du *just*.

I've just passed my English test.
He has just walked into a lamp post.

Bildung: have/has + *past participle* (3. Form) of the verb

He has fallen off his bike.
We've just moved house.

They've just scored a goal.

Past participles

Das *past participle* findest du in der dritten Spalte der Verblisten. Bei regelmäßigen
Verben hat das *past participle* die gleiche Form wie das Past simple. Hänge einfach
-ed (oder -d) an die Nennform an.

pass	pass**ed**	pass**ed**
walk	walk**ed**	walk**ed**
move	move**d**	move**d**

Die Formen der unregelmäßigen Verben solltest du am besten auswendig lernen
(siehe auch S. 144):

go	went	**gone**		lose	lost	**lost**
buy	bought	**bought**		cut	cut	**cut**
fall	fell	**fallen**		hurt	hurt	**hurt**
break	broke	**broken**		win	won	**won**
find	found	**found**		see	saw	**seen**

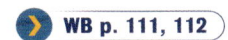 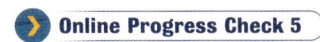

Kids in NYC 3

The city quiz

Before you watch

1 Write the words under the pictures.

an internet café
a library
a prize
a quiz

1 .... 2 .... 3 .... 4 ....

2 In what order do you think these pictures come in the DVD?
Write 1–4 in the boxes.

Watch the story

3 Check your answers to **2**.

4 Circle T (*True*) or F (*False*).

1 The children have written a quiz.   T / F
2 There are 20 questions in the quiz.   T / F
3 The children can win a prize in the quiz.   T / F
4 The children have three hours to do the quiz. T / F

5 **Complete the dialogue.**

with
idea
way
off
crazy
together

Jenny Come on – let's all do the quiz ¹..................................... .

Gerry No ²..................................... ! I'm going to the internet café over here.
I'm going to get all my answers ³..................................... the internet.

Emma Great ⁴..................................... , Gerry. Can I come ⁵..................................... you?

Gerry Sure. We can get a coffee too.

Steve You're ⁶..................................... . What if the teacher sees you?

Gerry Ah! Who cares?

Jenny Come on, Steve. Let's start. Bye, you guys. See you at two!

6 **Answer the questions.**

1 What time do the children have to be back at the park?

....

2 What does Gerry order at the internet café?

....

3 Which street is the New York Public Library on?

....

7 **Complete the list of places that Steve and Jenny see.**

St Patrick's Cathedral, ...

....

Everyday English

8 **Complete the dialogues.**

Let's see
have fun
Who cares?
I have no clue.

OK? I want you back here at two o'clock
and .... , everybody!

You're crazy! What if the teacher sees you?

Ah! ....

What did she mean?

....

What's the lunch special number four on the menu at Flor's Kitchen?

.... – grilled chicken over salad.

UNIT 16 Light rain in the north

1 Look at the map and read the text. Change the Fahrenheit temperatures into Celsius. Use this scale to help you.

F	0	10	20	30	40	50	60	70	80	90	100
C	-18	-12	-7	-1	4	10	16	21	27	32	38

Note:
To change Fahrenheit to Celsius, use this formula:
$(°F - 32) \times \frac{5}{9} = °C$
$0°F = -18°C$

The weather today

The good weather continues. Early morning clouds give way to lots of sunshine. Nicely cool and dry at the coast with lower temperatures in the North. Very hot in the South with temperatures in the 100s Fahrenheit.

78 SAN FRANCISCO
92
SAN JOSE   84
FRESNO
100
LOS ANGELES
104
SAN DIEGO

Vocabulary Weather

CD4 6

SbX

2 Listen and look. Then fill in the numbers. Test your partner.

☐ hot ☐ cold ☐ cloudy ☐ thunderstorm ☐ snowy ☐ foggy ☐ rainy ☐ sunny ☐ windy

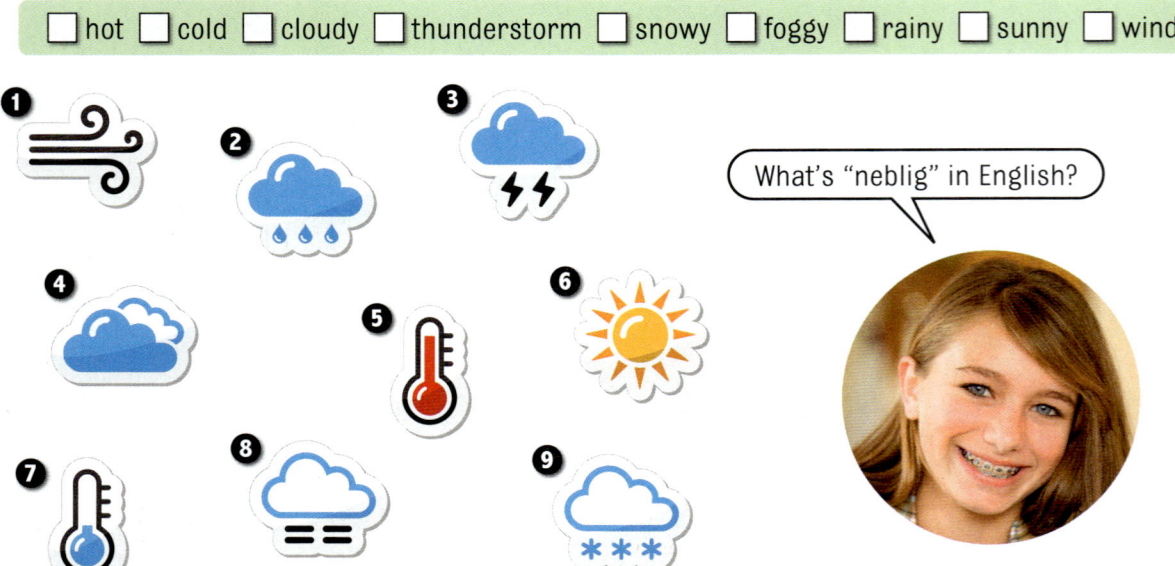

What's "neblig" in English?

> WB p. 114, 115   CYBER Homework 45 Revision

3 Listen to the weather forecast.
Then read it and draw the missing symbols on the maps.

Note:
° = degrees

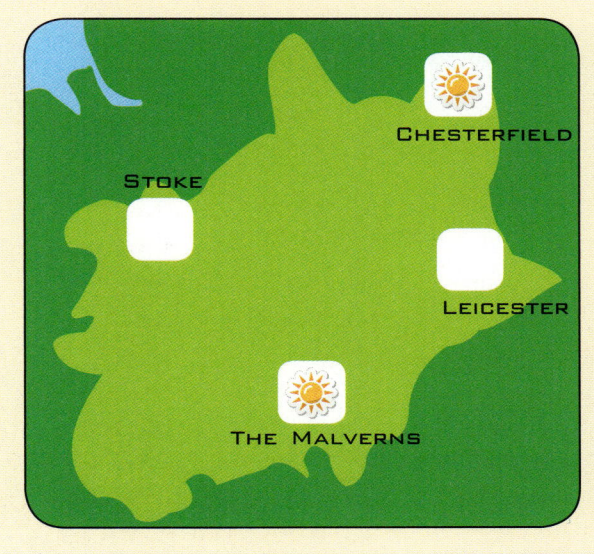

Today:
Sunny, some clouds north of Leicester.
Thick fog in the Stoke area will clear up
later. Temperatures between 3°C and 12°C.
Winds 10–20 mph.

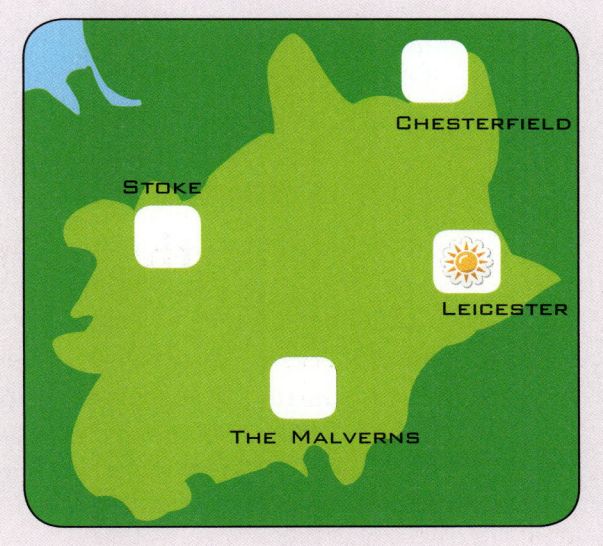

Outlook for tomorrow:
Light rain in the Stoke area. Sunny in the
Leicester area. More rain in the Malverns
and thunderstorms coming from the north
in the evening. Strong winds. Temperatures
between 8°C and 15°C.

4 Look at the maps of the UK. Listen to the weather forecasts and draw the symbols.

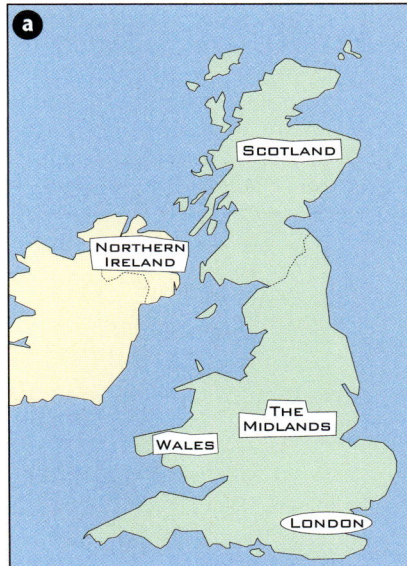

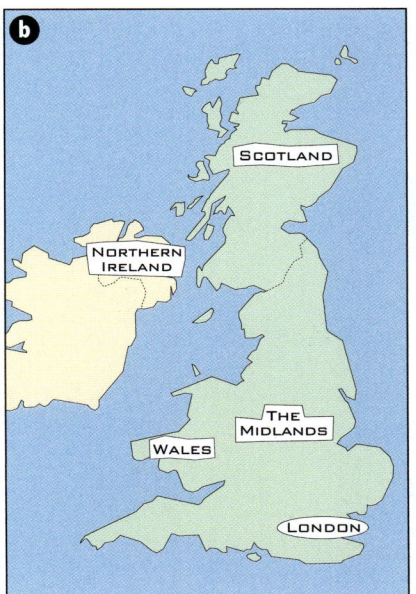

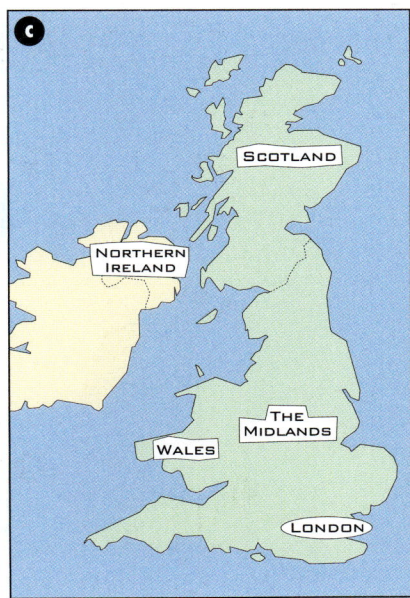

⑤ CHOICES

CD4 9 Listen to the dialogues. Then read them. Make some changes and act them out.

A DIALOGUE 1: Weather small talk

Monica	Nice day today.
Robert	That's right. It's really nice. But …
Monica	But what?
Robert	They say it'll rain later.
Monica	Oh, really. That's bad.
Robert	Why's that?
Monica	I wanted to go for a walk with you.
Robert	Really? Let's go. But …
Monica	But what?
Robert	I'll get an umbrella.

B DIALOGUE 2: Planning a trip

Receptionist	Highland Hotel Aviemore. Can I help you?
Tourist	Yes, I'd like to ask you about a hiking holiday*.
Receptionist	Yes.
Tourist	What's the weather like at your place right now?
Receptionist	Well, it's raining, and it's pretty cold.
Tourist	What about next week?
Receptionist	They say it'll be a bit warmer.
Tourist	But are you sure?
Receptionist	Well, I can't promise, of course. They say it'll be warmer and less windy. And towards the end of the week it'll be very sunny.
Tourist	Lovely. Thank you.

VOCABULARY: *hiking holiday – Wanderurlaub

Get talking Asking about the weather

 6 Work in pairs. Look at the map and say what the weather is like in an area. Your partner tries to guess the place.

A There is thick fog and the temperature is 10°C.

B You're in London.

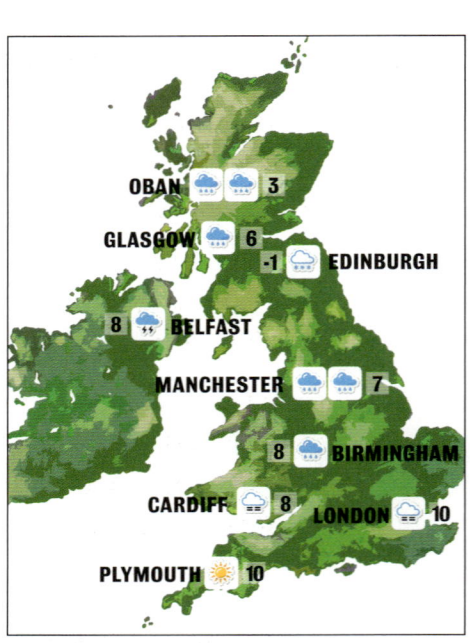

❯ WB p. 115, 117

Time for a sketch

7 **Read the sketch.**

"And the weather for tomorrow ..."

Dad OK, have we finished packing? Has everybody got their swimming trunks and bathing suits?

Jane Yes, Dad. Do I need a sweater?

Dad I don't think so. It won't be very cold in the evenings. *(Turns to Jamie.)* Jamie, turn off the TV. We're leaving in a few minutes.

Jamie Just a second, Dad. The weather report is coming on. Hey, Dad, listen to this.

(He turns up the volume.)

Weatherman

... In the south of England showers will be quite heavy and the sun won't come out for another few days. Temperatures will drop to 10° Celsius during the night and only go up to 17° Celsius during the day. There might also be a few thunderstorms. The weather situation will only get better after the weekend – and that's all from us for today.

Mum Turn it down, Jamie. Come here, and help with the unpacking.

Jane Oh, Mum. Why do we have to unpack?

Dad Your mum's right. We have to take out all the swimming things and put in a few sweaters. Come on, kids, it's a long way to the coast.

(They start unpacking.)

Jane What about my sweater? Will I need it?

Mum Yes, of course. And the raincoat too.

(15 minutes later.)

Dad Right. Have we got everything? And Jamie!!! Turn off the TV!

Jamie But Dad ...

Dad Turn it off!

Jamie Look, the weatherman is on again.

Mum Let's hear what he's got to say.

(Jamie turns up the volume.)

Weatherman

... have to apologise. I'm very sorry, but I gave you last week's weather report. I'm very sorry. Now here's the correct weather report for the next few days. Sunshine wherever we look, with temperatures going up to 25 to 30° Celsius. Some light cloud in the evenings, but there's nothing to worry about.

Dad OK! Let's start again!

8 **How many of these tasks can you do?**

1 The family are packing for a holiday.   T / F

2 Dad thinks Jane doesn't need a sweater.   T / F

3 The family are leaving tomorrow.   T / F

4 Mum asks Jamie to ☐ help pack. ☐ turn down the TV. ☐ watch the weather forecast.

5 The family are going to the ☐ mountains. ☐ seaside. ☐ countryside.

6 After the first weather report, Jane asks if she needs to take
☐ a bathing suit. ☐ an umbrella. ☐ a sweater.

7 Why doesn't Jamie want to turn off the TV? ....

8 Why does Jamie turn up the volume? ....

9 What mistake did the weatherman make? ....

   9 **Check your answers with a partner. Then listen to the sketch and act it out.**

 WB p. 116

10 Read the two texts and convert the numbers from Fahrenheit to Celsius, feet to metres and inches to centimetres.

> **Note:**
> 1 ft (foot) = 30.48 centimetres
> 1 inch = 2.54 centimetres

The hottest place in the USA

Death Valley is generally sunny, dry and clear throughout the year. The winters are mild, but summers are very hot and dry. In fact, Death Valley is one of the hottest places on earth. The highest temperature ever recorded in the USA was 134°F on July 10th, 1913. Summer high temperatures are usually around 120°F. The average rainfall each year is two inches.
Death Valley has the lowest point in the western world – 282 feet below sea level near Badwater – as well as many high mountains such as Telescope Peak at over 11,000 feet.

The wettest place in England

The wettest place in England is in the Lake District. It is a small village called Seatoller. Seatoller is the starting point for some great walks. But bring good clothes against the rain. The average rainfall each year is 120 inches. Some people say there is even more rainfall in Seathwaite (one mile away): 130 inches.
Seatoller doesn't have more rainy days than other places – but when it rains, it rains more.

Writing for your Portfolio

11 Read Carina's email to Tony. Draw a line where she should start a new paragraph.

To:	tony@home.uk
Subject:	bad weather :(

SEND

Hi Tony,
I'm sitting at the computer in the hotel lobby – guess why? No swimming, no lying in the sun. Outside it's raining, raining, raining. It all started with a thunderstorm yesterday. Then it got colder and then the heavy rain came. No tan* when I come back! ☹ And the outlook? More rain!! How boring. Hope I can catch a movie in town. How are things with you? Alright? Write back. Maybe we can chat a bit.
Love,
Carina

VOCABULARY: *tan – Bräune

12 Think back on your holidays and write an email about what it was like.
Write as much as possible about the weather (60–80 words).

WB p. 116

Sounds right /l/

13 Listen. Number the sentences as you hear them.

- ☐ I do it every day.
- ☐ I'll speak English to her.
- ☐ We tell jokes a lot.
- ☐ I speak English quite well.

- ☐ They see us on Fridays.
- ☐ We'll tell you a joke.
- ☐ They'll see us on Friday.
- ☐ I'll do it my way.

SbX GRAMMAR *will*-future

Mithilfe der *will*-future drückst du Erwartungen, Vermutungen und Hoffnungen für die Zukunft aus:

*We **will meet** again. (We**'ll meet** again.)*
*I **will not go** away for a very long time. (I **won't go** away for a very long time.)*

Du verwendest die *will*-future auch dann, wenn du etwas vorhersagen willst:

*Some heavy rain **will come** in from Northern Scotland.*
*The south of England **will have** quite a lot of fog near the coast.*
*The sun **won't come** out for another few days.*

Du verwendest die *will*-future auch dann, wenn du dich spontan entschließt oder spontan versprichst, etwas zu tun:

*Maybe **I'll try** sailing, too.*
***I'll help** you with your homework tonight.*

Complete with 'll / will / won't.

Bildung: person + [1].....................*(not)* + *base form* of the verb
Kurzformen: I will = I [2].....................
  I will not = I [3].....................

There'll be some showers today.

MORE fun with Fido!

I love rainy days!

I love really hot days!

But only on TV!

 WB p. 117–120

 CYBER Homework 47

UNIT 17 Get active!

You learn
- about the present perfect with *ever / never / yet / already*
- sports words

You can
- talk about your favourite sport
- write a text about your favourite sport

Vocabulary Sports

SbX **1** **Write the numbers of the sports in each picture.**

play		go					
1	football	5	mountain climbing	9	ice skating	13	surfing
2	tennis	6	cycling	10	skateboarding	14	windsurfing
3	basketball	7	mountain biking	11	swimming	15	skiing
4	volleyball	8	roller-skating	12	snowboarding	16	running

 A
 B
 C
 D
 E
 F
 G
 H
 I
 J
 K
 L
 M
 N
 O
 P

CD4 13 **2** **Listen and check your answers.**

WB p. 122, 123

CYBER Homework 48 Revision

Get talking Sports

 Ask and answer questions about some of the sports in .

Do you like … ?
What's your favourite … team?
Do you play/go … ?

How often do you … ?
Do you like watching … on TV?
Who's your favourite sportsman/sportswoman?

CD4
14
SbX

 Listen to the interviews with these two American teenagers and complete the profiles.

This is 14-year-old Danni from California. Her favourite sport is surfing. She started surfing when she was [1] …………………………… years old. She lives near the [2] …………………… in Santa Barbara. She goes surfing [3] …………………………… a day.

This is 14-year-old Ricky from Colorado. His favourite sport is mountain climbing. He started climbing when he was [4] …………………… years old. He always goes climbing with his [5] ……………………… . They go about [6] ……………………. times a month. They usually go climbing in the Rocky Mountains. They live [7] ……………………. miles away from the Rocky Mountains National Park.

Look at the questions below from the interviews. Which questions do you think are for Danni and which are for Ricky? Write D or R in the boxes.

1 Have you ever won any competitions? ☐
2 Have you ever got lost in the mountains? ☐
3 Have you ever seen a shark? ☐
4 Have you ever had an accident? ☐
5 Have you ever climbed the Matterhorn? ☐
6 Have you ever been to Australia? ☐

CD4
15

Listen and check. Then listen again. Are their answers to the questions yes or no?

WB p. 123, 126

Get talking Asking questions with *Have you ever ... ?*

7 Work in small groups. Ask and answer questions to find someone who has ...

1 met a famous person.
2 won a competition.
3 appeared on television.
4 found some money.

5 lived in another country.
6 been to a pop concert.
7 fallen asleep in a lesson.
8 written a poem.

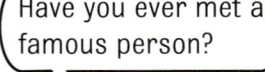
Have you ever met a famous person?

A Have you ever met a famous person?
B Yes, I have.
A Who?

B ...
A When was that?
B ...

CD4 16

8 Listen to the poem. Then read it.

The game

Eleven of us were on the field.
The other team looked scared.
"We're going to win," our trainer said.
"We're really well prepared."

Then Johnny kicked the ball to Paul
and Paul kicked it to Sue,
when Sue's mum shouted, "Come home,
Sue, there's work for you to do."

Ten of us were on the field
and Helen tackled Eddie.
Then Mr Sutton arrived and said,
"Triplets, your dinner's ready."

Seven of us were on the field.
The other team then scored.
And Tom and Helen said, "We're off,
we're getting really bored."

Five of us were on the field,
when Roland hurt his knee.
He left. And Lisa went with him.
And then we were only three.

Three of us were on the field.
The score was twenty – nil.
"I've had enough. It's a waste of time."
And off the field went Phil.

Two of us were on the field
and we tried our very best.
But then Johnny turned to me and said,
"I'm off, I need a rest."

So there I was all on my own,
a goalie without a team.
Then Dad called out, "Wake up! You're late."
Thank God – it was just a dream.

Sounds right /ɔː/ /əʊ/

9 **Which is the odd one out? Listen and check.**

1 a) m**o**re   b) b**oa**rd   c) c**oa**t
2 a) d**oo**r   b) g**o**   c) sl**ow**
3 a) f**ou**r   b) kn**ow**   c) s**aw**
4 a) sp**o**rt   b) b**ou**ght   c) t**oe**

10 **CHOICES**

A **Read the text and match the sentence halves.**

Extreme sports profile

ACTION WOMAN

Who is she?
Emma Sanderson, from England.

What does she do?
She's a yachtswoman.

Tell me more.
She sails a yacht, in team races or alone.

What competitions has she won?
She won the Round Britain and Ireland Race in 2000 at the age of 25 and also the Europe 1 New Man Star from Plymouth to Rhode Island, USA.

What is she most famous for?
She won the Around Alone race in 2002/03. She was the youngest woman and first British person to complete the 29,000 mile solo around-the-world yacht race. She was at sea for over 135 days. She had to face a hurricane, pirates and the extreme weather of the Southern Ocean – and, of course, she was alone at sea for four and a half months.

What does she say about her sport?
"I love the challenge. I don't really like being alone for a long time – I'm a people person. But I really wanted to be in the Around Alone race. I'm also in a global education programme and now I can tell kids about my sailing. I really enjoy that."

1 Emma Sanderson is an   ☐ complete the 29,000 mile solo race.
2 She sails in   ☐ about her sailing.
3 She won many team races,   ☐ team races or alone.
4 She was the youngest woman to   ☐ English yachtswoman.
5 She doesn't like being   ☐ but she's really famous for the Around Alone race.
6 Now she enjoys telling kids   ☐ alone for such a long time, but she loves the challenge.

▶ WB p. 124

B Read the text and complete the sentences.

Tommy Caldwell, Master of Rock

Who is he?
Tommy Caldwell (born August 11th, 1978 in Estes Park, Colorado) is an American rock climber.

What does he do?
traditional climbing, big wall speed-climbing, big wall free climbing

What is a big wall?
A big wall is a huge cliff usually around 300 metres high. But there are some much higher ones, such as El Capitan or Dawn Wall in Yosemite National Park. They are 900 metres. Climbers often go up in pairs; sometimes it takes a few days to get to the top.

So what has he already climbed?
He has already climbed walls like The Nose several times. He climbed it with his former wife in four days. He has also speed-climbed it in less than twelve hours. For many years his greatest challenge was to climb the Dawn Wall of the El Capitan Mountain in Yosemite National Park in California. In January 2015, after several attempts, he finally managed to get to the top.

How important is climbing for him?
Very important, of course. He likes the adventure and the thrill. But he also likes the fact that it has given him a chance to travel and to see the world. He has already been to so many beautiful places and he thinks he's living a full and exciting life. Climbing has also taught him to live without fear.

What does he think about his sport?
He loves it. He enjoys pushing himself, and he enjoys the freedom. He thinks life doesn't get any better than this. But he also sees the dangers. One danger is to become too obsessed and forget your friends and family. He says: "I've learned that I love climbing, but I love people more."

What are his goals for the future?
To be a good husband and a good dad and to share his love of climbing with others all over the world.

1 Tommy Caldwell is from ....

2 His sports are ....

3 Caldwell has already climbed ....

4 He doesn't only like the adventure of climbing, but also ....

5 He loves climbing, but he says it's more important ....

6 One goal for his future is ....

 WB p. 125

Read the text about someone's favourite sport.

I love volleyball. I love playing it and I love watching it on TV too. There are some great teams like Brazil and Italy. I like playing it because it's a fantastic team sport. It's also a brilliant way to make friends. I play in the school team. We're very good. Last year we won 18 out of 20 games. Once I broke my arm playing volleyball. I couldn't play for three months. My dream is to play professional volleyball.

Write a text about your favourite sport (60–80 words). Think about:

- what sport it is
- why you like it
- where / when / how often you play it
- how good you are / how good your team is

SbX # GRAMMAR

 ## Present perfect with *already* and *yet*

Zur Erinnerung: Du verwendest das Present perfect oft dann, wenn du nicht über einen bestimmten Zeitpunkt in der Vergangenheit sprichst.

*I***'ve heard** *about it.* (= Ich hab davon gehört, jemand hat mir irgendwann davon erzählt.)
She **has gone** *home.* (= Sie ist nach Hause gegangen, aber es ist unwichtig oder unbekannt, wann das war.)

Wenn du sagen willst, dass jemand etwas schon gemacht hat, kannst du das Present perfect mit dem Wort *already* verwenden. Das Wort *already* steht zwischen *has / have* und dem *past participle* (3. Form des Verbs).

He **has already climbed** *walls like The Nose several times.*
He **has already been** *to so many beautiful places.*

Wenn du sagen willst, dass etwas noch nicht geschehen ist, verwendest du *not yet* mit Present perfect. Das Wort *yet* kommt an das Satzende.

He **hasn't reached** *the top* **yet**.
There's a new film at the cinema, but I **haven't seen** *it* **yet.**

 ## Present perfect with *ever* and *never*

Wenn du fragen willst, ob jemand *irgendwann* in der Vergangenheit etwas getan oder erlebt hat, dann verwendest du meist das Present perfect.
Du verwendest es auch um auszudrücken, dass du etwas *nie* getan oder erlebt hast.
Häufig verwendest du in diesen Situationen die Wörter *ever* und *never*.

Have *you* **ever seen** *a shark?*
Have *you* **ever won** *a competition?*

*I***'ve never had** *an accident.*
*I***'ve never met** *a famous person.*

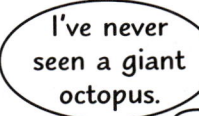

I've never seen a giant octopus.

DEVELOPING SPEAKING COMPETENCIES

DVD

Language function
● making requests and offers (*einen Wunsch äußern und Vorschläge machen*)

Speaking strategy
● responding to requests and offers (*auf Wünsche und Vorschläge reagieren*)

The sports party

Vocabulary Sports

  CD4 18

1 Match the sports and the pictures. Listen and check.

football
rugby
tennis
cricket
golf
swimming

❶ ....

❷ ....

❸ ....

❹ ....

❺ ....

❻ ....

  CD4 19

2 Watch or listen to the dialogue. Then read it. What sports do Lucy and Leo want at their party?

Lucy So we're having a sports party for our birthday this year.

Leo Yeah. Football and tennis. It's going to be cool.

Lucy Why don't I write the invitations?

Leo That's great. And I'll organise the equipment.

Lucy Fantastic. What else do we need to do?

Leo Well, Mum has already booked the sports centre.

Lucy What about food? Can you make a list of the food?

Leo Sure, no problem. And could you organise the drinks?

Lucy Of course.

Leo Football, tennis, food and drink. This is going to be the best party ever.

Lucy I just hope the weather's good.

Leo Don't be so silly. I checked the forecast. It's going to be sunny all day.

WB p. 127

3 Read the to-do list for Lucy and Leo's party and tick (✓) for 'done' or cross (X) for 'to do'.

1 Decide what kind of party to have. ☐
2 Write the invitations. ☐
3 Organise the equipment. ☐
4 Hire the sports centre. ☐
5 Make a list of food and drink. ☐
6 Check the weather forecast. ☐

Useful phrases Making requests and offers

4 Read the sentences. Write R (*Request*) or O (*Offer*).

1 I'll organise the equipment. ☐
2 Can you make a list of the food? ☐
3 Could you organise the drinks? ☐
4 Why don't I write the invitations? ☐

? What do you think? Answer the questions.

- Is the party a success?   • Why (not)?

Mobile homework

Watch part 2 of the video and answer the questions.

1 What other sports does Lucy suggest? ....
2 What does Leo think about these suggestions? ....
3 What's the weather like on the day of the party? ....
4 What sports do they play at the party? ....
5 Is the party a success? ....

Speaking strategy Responding to requests and offers

5 Match the responses with sentences 1–4 in **4** . Check with the dialogue in **2** .

Of course.

Fantastic.

Sure, no problem.

That's great.

6 **CHOICES**

A Work in pairs. Use the prompts.

A Make a request or offer. ➝ B Respond.

request	offer
make me / sandwich	play tennis / you
take me to / party	do / washing up
help me with / homework	wash / car

A Can you make me a sandwich?

B Of course.

B ROLE PLAY: Work in pairs.

You are organising a party.

- Make a list of all the things you need to organise (e.g. what kind of party, food, drink, music, invitation, etc.).
- Discuss the list. Make offers and requests.

You learn
- words for looking after a pet
- how to use *so do/have I* and *neither do/have I*

You can
- ask about pets
- agree/disagree with someone

Vocabulary Looking after your pet

 CD4 20

 SbX

1 **Listen and look at the pictures. Then number the words.**

- ☐ play with your pet
- ☐ clean out your pet's cage
- ☐ brush your pet
- ☐ feed your pet
- ☐ dry your pet
- ☐ stroke your pet
- ☐ walk your pet
- ☐ give your pet a bath
- ☐ take your pet to the vet
- ☐ clean out the litter tray

2 **Play a memory game.**

What did you do yesterday?

5, 2, 9.

Ah, you fed your pet, you walked your pet and you took your pet to the vet.

That's right.

WB p. 129   CYBER Homework 51 Revision

3 Listen to the interviews and tick the correct answers.

Megan

1 What is Megan's pet? ☐ a cat ☐ a hamster ☐ a dog

2 What colour is she? ☐ black and white ☐ black and grey ☐ black, grey and brown

3 Where does she sleep? ☐ in Megan's room ☐ in the bathroom ☐ in the living room

4 How often does she feed her? ☐ once a day ☐ twice a day ☐ three times a day

5 How much time a day does she spend on her? ☐ 15 minutes ☐ 50 minutes ☐ 90 minutes

David

6 What is David's pet? ☐ a cat ☐ a hamster ☐ a dog

7 What colour is he? ☐ black ☐ brown ☐ brown and white

8 How often does he feed him? ☐ once a day ☐ twice a day ☐ three times a day

9 How much time a day does he spend on him? ☐ 15 minutes ☐ 50 minutes ☐ 90 minutes

10 Where does he sleep? ☐ in the hall ☐ in David's room ☐ in the living room

4 Listen to the interviews again and complete the sentences.

1 Megan doesn't often …

2 When Megan does her homework, Princess …

3 Megan doesn't like to …

4 When it rains, David has to …

5 David's sister doesn't …

6 David plays a lot with Buddy when he …

Get talking Asking about pets

5 Hold interviews. Ask two classmates. Take notes.

Questions:

Have you got a pet?
What is it?
What colour is it?
How often do you feed it?
Where does it sleep?
How much time a day do you spend on it?

What would you like?

Answers:

Yes, I have. A mouse / …

No, I don't. A …

6 Report to the class.

Nathalie has got a … . It's … . It sleeps … . She feeds it … . She spends … minutes on it.

7 Read the picture story. Then listen to it.

A new pet

Bob Do you know what this house needs, Alice?
Alice What does it need, Bob?
Bob A pet. This house needs a pet. A pet to keep us company.
Alice That's a great idea. Let's get one.

Alice "The Animal Shelter". I think we're going to find something in here.
Bob So do I. Something very special to make our house the perfect home.

Alice How about a dog? They've got some lovely dogs here.
Bob Hmm, I'm not too sure. Think of the mess they make and the noise. Then we need to take them for walks …
Alice Yes, that's a good point. Let's look at the cats.

Bob Cats. They're cleaner than dogs, but they're not very good company. I don't really like cats.
Alice Neither do I. Let's forget about cats and look for something else.
Bob Let's go to the pet shop.

Bob "The Perfect Pet". The best pet shop in town. What are these?
Alice Rats! No way. I've got a fear of rats.
Bob So have I. There's no way I want a rat in the house.

Alice What about a budgie? They're easy to look after and they're great company.
Bob No. I don't really like the idea of birds in cages. Birds need to fly.

WB p. 131, 133

7

Bob   Snakes. Hmm. Interesting. They're easy to look after, for sure. And they'll keep the house safe. Nobody's going to break into a house with a snake like this in it. It's going to need a big glass cage, but we've got lots of space in the living room.
Alice   No way! I'm scared of snakes.
Bob   So what are we going to get, Alice?
Alice   Come with me. I think I've got the perfect pet for us.

8

Bob   A goldfish. Perfect.
Alice   Isn't it beautiful?
Bob   I haven't thought of a name for it yet.
Alice   Neither have I. But we've got all day to think of one.

8   Read the picture story again and answer the questions.

1   Why does Bob say they need a pet?
2   Why doesn't Bob want a dog?
3   Why don't Bob and Alice want a cat?
4   Why don't Bob and Alice want a rat?
5   Why doesn't Bob want a bird?
6   Why does Bob think a snake might be a good idea?

A Song 4 U

CD4 23/24

9   Listen and sing.

Getting a pet

*We've got to get a pet,
something for our home.
We've got to get a pet.
Don't want to be alone.*

Shall we get a cat?
Or shall we get a dog?
Shall we get a snake?
Or shall we get a frog?
Hmmmmmmmm ...

A dog is too much work.
A cat is much too proud.
A snake's too dangerous.
A frog is much too loud.

*We've got to get a pet,
something for our home.
We've got to get a pet.
Don't want to be alone.*

Shall we get a bird?
Or shall we get a rat?
Or shall we get a goldfish, dear?
What do you say to that?
Hmmmmmmmmmm ...

Bird in a cage? No way!
I've got a fear of rats.
I'd really love a goldfish, dear.
So would the neighbours' cats.

10 **Read the story.**

The story of Happy Feet

In June 2011, some people found an emperor penguin on a beach in New Zealand. It was really unusual because there are no emperor penguins in New Zealand. The penguin was more than 2,500 kilometres from home! Penguins are excellent swimmers, but that's a very long way to swim, even for a penguin. The people saw that the penguin ate sand. They also saw that the bird was quite sick. Why did he eat sand? Because the poor bird thought it was snow.

They took the penguin to the zoo in Wellington, the capital of New Zealand. They called the emperor penguin "Happy Feet". Happy Feet soon became a star. Lots of people wanted to see him. At the zoo they fed Happy Feet fish and after some months Happy Feet was fine again. They decided to take him back home.

Did you know?
The emperor penguin is the tallest and heaviest of all penguins. They can be 120 cm tall and weigh up to 45 kilos. They eat fish and other small animals that live in the Arctic Sea.

They fixed a transmitter* to the bird and put him on a ship. They took him about 600 km south. Then they said goodbye to him and put him in the sea to swim home.
But what happened to Happy Feet? After five days there was no signal from the transmitter any more. Did he get home? Did a shark eat him? We will never know.

VOCABULARY: *transmitter – Sender

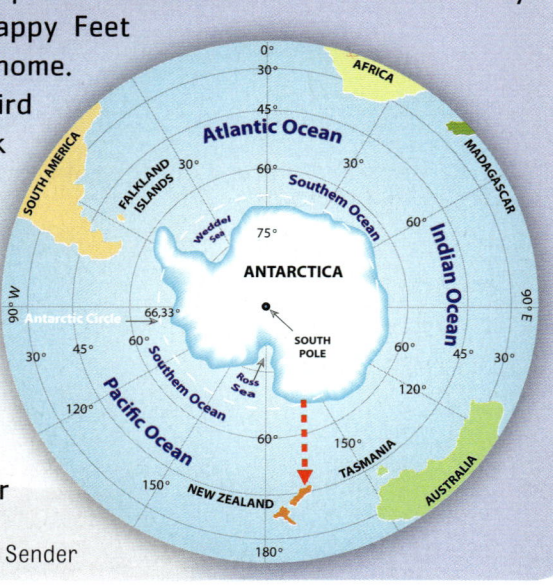

11 **How many of these tasks can you do?**

1 The penguin wasn't a very long way from home.   T / F
2 Penguins often swim more than 2,500 km.   T / F
3 The penguin was trying to eat sand.   T / F

4 The penguin was quite sick because he ....
5 The penguin stayed .... for a while.
6 Before they let Happy Feet go, they .... on him.

7 Where did they release Happy Feet? ....
8 What happened to Happy Feet? ....
9 How are emperor penguins different from other penguins? ....

CD4 25/26

12 **Check your answers with a partner. Then listen to the story.**

 WB p. 132

Writing for your Portfolio

Read the texts. Then write your own text.

A

I haven't got a pet. We live in a flat and my parents always say no. I'd like a dog. My parents say dogs are a lot of work, but I don't think so. One of my friends has got a dog. He doesn't spend a lot of time on it. We sometimes play with it in the park.

B

My pet is a rat. He's brown and his name is Fluff. I often play with Fluff. He likes it when I put him inside my shirt. Some of my friends are scared of Fluff. When I take Fluff out of my shirt or jacket, they run away. I don't understand that. I clean the cage every second day and I put in clean water twice every day. At night, Fluff sleeps in his cage. When I get up at the weekend, I put him in the pocket of my pyjamas. Then I go into the kitchen and hug my mum. When she feels Fluff, she screams.

 GRAMMAR *So do/have I. – Neither do/have I.*

Read the examples.

A *Rats! No way.* **I've got** *a fear of rats.*
B **So have** *I.*

A *I* **haven't thought** *of a name for her yet.*
B **Neither have** *I.*

A *I* **think** *we're going to find something in here.*
B **So do** *I.*

A *I* **don't** *really* **like** *cats.*
B **Neither do** *I.*

 Complete the sentences with *neither* or *so*.

Du verwendest [1]............................ *do/have I*, um einer positiven Aussage zuzustimmen.

Du verwendest [2]............................ *do/have I*, um einer negativen Aussage zuzustimmen.

MORE fun with **Fido!**

Why doesn't she clean my bowl?

Why doesn't he tidy up my basket?

I have to do everything myself.

Kids in NYC 4

The missing cat

Before you watch

1 Write the words under the pictures.

> **Note:**
> cell phone = American English
> mobile (phone) = British English

market
cell phone
reward

1 ....   2 ....   3 ....

2 In what order do you think these pictures come in the DVD? Write 1–4 in the boxes.

MISSING

Three year-old tabby cat called Tiger.

If you find my cat, please phone
(646) 859-1237.

BIG REWARD!

3 In pairs, invent a story that goes with the pictures in **2**.

Watch the story

DVD **4** Check your answers to **2**.

5 Complete the sentences.

1 Steve and Jenny see ....

2 They want to ....

3 First they want to look .... and ....

4 Then Jenny has an idea. She wants to look for the cat ....

5 She thinks they might find the cat there because ....

6 Complete the dialogue.

| think |
| look |
| see |
| get |
| check |

Jenny ¹........................... that cat? Doesn't it ²........................... like Tiger?

Steve No. I don't ³........................... so. But look. There, behind that box. Let's ⁴........................... with the picture.

Jenny Yeah, it looks a bit like Tiger. ⁵........................... him.

Steve Here, kitty, kitty. Here, kitty. Got you, Tiger.

7 Circle T (*True*) or F (*False*).

1 Jenny and Steve find Tiger at the fish market.   T / F

2 They find Tiger under a car.   T / F

3 They put Tiger in a bag.   T / F

4 The man at the fish market has a cat and a dog.   T / F

5 Jenny and Steve give Tiger to the man.   T / F

6 The woman gives Jenny and Steve a $20 reward.   T / F

Everyday English

8 Complete the dialogues.

| I don't get it. |
| Got you, |
| What for? |
| Right here. |

Take a photo of the cat.

....

Have you got the photo?

....

I'm hungry.

The Fulton Fish Market? ....

Hungry! That's it! We have to go to the Fulton Fish Market.

.... Tiger.

1 **Everybody is waiting for the holidays. So is Marcus White. Read his diary. What day of the week do these things happen?**

1 Marcus wants a new best friend.
2 Marcus runs a race.
3 Marcus gets told off in the school assembly.

4 Marcus makes a list.
5 Marcus is late for school.
6 Marcus gets his test results.

Sunday

Fantastic. Great. Wonderful. Finally – it's here!
The last week of school for six weeks.
Six weeks of holiday!
Oh, what a happy week!
Things to do for my holidays
• Paint my bedroom black.
• Do karate lessons.
• Beat my dad at chess.
• Read all the Percy Jackson books – again!
• Get fit!
• Build a new go-kart with Sam
  (my best friend this week).
• Spend time with Jenny – this might be difficult
  because I've never spoken to her in my life.
  I'll definitely need a plan for this.

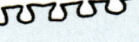

Monday

School was a bit boring.
I got my test results. 'C' for everything.
'C' isn't so bad. It's better than 'D'.
I explained this to Dad. He didn't
really understand. I don't think
he's very happy at the moment.
I think he has got problems at work.
I forgot to ask Jenny for her
phone number.
I must do this tomorrow.
Four days to go!

Tuesday

I had a big argument with my dad at
breakfast today. He says I can't paint my
bedroom black. It has got to be blue. Blue!
My dad doesn't understand teenagers.
I'm not going to speak to him for a week.
School was better. We played games
all day. I think our teachers are very tired.
There was one bad thing. Sam had some news
for me – Jenny is going to live in London.
She's not going to be at our school next term.
"What!?" I screamed.
Then Sam said it was a joke.
I think I need a new best friend.

That's me! :(

Wednesday

Another bad breakfast. I asked my dad for £10 to buy some wood for my go-kart. Dad said "Have you forgotten? You're not speaking to me." He's so smart. So I asked Mum because I'm still speaking to her. She said "Ask your dad." Parents are complicated.

It was Sports Day at school today. I was in the 2,000 metres – five times around the running track! I got a new school record – the slowest time in the history of Sports Day. It was the last race of the day. When I finished, nobody was there. That was a shame because I wanted to ask Jenny for her phone number. I must do this tomorrow.

Thursday

I got up half an hour late today because I didn't want to see Dad at breakfast. The plan worked. I didn't see him. The only problem was I was half an hour late for school.
My teacher wasn't happy.
We had the school play this afternoon.
I don't really remember what the story was about. But Jenny was in it. She was great. After the play everybody wanted to talk to her. I couldn't ask her for her phone number. There were too many people. I'm going to be in the school play next year.

JENNY

Friday

Today we had the final assembly with Mr Hill, the headmaster. He read out all the names of the best students. The best students at Maths, the best students at Science, at Sport, at French, etc. Then he shouted out my name – not because I'm best at anything (unfortunately), but because I was talking to my friend. Everyone looked at me. Jenny looked at me. I think she smiled. I went red. I didn't ask Jenny for her phone number, but I've got a new plan. I'm going to talk to Jenny next term. I'll be thirteen then. I read in a book that talking to girls is easier when you're thirteen! But I wrote a holiday song for her and uploaded it on the internet. I hope Jenny likes it.

School life in the USA

1 Read about the different methods of schooling in the USA.

The American school system

School	Age
Elementary school (Grades 1–8)	6–13
High school (Grades 9–12)	14–17

Home schooling

In the United States, there are thousands of children who don't go to school but learn from home. In 2012, there were 1.8 million children 'home schooling'.

The school system

Hi, my name's Susannah and I'm American. There are five types of schools in America: public schools, charter schools, private schools, religious schools and home schooling.
I go to a charter school. Charter schools are run by* a private organization and you don't pay. There are over 6,100 of these schools in America now.

VOCABULARY
*run by – geführt von

Home schooling

Hello, my name is Mark and I have home schooling. It's fantastic! I do all my lessons at home on the computer. I don't have to wear a uniform and I don't have to catch the school bus. And of course I don't have homework after school!

CD4 27

2 Listen to Amy talk about her high school prom and answer the questions.

The high school prom

Did you know?

* In American schools, there is a junior and a senior prom.
* The senior prom is at the end of the last year of high school.
* Traditionally, boys wear suits and ties and girls wear ball gowns*.
* The girl's date* for the evening gives her flowers to wear.

VOCABULARY: *ball gown – Ballkleid; **date** – Verabredung

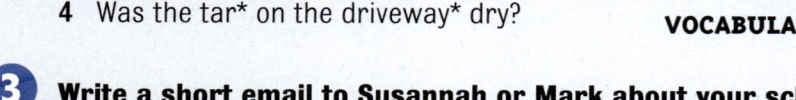

1 What did Amy wear to the prom?
2 Who asked her to the prom?
3 How did she travel to her date's house?
4 Was the tar* on the driveway* dry?

5 How much did her shoes cost?
6 How long did it take her mother to get the tar out of her hair?

VOCABULARY: *tar – Teer; **driveway** – Auffahrt/Einfahrt

3 Write a short email to Susannah or Mark about your school.

POPULAR AMERICAN SPORTS

 1 Match the sports to the correct pictures.

> **1** baseball **2** American football **3** basketball

 2 Do the quiz. Then listen and check your answers.

CD4 28

1 Which sport is the oldest?
  a) American football
  b) basketball
  c) baseball

2 Which sport are these terms from: a pitcher, a home run and a pennant?
  a) baseball   b) football   c) rounders

3 There are ... players in a basketball team.
  a) 5   b) 6   c) 7

4 How long does a baseball match usually last?
  a) 50 minutes
  b) 90 minutes
  c) more than three hours

5 What is a baseball field called?
  a) a star   b) a diamond   c) a square

6 The Cincinnati Red Stockings were the first professional ... team.
  a) basketball
  b) baseball
  c) American football

7 How many points do you score for a 'touchdown' in American football?
  a) 5   b) 6   c) 1

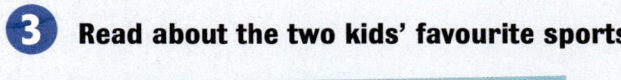 **3** Read about the two kids' favourite sports.

> **Note:**
> favorite = American English; favourite = British English

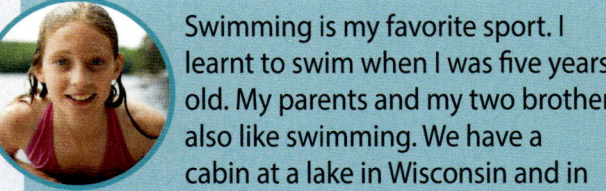 Swimming is my favorite sport. I learnt to swim when I was five years old. My parents and my two brothers also like swimming. We have a cabin at a lake in Wisconsin and in summer we spend three weeks there. We swim before breakfast and in the afternoon. I also love swimming in the lake when there is a full moon. I love swimming because it is good for my body. And there is another thing: when I swim slowly in our lake, good ideas often come to my mind.

 My favorite sport is badminton. I love badminton because it is good exercise and a lot of my best friends play. I also love to watch badminton matches on TV. Unfortunately, the US have not won any medals in badminton at the Olympic Games. We have a school team that plays against other schools, but I'm not on it. I train hard so maybe I will be on the team next year.

 4 Now write a short text about your favourite sport.

Life in the USA

American national parks

THE REDWOOD NATIONAL PARK

The Redwood Trees

Height:

Number of years to grow:

Age:

CD4 29

1 Listen to Emma talking about her visit to the Redwood National Park. Complete the information about the trees.

2 Read about the Colorado Rockies and Yellowstone National Park. Then answer the questions.

1 Who lived in the Rocky Mountains?
2 How many mountains are there in the Rocky Mountain chain?
3 Why are the Colorado Rockies called 'the roof of America'?
4 What is Yellowstone famous for?
5 How often does Yellowstone erupt?

Did you know?

The first national park in the USA was Yellowstone Park. It opened in 1872 and was the first national park in the world.

THE COLORADO ROCKIES

The Rocky Mountains were the home of the Apache, Blackfoot and Sioux, and stretch from* Alaska to New Mexico. The Rockies are high! There are 107 mountains in the range* which are over 3,000 meters. The Colorado Rockies are the tallest. People call them 'the roof of America' because the tops of the mountains here are more than 4,000 meters. The Colorado Rockies are a popular area to go mountain climbing, fishing, hunting and skiing.

VOCABULARY: *stretch from – erstrecken sich von; range – Gebirgskette

YELLOWSTONE NATIONAL PARK

This park is in Wyoming and is older than the other national parks in America. It is famous for its hot springs* and for its grizzly bears. Some of the bears are huge. They can weigh 700 kg. There are also wolves and bison in the park.

The park is 8,980 square km. Before human history, a huge volcanic eruption* covered* the area with ash*. Yellowstone is the name of a volcano too and it usually erupts every 600,000 years. The last eruption was 640,000 years ago!

VOCABULARY: *hot springs – heiße Quellen; volcanic eruption – Vulkanausbruch; covered – bedeckt; ash – Asche

3 Work in groups. Choose an Austrian national park. Collect pictures and information and do a poster presentation.

Extreme weather

1 Which photograph shows a hurricane and which a tornado?

HURRICANES
– THE FACTS –

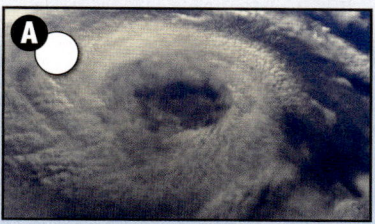

- Hurricanes come from the sea.
- They travel at 119 km per hour.
- They can be from 100 to 1,600 km wide.
- Hurricanes are given girls' and boys' names, for example Hurricane Andrew.

2 TORNADOES
– THE FACTS –

- There are about 800 to 1,200 tornadoes a year in America.
- They are usually in Northwest Texas, Oklahoma and Kansas.
- They circle around* at speeds of 320 to 800 km per hour.
- They are a dark grey colour because they pick up* soil and other objects.

VOCABULARY: *circle around – sich drehen; **pick up** – aufheben/mitnehmen

2 Read Mary Ann's story and answer the questions.

1 When did Hurricane Katrina hit Florida?
2 What happened after the rooms were filled with water?
3 What happened to the building?
4 How fast was the wind?
5 How far did the water carry Mary Ann?

CD4 30

3 Listen and circle T (*True*) or F (*False*).

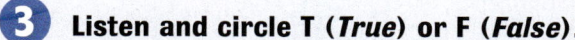

The Storm Chasers!
Most people run away or hide from hurricanes and tornadoes but some people in America chase them! You can even go on a storm-chasing holiday!

1 The storm-chasing tours are not safe.	T / F
2 There is a good chance you will see a tornado.	T / F
3 The tornadoes are always far from the hotel.	T / F
4 You can't take photos of the tornadoes.	T / F
5 If there aren't any tornadoes, they go sightseeing.	T / F

Mary Ann's Story

In 2005, Hurricane Katrina hit my three-storey block of flats near Hallandale Beach in Florida. First, the sea hit the building and all the windows broke. Then the room filled with water. Five minutes later, my bed was up by the ceiling. Then it went out of the window. It was dark and the wind was making a really loud noise. I was terrified. The building was falling down* all around me. The wind was awful. It reached a speed* of more than 300 km per hour. I was cut and bleeding* from head to toe. Finally, someone found me 8 km from my house and they took me to hospital.

VOCABULARY
*was falling down – stürzte ein; **reach a speed** – eine Geschwindigkeit erreichen; **was bleeding** – blutete

GRAMMAR

PRESENT TENSE

Present simple (Einfache Gegenwartsform)

Die Form des Present simple ist für alle Personen gleich.

Ausnahme: In der 3. Person Singular wird ein **-s** angehängt.

Positive Aussagen	Negative Aussagen	Fragen	Kurzantworten	
I **like** London.	I **don't (do not) like** London.	**Do/Don't** I **like** London?	Yes, I **do**.	No, I **don't**.
You **like** London.	You **don't (do not) like** London.	**Do/Don't** you **like** London?	Yes, you **do**.	No, you **don't**.
He **likes** London.	He **doesn't (does not) like** London.	**Does/Doesn't** he **like** London?	Yes, he **does**.	No, he **doesn't**.
She **likes** London.	She **doesn't (does not) like** London.	**Does/Doesn't** she **like** London?	Yes, she **does**.	No, she **doesn't**.
It **likes** fish.	It **doesn't (does not) like** fish.	**Does/Doesn't** it **like** fish?	Yes, it **does**.	No, it **doesn't**.
We **like** London.	We **don't (do not) like** London.	**Do/Don't** we **like** London?	Yes, we **do**.	No, we **don't**.
You **like** London.	You **don't (do not) like** London.	**Do/Don't** you **like** London?	Yes, you **do**.	No, you **don't**.
They **like** London.	They **don't (do not) like** London.	**Do/Don't** they **like** London?	Yes, they **do**.	No, they **don't**.

Present continuous / progressive (Verlaufsform, -ing-Form)

Das Present continuous wird mit der richtigen Form von **be** und der **-ing**-Form des Verbs gebildet.

Positive Aussagen	Negative Aussagen	Fragen	Kurzantworten	
I'm (I am) **playing** golf.	I'm **not** (I am **not**) **playing** golf.	**Am** I / **Am** I **not playing** golf?	Yes, I **am**.	No, I'm **not**.
You're (You are) **playing** golf.	You **aren't** (You're **not**) **playing** golf.	**Are/Aren't** you **playing** golf?	Yes, you **are**.	No, you **aren't**. / No, you're **not**.
He's (He is) **playing** golf.	He **isn't** (He's **not**) **playing** golf.	**Is/Isn't** he **playing** golf?	Yes, he **is**.	No, he **isn't**. / No, he's **not**.
She's (She is) **playing** golf.	She **isn't** (She's **not**) **playing** golf.	**Is/Isn't** she **playing** golf?	Yes, she **is**.	No, she **isn't**. / No, she's **not**.
It's (It is) **raining**.	It **isn't** (It's **not**) **raining**.	**Is/Isn't** it **raining**?	Yes, it **is**.	No, it **isn't**. / No, it's **not**.
We're (We are) **playing** golf.	We **aren't** (We're **not**) **playing** golf.	**Are/Aren't** we **playing** golf?	Yes, we **are**.	No, we **aren't**. / No, we're **not**.
You're (You are) **playing** golf.	You **aren't** (You're **not**) **playing** golf.	**Are/Aren't** you **playing** golf?	Yes, you **are**.	No, you **aren't**. / No, you're **not**.
They're (They are) **playing** golf.	They **aren't** (They're **not**) **playing** golf.	**Are/Aren't** they **playing** golf?	Yes, they **are**.	No, they **aren't**. / No, they're **not**.

Present perfect – Regular verbs (Regelmäßige Verben)

Das Present perfect wird gebildet mit **has** / **have** und der dritten Form (*past participle* Form) des Verbs (siehe "irregular verbs").

Positive Aussagen		Negative Aussagen			Fragen			Kurzantworten	
I've (I have)		I	**haven't (have not)**		Have/ Haven't	I		Yes, I **have**.	No, I **haven't**.
You've (You have)		You				you		Yes, you **have**.	No, you **haven't**.
He's (He has)		He				he		Yes, he **has**.	No, he **hasn't**.
She's (She has)	finished.	She	**hasn't (has not)**	finished.	Has/ Hasn't	she	finished?	Yes, she **has**.	No, she **hasn't**.
It's (It has)		It				it		Yes, it **has**.	No, it **hasn't**.
We've (We have)		We				we		Yes, we **have**.	No, we **haven't**.
You've (You have)		You	**haven't (have not)**		Have/ Haven't	you		Yes, you **have**.	No, you **haven't**.
They've (They have)		They				they		Yes, they **have**.	No, they **haven't**.

Present perfect + *already / yet*

Already stellst du zwischen **have / has** und die dritte Form des Verbs, **yet** stellst du an das Satzende.

I've **already washed** the car.	We've **already seen** this film.	I **haven't done** my homework **yet**.	She **hasn't told** him **yet**.

Present perfect + *ever / never*

Ever und **never** stellst du zwischen **have / has** und die dritte Form des Verbs.

Have you **ever been** to Hollywood?	**Has** she **ever met** a famous person?	I've **never been** to Hollywood.	She **has never met** a famous person.

PAST TENSE

Past simple – *was / were* (Einfache Vergangenheitsform)

Das Past simple von **be** wird wie folgt gebildet:

Positive Aussagen	Negative Aussagen	Fragen	Kurzantworten	
I **was** tired.	I **wasn't (was not)** tired.	**Was/Wasn't** I tired?	Yes, I **was**.	No, I **wasn't (was not)**.
You **were** tired.	You **weren't (were not)** tired.	**Were/Weren't** you tired?	Yes, you **were**.	No, you **weren't (were not)**.
He **was** nice.	He **wasn't (was not)** nice.	**Was/Wasn't** he nice?	Yes, he **was**.	No, he **wasn't (was not)**.
She **was** nice.	She **wasn't (was not)** nice.	**Was/Wasn't** she nice?	Yes, she **was**.	No, she **wasn't (was not)**.
It **was** blue.	It **wasn't (was not)** blue.	**Was/Wasn't** it blue?	Yes, it **was**.	No, it **wasn't (was not)**.
We **were** busy.	We **weren't (were not)** busy.	**Were/Weren't** we busy?	Yes, we **were**.	No, we **weren't (were not)**.
You **were** busy.	You **weren't (were not)** busy.	**Were/Weren't** you busy?	Yes, you **were**.	No, you **weren't (were not)**.
They **were** busy.	They **weren't (were not)** busy.	**Were/Weren't** they busy?	Yes, they **were**.	No, they **weren't (were not)**.

Past time markers

Bei diesen Wörtern verwendest du beim Erzählen das Past simple:

then	ago	later	after	one day	finally

Past simple – Regular verbs (Regelmäßige Verben)

Das Past simple wird bei regelmäßigen Verben mit **-ed** gebildet, bei unregelmäßigen Verben mit der zweiten Form (siehe "irregular verbs").

Positive Aussagen	Negative Aussagen
I lik**ed** London.	I **didn't (did not) like** London.
You laugh**ed** a lot.	You **didn't (did not) laugh** a lot.
He walk**ed** home.	He **didn't (did not) walk** home.
She look**ed** good.	She **didn't (did not) look** good.
It turn**ed** around.	It **didn't (did not) turn** around.
We jump**ed** into the water.	We **didn't (did not) jump** into the water.
You cook**ed** dinner.	You **didn't (did not) cook** dinner.
They lov**ed** the film.	They **didn't (did not) love** the film.

Irregular verbs (Unregelmäßige Verben)

Hier findest du eine Liste mit einer Auswahl der wichtigsten unregelmäßigen Verben:

Present	Past simple	Past participle	Übersetzung
be	was/were	been	*sein*
become	became	become	*werden*
begin	began	begun	*beginnen*
blow	blew	blown	*blasen*
break	broke	broken	*brechen*
bring	brought	brought	*bringen*
build	built	built	*bauen*
buy	bought	bought	*kaufen*
catch	caught	caught	*fangen*
choose	chose	chosen	*(aus-)wählen*
come	came	come	*kommen*
cut	cut	cut	*schneiden*
dig	dug	dug	*graben*
do	did	done	*tun, machen*
draw	drew	drawn	*zeichnen*
dream	dreamt (dreamed)	dreamt (dreamed)	*träumen*
drink	drank	drunk	*trinken*
drive	drove	driven	*fahren; treiben*
eat	ate	eaten	*essen*
fall (asleep)	fell (asleep)	fallen (asleep)	*fallen (einschlafen)*
feel	felt	felt	*fühlen*
fight	fought	fought	*kämpfen*
find	found	found	*finden*
fly	flew	flown	*fliegen*
forget	forgot	forgotten	*vergessen*
get	got	got	*bekommen; werden*
get up	got up	got up	*aufstehen*
give	gave	given	*geben*
go	went	gone	*gehen, fahren*
hang	hung	hung	*hängen*
have	had	had	*haben*
hear	heard	heard	*hören*
hide	hid	hidden	*(sich) verstecken*
hit	hit	hit	*schlagen*
hold	held	held	*(fest-)halten*
hurt	hurt	hurt	*(sich) verletzen, schmerzen*
know	knew	known	*wissen; kennen*

Present	Past simple	Past participle	Übersetzung
lay	laid	laid	*legen*
learn	learnt (learned)	learnt (learned)	*lernen*
leave	left	left	*verlassen*
let	let	let	*lassen*
lie	lay	lain	*liegen*
lose	lost	lost	*verlieren*
make	made	made	*machen*
meet	met	met	*treffen*
put	put	put	*legen; setzen; stellen*
read	read [red]	read [red]	*lesen*
ride	rode	ridden	*reiten; fahren*
ring	rang	rung	*läuten*
run	ran	run	*laufen*
say	said	said	*sagen*
see	saw	seen	*sehen*
send	sent	sent	*senden, schicken*
shoot	shot	shot	*schießen*
show	showed	shown (showed)	*zeigen*
sing	sang	sung	*singen*
sink	sank (sunk)	sunk	*untergehen, sinken*
sit	sat	sat	*sitzen, sich setzen*
sleep	slept	slept	*schlafen*
smell	smelt (smelled)	smelt (smelled)	*riechen*
speak	spoke	spoken	*sprechen, sagen*
spend	spent	spent	*verbringen; ausgeben*
stand	stood	stood	*stehen*
steal	stole	stolen	*stehlen*
swim	swam	swum	*schwimmen*
take off	took off	taken off	*ausziehen*
take	took	taken	*nehmen*
teach	taught	taught	*lehren, unterrichten*
tell	told	told	*sagen, erzählen*
think	thought	thought	*denken*
wake (up)	woke (up)	woken (up)	*(auf-)wachen*
win	won	won	*gewinnen*
write	wrote	written	*schreiben*

FUTURE TENSE

going to-future (Zukunft mit *going to*)

Die *going to*-future wird mit einer Form von **be** und **going to** und der Grundform des Vollverbs gebildet.

Positive Aussagen		Negative Aussagen		Fragen		Kurzantworten
I'm		I'm not		Am I / Aren't I		Yes, I **am**. / No, **I'm not**.
You're		You **aren't** (You're **not**)		Are/Aren't you		Yes, you **are**. / No, you **aren't** (you're **not**).
He's	going to play football.	He **isn't** (He's **not**)	going to play football.	Is/Isn't he	going to play football?	Yes, he **is**. / No, he **isn't** (he's **not**).
She's		She **isn't** (She's **not**)		Is/Isn't she		Yes, she **is**. / No, she **isn't** (she's **not**).
We're		We **aren't** (We're **not**)		Are/Aren't we		Yes, we **are**. / No, we **aren't** (we're **not**).
You're		You **aren't** (You're **not**)		Are/Aren't you		Yes, you **are**. / No, you **aren't** (you're **not**).
They're		They **aren't** (They're **not**)		Are/Aren't they		Yes, they **are**. / No, they **aren't** (they're **not**).

will-future

Die *will*-future verwendest du, wenn du etwas vorhersagen möchtest oder versprichst.

Positive Aussagen	Negative Aussagen	Fragen	Kurzantworten	
I'll (I will) see you tomorrow.	I **won't** (will **not**) see you tomorrow.	**Will** I see you tomorrow?	Yes, I **will**.	No, I **won't** (will **not**).
You'll (You will) see me tomorrow.	You **won't** (will **not**) see me tomorrow.	**Will** you see me tomorrow?	Yes, you **will**.	No, you **won't** (will **not**).
He'll (He will) see her tomorrow.	He **won't** (will **not**) see her tomorrow.	**Will** he see her tomorrow?	Yes, he **will**.	No, he **won't** (will **not**).
She'll (She will) see him tomorrow.	She **won't** (will **not**) see him tomorrow.	**Will** she see him tomorrow?	Yes, she **will**.	No, she **won't** (will **not**).
It'll (It will) rain tomorrow.	It **won't** (will **not**) rain tomorrow.	**Will** it rain tomorrow?	Yes, it **will**.	No, it **won't** (will **not**).
We'll (We will) see you tomorrow.	We **won't** (will **not**) see you tomorrow.	**Will** we see you tomorrow?	Yes, we **will**.	No, we **won't** (will **not**).
You'll (You will) see me tomorrow.	You **won't** (will **not**) see me tomorrow.	**Will** you see me tomorrow?	Yes, you **will**.	No, you **won't** (will **not**).
They'll (They will) see you tomorrow.	They **won't** (will **not**) see you tomorrow.	**Will** they see you tomorrow?	Yes, they **will**.	No, they **won't** (will **not**).

BESONDERE VERBEN

to be – affirmative, negative

Das Verb **be** wird wie das deutsche Verb **sein** verwendet.

Positive Aussagen	Negative Aussagen
I'm (**I am**) tired.	I'm **not** tired.
You're (**You are**) clever.	You **aren't**/You're **not** clever.
He's (**He is**) nice.	He **isn't**/He's **not** nice.
She's (**She is**) in class 3B.	She **isn't**/She's **not** in class 3B.
It's (**It is**) blue.	It **isn't**/It's **not** blue.
We're (**We are**) busy.	We **aren't**/We're **not** busy.
We're (**We are**) busy.	We **aren't**/We're **not** busy.
They're (**They are**) twelve.	They **aren't**/They're **not** twelve.

Questions with *to be*

Fragen	Kurzantworten	
Am I tired?	Yes, I **am**.	No, I'**m not**.
Are/Aren't you tired?	Yes, you **are**.	No, you **aren't**. / No, you'**re not**.
Is/Isn't he nice?	Yes, he **is**.	No, he **isn't**. / No, he'**s not**.
Is/Isn't she in class 3B?	Yes, she **is**.	No, she **isn't**. / No, she'**s not**.
Is/Isn't it blue?	Yes, it **is**.	No, it **isn't**. / No, it'**s not**.
Are/Aren't we busy?	Yes, we **are**.	No, we **aren't**. / No, we'**re not**.
Are/Aren't you busy?	Yes, you **are**.	No, you **aren't**. / No, you'**re not**.
Are/Aren't they twelve?	Yes, they **are**.	No, they **aren't**. / No, they'**re not**.

have got / haven't got

Have got wird wie das deutsche Verb **haben** (besitzen) verwendet.
Die richtige Form für die 3. Person der Gegenwart (**he**/**she**/**it**) ist **has got**.

Positive Aussagen	Negative Aussagen	Fragen	Kurzantworten	
I'**ve got** (I **have got**) a dog.	I **haven't got** (**have not got**) a dog.	**Have/Haven't** I **got** a dog?	Yes, I **have**.	No, I **haven't**.
You'**ve got** (You **have got**) a dog.	You **haven't got** (**have not got**) a dog.	**Have/Haven't** you **got** a dog?	Yes, you **have**.	No, you **haven't**.
He'**s got** (He **has got**) a dog.	He **hasn't got** (**has not got**) a dog.	**Has/Hasn't** he **got** a dog?	Yes, he **has**.	No, he **hasn't**.
She'**s got** (She **has got**) a dog.	She **hasn't got** (**has not got**) a dog.	**Has/Hasn't** she **got** a dog?	Yes, she **has**.	No, she **hasn't**.
It'**s got** (It **has got**) big ears.	It **hasn't got** (**has not got**) big ears.	**Has/Hasn't** it **got** big ears?	Yes, it **has**.	No, it **hasn't**.
We'**ve got** (We **have got**) a dog.	We **haven't got** (**have not got**) a dog.	**Have/Haven't** we **got** a dog?	Yes, we **have**.	No, we **haven't**.
You'**ve got** (You **have got**) a dog.	You **haven't got** (**have not got**) a dog.	**Have/Haven't** you **got** a dog?	Yes, you **have**.	No, you **haven't**.
They'**ve got** (They **have got**) a dog.	They **haven't got** (**have not got**) a dog.	**Have/Haven't** they **got** a dog?	Yes, they **have**.	No, they **haven't**.

there is / there are

There is / **there are** wird verwendet, um auszudrücken, dass etwas vorhanden ist, oder dass es etwas gibt.

There's a monster in the tree. (= **There is** a monster in the tree.)
There are three frogs on the table.

Modal verbs (Modalverben)

Die wichtigsten Modalverben sind **should** / **shouldn't**, **have to** / **don't have to**, **might** / **might not**, **must** / **mustn't**, **can** / **can't**, **could** / **couldn't**, **will** / **won't**, **would** / **wouldn't**, **shall** / **shall not**, and **may** / **may not**.

I			I	have to/don't have to	
You	can/can't (cannot)		You		
He			He		
She	must/mustn't	come today.	She	has to/doesn't have to	go to school.
It	should/shouldn't		It		
We			We		
You	might/might not (mightn't)		You	have to/don't have to	
They			They		

can / can't

Can ist ein Modalverb und wird deshalb immer in Verbindung mit einem Vollverb verwendet.
Die Verneinung wird gebildet als **cannot** oder **can't**.

Positive Aussagen	Negative Aussagen	Fragen	Kurzantworten	
I **can speak** French.	I **can't** (**cannot**) **speak** French.	**Can/Can't** I speak French?	Yes, I **can**.	No, I **can't**.
You **can speak** French.	You **can't** (**cannot**) **speak** French.	**Can/Can't** you speak French?	Yes, you **can**.	No, you **can't**.
He **can speak** French.	He **can't** (**cannot**) **speak** French.	**Can/Can't** he speak French?	Yes, he **can**.	No, he **can't**.
She **can speak** French.	She **can't** (**cannot**) **speak** French.	**Can/Can't** she speak French?	Yes, she **can**.	No, she **can't**.
It **can run** fast.	It **can't** (**cannot**) **run** fast.	**Can/Can't** it run fast?	Yes, it **can**.	No, it **can't**.
We **can speak** French.	We **can't** (**cannot**) **speak** French.	**Can/Can't** we speak French?	Yes, we **can**.	No, we **can't**.
You **can speak** French.	You **can't** (**cannot**) **speak** French.	**Can/Can't** you speak French?	Yes, you **can**.	No, you **can't**.
They **can speak** French.	They **can't** (**cannot**) **speak** French.	**Can/Can't** they speak French?	Yes, they **can**.	No, they **can't**.

like (doing)

Mit **like doing** sagst du, ob jemand gerne etwas macht oder sich gerne mit etwas beschäftigt. Gebildet wird es mit der einfachen Gegenwartsform von **like** + der **-ing**-Form des folgenden Verbs.

Samantha **doesn't like reading**, but she **likes listening** to music.	James **likes running**, but he **doesn't like swimming**.

ADVERBS (ADVERBIEN)

Adverbs of manner (Adverbien der Art und Weise)

Mit Adverbien der Art und Weise beschreibst du, wie jemand etwas macht. Regelmäßige Adverbien werden mit **-ly** gebildet.

Regular (+ -ly) (Regelmäßig)				Irregular (Unregelmäßig)	
bad – bad**ly**	quiet – quiet**ly**	happy – happi**ly**		fast – fast	good – well

Adverbs of frequency (Häufigkeitsadverbien)

0%	→	→	→	100%		
never	sometimes	often	usually	always	We **sometimes** go to the cinema on Fridays.	
					She's **always** happy.	

IMPERATIVES (IMPERATIV / BEFEHLSFORMEN)

Die Befehlsform ist immer gleich wie die Grundform des Verbs (ohne **to**).
Die Verneinung wird mit **do not** (**don't**) + Grundform gebildet.

Run!	Don't run!
Sit down.	Don't sit down.
Open the window.	Don't open the window.

Indefinite article (Unbestimmter Artikel)

Der unbestimmte Artikel **a** wird vor einem zählbaren Hauptwort verwendet, **an** wird vor Selbstlauten verwendet.

a bike		Vor den Vokalen (Selbstlauten): a, e, i, o, u
a teacher		an egg [ən ˈeg]
a dog		an apple [ən ˈæpl]

Definite article (Bestimmter Artikel)

Der bestimmte Artikel, der wie **der/die/das** im Deutschen verwendet wird, ist im Englischen immer **the**.

the bike	**the** teacher	**the** dog

NOUNS (HAUPTWÖRTER)

Plural nouns – Irregular plurals (Pluralformen)

Regelmäßige Pluralformen werden gebildet, indem ein **-s** angehängt wird.
Bei unregelmäßigen Formen wird am Wortende **-y** zu **-ies** (Vokal vor **-y** bleibt **-y**) und **-f** oder **-fe** zu **-ves**.
Aber es gibt auch Ausnahmen, die ganz andere Formen haben und keiner Regel folgen. Diese lernst du am besten auswendig, um sie dir gut zu merken.

Regelmäßig		
dog – dog**s**	snake – snake**s**	cat – cat**s**

Unregelmäßig						
baby – bab**ies**	leaf – lea**ves**	woman – women	person – people	mouse – mice	foot – feet	child - children

whose + possessive 's (Genitiv)

Wenn du fragen willst, wem etwas gehört, verwendest du **whose**.
Wenn du mit einem Namen oder Nomen antwortest, fügst du das Possessive **'s** an.
Wenn der Name oder das Nomen im Plural steht oder auf **-s** endet, setzt du ans Ende des Wortes ein **'** (Apostroph).
Bei Wörtern mit unregelmäßiger Pluralform hängst du ebenfalls das Possessive **'s** an.

Whose is this book?	It's **Amanda's** (book).	**Whose** is this room?	It's the **teachers'** (room).
Whose book is this?	It's **Les'** (book).	**Whose** is this room?	It's the **children's** (room).

Personal pronouns – Subject and object pronouns (Personalpronomen)

Personalpronomen können als Subjekt oder Objekt eines Satzes verwendet werden.

Das unpersönliche deutsche **man** kann im Englischen durch **you**, **they** oder **one** ausgedrückt werden.

Subjekt	I	you	he	she	it	we	you	they	Objekt	me	you	him	her	it	us	you	them

Possessives

Possessives stehen immer vor dem Hauptwort und zeigen an, wem oder zu wem etwas gehört.

I	you	he	she	it	we	you	they
my	your	his	her	its	our	your	their

Possessive pronouns (Possessivpronomen)

Besitzanzeigende Fürwörter zeigen an, wem etwas gehört.

It's my book. It's **mine**.	It's his book. It's **his**.	It's our book. It's **ours**.
It's your book. It's **yours**.	It's her book. It's **hers**.	It's their book. It's **theirs**.

Question words (Fragewörter)

Who	What	Where	How often
Who is she?	**What**'s your name?	**Where** are you now?	**How often** do you go to the cinema?
Who are you?	**What** eats insects?	**Where** do you live?	
Who likes ice cream?	**What** does your dog eat?		
Who do you like?			

this / that – these / those

This / **that**, **these** / **those** sind Demonstrativpronomen, die verwendet werden, um Nähe oder Ferne auszudrücken.

This / **these** beschreibt etwas in der Nähe, **that** / **those** etwas weiter Entferntes.

I like **this** sweater here.	I like **that** sweater over there.	I like **these** shoes here.	I like **those** shoes over there.

one – ones

Wenn du ein Hauptwort nicht wiederholen willst, kannst du es durch **one** / **ones** ersetzen.

What **book** are you reading? **One** about a man travelling around Africa.
What **kind of books** do you like? **Ones** about travel.

some – any

Wenn du etwas Unzählbares beschreibst oder nach etwas fragst, von dem du weißt, dass es vorhanden ist, verwendest du **some**.

Wenn du fragen willst, ob es etwas gibt, oder wenn du sagen willst, dass es etwas nicht gibt, verwendest du **any**.

some	any	
We've got **some** cheese.	We haven't got **any** cheese.	Is there **any** milk in the fridge?
I've got **some** money.	I haven't got **any** money.	Have we got **any** strawberries?
Can I have **some** soup?	There aren't **any** onions in the kitchen.	Do they sell **any** sweets?

PREPOSITIONS (PRÄPOSITIONEN)

Präpositionen stehen vor einem Hauptwort oder Pronomen und zeigen die Richtung, den Ort (siehe "prepositions of place"), oder die Zeit (siehe "time prepositions") an.

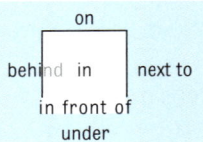

Time prepositions (Präpositionen der Zeit)

My birthday is **on** February 12th / May 28th / September 5th.	The film starts **at** 7 o'clock / half past eight / six forty-five.
The concert's **on** Thursday, July 15th.	We have Maths **in** the morning / **in** the afternoon.
My sister's birthday is **in** December / April / June.	We go to bed late **at** night.

Prepositions of place (Directions) (Präpositionen des Ortes)

at	by	behind	in	in front of	inside	near
next to	on	opposite	outside	over	round	under

ADJECTIVES (ADJEKTIVE)

as ... as

Wenn du sagen willst, dass etwas (nicht) gleich ist wie etwas anderes, verwendest du **(not) as ... as**.

I am **as** intelligent **as** my sister.	He is **not as** tall **as** his father.

Comparatives & Superlatives (Vergleiche & Steigerung der Adjektive)

Einsilbige Adjektive steigerst du mit **-er** und **-est**. Bei mehr als zwei Silben steigerst du mit **more** und **most**. Eine Auflistung der am häufigsten verwendeten Adjektivsteigerungen findest du hier.

My bike is big**ger** than your bike.	My mum is **the most intelligent** person in our family.

Adjective	Comparative	Superlative
bad	**worse**	**worst**
big	big**ger**	big**gest**
cold	cold**er**	cold**est**
fast	fast**er**	fast**est**
good	**better**	**best**
hot	hot**ter**	hot**test**
long	long**er**	long**est**
new	new**er**	new**est**
old	old**er**	old**est**
rich	rich**er**	rich**est**
safe	saf**er**	saf**est**
small	small**er**	small**est**
strong	strong**er**	strong**est**
tall	tall**er**	tall**est**
young	young**er**	young**est**

Adjective	Comparative	Superlative
easy	easi**er**	easi**est**
funny	funni**er**	funni**est**
happy	happi**er**	happi**est**
heavy	heavi**er**	heavi**est**
pretty	pretti**er**	pretti**est**
ugly	ugli**er**	ugli**est**

beautiful	**more** beautiful	**most** beautiful
boring	**more** boring	**most** boring
dangerous	**more** dangerous	**most** dangerous
difficult	**more** difficult	**most** difficult
exciting	**more** exciting	**most** exciting
expensive	**more** expensive	**most** expensive
handsome	**more** handsome	**most** handsome
important	**more** important	**most** important
intelligent	**more** intelligent	**most** intelligent
poisonous	**more** poisonous	**most** poisonous
popular	**more** popular	**most** popular
relaxing	**more** relaxing	**most** relaxing

Linking words (*and, but, because*)

Konjunktionen verbinden Hauptsätze und Nebensätze miteinander.

We went to the cinema **and** watched a great film.	
but it was closed.	
because we had free tickets.	

So do/have I – Neither do/have I

Wenn du jemandem zustimmen willst („ich auch"), verwendest du **So do I**. Bei einer negativen Aussage, der du zustimmst („ich auch nicht"), verwendest du **Neither do I**.
Bei Modalverben und **have** wiederholst du das Verb, ansonsten verwendest du **do**.

I **like** rap. – **So do I.**	I **don't like** rock. – **Neither do I.**
I**'ve got** a laptop. – **So have I.**	I **haven't got** a laptop. – **Neither have I.**
I **can** play the piano. – **So can I.**	I **can't play** the piano. – **Neither can I.**
I **went** to the cinema last night. – **So did I.**	I **didn't go** to the cinema last night. – **Neither did I.**

why – because

Um die Ursache von etwas zu erfragen bzw. zu begründen, verwendest du **why** bzw. **because**.

Why did you go to the store? – **Because** I needed bread.

How much is / are ... ?

Mit **how much** wird nach der Menge (bei nicht zählbaren Hauptwörtern) oder nach dem Preis gefragt.

How much ice cream do you eat every day?	**How much** is the ice cream?	**How much** money have you got?	**How much** are the trainers?

Ordinal numbers

Cardinal	Ordinal	Cardinal	Ordinal
1 one	**first**	16 sixteen	sixteen**th**
2 two	**second**	17 seventeen	seventeen**th**
3 three	**third**	18 eighteen	eighteen**th**
4 four	four**th**	19 nineteen	nineteen**th**
5 five	fif**th**	20 twenty	twentie**th**
6 six	six**th**	21 twenty-one	twenty-**first**
7 seven	seven**th**	30 thirty	thirtie**th**
8 eight	eigh**th**	40 forty	fortie**th**
9 nine	nin**th**	50 fifty	fiftie**th**
10 ten	ten**th**	60 sixty	sixtie**th**
11 eleven	eleven**th**	70 seventy	seventie**th**
12 twelve	twelf**th**	80 eighty	eightie**th**
13 thirteen	thirteen**th**	90 ninety	ninetie**th**
14 fourteen	fourteen**th**	100 hundred	hundred**th**
15 fifteen	fifteen**th**	101 a/one hundred and one	**the (one) hundred and first**

CLASSROOM LANGUAGE

Can you understand your teacher?

We have plenty of time.

Have a go.

Have a guess.

Don't worry about your pronunciation.

Don't worry, it'll get better.

Maybe this will help you.

Can anybody correct this sentence?

That's very good.

Well done.

That's nice.

I like that.

You did a great job.

That's correct.

That's quite right.

Yes, you've got it.

That's much better.

That's a lot better.

You didn't make a single mistake.

Your pronunciation is very good.

You're getting better all the time.

Work in pairs/threes/fours/fives.

Work in groups of two/three/four.

Stand up and find another partner.

Have you finished?

Do the next activity.

Let's check the answers.

Come out and write it on the board.

Repeat after me.

Again, please.

Would you like to answer question 3?

Right. Now we will go on to the next exercise.

Next one, please.

You have ten minutes to do this.

Your time is up.

Are you ready?

Any questions?

I'm afraid it's time to finish now.

We'll have to stop here.

Hang on a moment.

Just a moment, please.

One more thing before you go.

This is your homework.

Do exercise 11 on page 22 for your homework.

There is no homework today.

When you have a problem, say this:

Sorry? / Pardon?

Can you help me, please?

What's … in English, please?

I don't understand this.

Sorry, I've forgotten my … .

Sorry, what's our homework?

ENGLISH SOUNDS

[ɑː] **ar**m
[ʌ] f**u**n
[e] d**e**sk
[ə] **a**, an
[ɜː] g**ir**l, b**ir**d
[æ] **a**pple
[ɪ] **i**n, **i**t
[i] ever**y**
[iː] **ea**sy, **ea**t
[ɒ] **o**range, s**o**rry
[ɔː] **a**ll, c**a**ll
[ʊ] l**oo**k
[u] Febr**u**ary
[uː] f**oo**d
[aɪ] **eye**, b**uy**
[aʊ] **ou**r

[eə] th**ere**
[eɪ] t**a**ke, th**ey**
[ɪə] h**ere**
[ɔɪ] b**oy**
[əʊ] g**o**, **o**ld
[ʊə] t**our**ist
[b] **b**ag, clu**b**
[d] **d**uck, car**d**
[f] **f**ish, lau**gh**
[g] **g**et, do**g**
[h] **h**ot
[j] **y**ou
[k] **c**an, du**ck**
[l] **l**ot, sma**ll**
[m] **m**ore, **m**um
[n] **n**ow, su**n**

[ŋ] so**ng**, lo**ng**
[p] **p**resent, to**p**
[r] **r**ed, **r**ight
[s] **s**ister, cla**ss**
[t] **t**ime, ca**t**
[z] no**s**e, dog**s**
[ʒ] televi**s**ion
[dʒ] oran**ge**
[ʃ] **s**ure, Engli**sh**
[tʃ] **ch**ild, **ch**eese
[ð] **th**ese, mo**th**er
[θ] **th**ink, mou**th**
[v] **v**ery, ha**v**e
[w] **wh**at, **w**ord

The English alphabet:

A   [eɪ]
B   [biː]
C   [siː]
D   [diː]
E   [iː]
F   [ef]
G   [dʒi]
H   [eɪtʃ]
I   [aɪ]
J   [dʒeɪ]
K   [keɪ]
L   [el]
M   [em]
N   [en]
O   [əʊ]
P   [piː]

Q   [kjuː]
R   [ɑː]
S   [es]
T   [tiː]
U   [juː]
V   [viː]
W   [ˈdʌbəljuː]
X   [eks]
Y   [waɪ]
Z   [zed/ziː]

WORDLIST

A

a / an MORE 1	[ə, eɪ / ən]	ein/e
above MORE 1	[ə'bʌv]	(dar-)über, oberhalb
absent-minded U12/15	[,æbsnt'maɪndɪd]	zerstreut
absolutely U9/10	[,æbsə'lu:tli]	absolut
accident MORE 1	['æksɪdənt]	Unfall
ache U15/3	[eɪk]	Schmerz/en
acrobat U11/3	['ækrəbæt]	Akrobat/in
across MORE 1	[ə'krɒs]	quer durch/über
active U17	['æktɪv]	aktiv
activity MORE 1	[æk'tɪvəti]	Aktivität
actually U11/2	['æktʃuəli]	eigentlich; tatsächlich
add U3/9	[æd]	hinzufügen
address (pl -es) MORE 1	[ə'dres]	Adresse, Anschrift
adopt U12/3	[ə'dɒpt]	adoptieren
adult MORE 1	['ædʌlt]	Erwachsene/r
adventure MORE 1	[əd'ventʃə]	Abenteuer, Erlebnis
advice U3/6	[əd'vaɪs]	Rat(schlag)
aeroplane U8/2	['eərəpleɪn]	Flugzeug
a few U3/1	[ə fju:]	ein paar
be afraid (of) U13/8	[bi: ə'freɪd əv]	Angst haben (vor)
I'm afraid (so/not) U13/S6	[aɪm ,ə'freɪd səʊ / nɒt]	leider / leider nicht
Africa U12/3	['æfrɪkə]	Afrika
(be) after U9/S4	[bi: 'a:ftə]	her sein hinter
after all U7/9	[a:ftər 'ɔ:l]	schließlich
against MORE 1	[ə'genst]	gegen
age MORE 1	[eɪdʒ]	Alter
aged (11) U4/3	[eɪdʒd]	(11) Jahre alt
(two days) ago MORE 1	[ə'gəʊ]	vor (zwei Tagen)
agree (with sb) U18	[ə'gri: wɪð 'sʌmbədi]	(jemandem) zustimmen
air MORE 1	[eə]	Luft
airplane U9/9	['eəpleɪn]	Flugzeug
airport U6/6	['eəpɔ:t]	Flughafen
alarm U2/2	[ə'la:m]	Angst; hier: Alarm
alien U3/4	['eɪliən]	Außerirdische/r
alive U4/S2	[ə'laɪv]	lebendig, am Leben
all day U1/12	['ɔ:l deɪ]	den ganzen Tag
all the time U5/1	['ɔ:l ðə 'taɪm]	die ganze Zeit
all over U12/3	['ɔ:l 'əʊvə]	überall auf/in
almost U2/S1	['ɔ:lməʊst]	fast, beinahe
alone MORE 1	[ə'ləʊn]	alleine
along U3/DSC1	[ə'lɒŋ]	entlang
the Alps U17/6	[ði ælps]	die Alpen
already U2/2	[ɔ:l'redi]	schon
altar U11/2	['ɔ:ltə]	Altar
amazing MORE 1	[ə'meɪzɪŋ]	erstaunlich
Amazon U11/2	['æməzən]	Amazonas
America C/p.138	['əmerɪkə]	Amerika
American U12/3	['əmerɪkən]	Amerikaner/in; amerikanisch
American football C/p.139	['əmerɪkən 'fʊtbɔ:l]	(American) Football
anaconda U5/13	[,ænə'kɒndə]	Anakonda
ancient U11	['eɪnʃənt]	alt, antik
anecdote U12/15	['ænɪkdəʊt]	Anekdote
Angola U12/9	[æŋ'gəʊlə]	Angola
angry MORE 1	['æŋgri]	verärgert, zornig, wütend
animal shelter U18/7	['ænɪməl ,ʃeltə]	Tierheim
ankle MORE 1	['æŋkl]	Fußgelenk, Knöchel
anorak U7/3	['ænəræk]	Anorak
another MORE 1	[ə'nʌðə]	ein/e andere/r/s; weitere/r/s
answer MORE! 1	['a:nsə]	antworten; Antwort
Antarctic U18/10	[ænt'a:ktik]	Antarktis
antelope U5/11	['æntɪləʊp]	Antilope
any MORE 1	['eni]	irgendein/e; etwas
(not) any longer U13/S6	[nɒt 'eni lɒŋə]	nicht mehr
(not) any more U7/7	[nɒt 'eni 'mɔ:]	nicht mehr
anyone U3/6	['eniwʌn]	irgendjemand
anyway MORE 1	[eniweɪ]	jedenfalls; sowieso
apologise U3/DSC1	[ə'pɒlədʒaɪz]	sich entschuldigen
appear U17/7	[ə'pɪə]	erscheinen
applause U2/2	[ə'plɔ:z]	Beifall
Arctic Sea U18/10	['aktɪk si:]	Arktischer Ozean
area U7/3	['eəriə]	Gebiet, Region
argument EU/1	['a:gjʊmənt]	Wortwechsel; Streit
armchair U14/3	['a:mtʃeə]	Sessel, Lehnstuhl
(eight-)armed U1/11	[a:md]	(acht-)armig
arrest U2/2	[ə'rest]	verhaften
arrive MORE 1	[ə'raɪv]	ankommen
art U1/2	[a:t]	Kunst
article MORE 1	['a:tɪkl]	(Zeitungs-)Artikel
as ... as MORE 1	[əz əz]	(genau)so ... wie

as much as U16/12	[əz mʌtʃ əz]	so viel wie	
as soon as U1/4	[əz suːn əz]	so bald (wie)	
as well as U16/10	[əz wel əz]	so wie; als auch	
as well U16/10	[əz wel]	auch, ebenfalls	
ash C/p.140	[æʃ]	Asche	
be ashamed U8/7	[ə'ʃeɪmd]	sich schämen	
Asia U5/10	['eɪʒə]	Asien	
(fall) asleep U17/7	[fɔːl əsliːp]	einschlafen	
assembly MORE 1	[ə'sembli]	Versammlung	
assistant U2/1	[ə'sɪstənt]	Assistent/in, Mitarbeiter/in	
astronaut U9/4	['æstrənɔːt]	Astronaut/in	
(not) at all U3/DSC1	[ət ɔːl]	gar nicht	
Atlantian U5/6	[ət'læntɪən]	Bewohner/in von Atlantis	
at least U13/12	[ət liːst]	mindestens	
attack U1/9	[ə'tæk]	angreifen	
attacker U1/8	[ə'tækə]	Angreifer/in	
attempt U17/10	[ə'tempt]	Versuch, Anlauf	
aunt MORE 1	[ɑːnt]	Tante	
Austrian U17/6	['ɒstriːən]	österreichisch	
avenue U15/NYC3	['ævənjuː]	(breite) Straße, Allee	
average U16/10	['ævərɪdʒ]	durchschnittlich	
awesome U3/8	['ɔːsəm]	beeindruckend	
away MORE 1	[ə'weɪ]	weg	
awful MORE 1	['ɔːfl]	schrecklich, scheußlich	

B

back MORE 1	[bæk]	zurück	
back U1/10	[bæk]	Rücken	
backache U15/3	['bækeɪk]	Rückenschmerzen	
background U2/2	['bækgraʊnd]	Hintergrund	
backside (informal) C/p.138	['bæksaɪd]	Hintern, Hinterteil	
bad MORE 1	[bæd]	schlecht, böse	
badly U15/4	['bædli]	schwer, schlimm	
badminton C/p.139	['bædmɪntən]	Federball	
ball gown C/p.138	['bɔːl ˌgaʊn]	Ballkleid	
bandage U11/8	['bændɪdʒ]	Verband	
bank MORE 1	[bæŋk]	Bank	
bank U7/S3	[bæŋk]	Ufer, Böschung	
bar U7/7	[bɑː]	Tafel, Riegel	
barefoot U11/3	['beəfʊt]	barfuß	
bark U9/1	[bɑːk]	bellen	
baseball U10/NYC2	['beɪsbɔːl]	Baseball	
basket U10/3	['bɑːskɪt]	Korb	
bat U10/NYC2	[bæt]	Schläger	

bath U11/2	[bɑːθ]	Bad	
bathing suit U16/7	['beɪðɪŋ suːt]	Badeanzug	
bathroom MORE 1	['bɑːθruːm]	Bad, Badezimmer	
(be) like U1/12	[biː laɪk]	wie etwas sein	
be lucky MORE 1	[biː 'lʌki]	Glück haben	
be scared MORE 1	[biː skeəd]	Angst haben	
be worried U3/1	[biː 'wʌrid]	sich Sorgen machen	
beach MORE 1	[biːtʃ]	Strand	
bear MORE 1	[beə]	Bär	
beat U12/S5	[biːt]	schlagen	
because of U3/6	[bɪkəz əv]	wegen, aufgrund	
become MORE 1	[bɪ'kʌm]	werden	
bedside table U14/3	['bedsaɪd 'teɪbl]	Nachttisch	
beef MORE 1	[biːf]	Rindfleisch	
beer U13/7	[bɪə]	Bier	
begin MORE 1	[bi'gɪn]	anfangen, beginnen	
beginner U2/F	[bɪ'gɪnə]	Anfänger/in	
behaviour U3/6	[bɪ'heɪvjə]	Benehmen, Verhalten	
behind MORE 1	[bɪ'haɪnd]	hinter	
believe MORE 1	[bɪ'liːv]	glauben	
belong U14	[bi'lɒŋ]	zugehören; hingehören	
below MORE 1	[bɪ'ləʊ]	unten; darunter	
belt U2/S1	[belt]	Gürtel	
beside U6/G	[bɪ'saɪd]	neben	
between MORE 1	[bɪ'twiːn]	zwischen	
bike MORE 1	[baɪk]	Fahrrad	
bird MORE 1	[bɜːd]	Vogel	
bison C/p.140	['baɪsən]	Bison	
bite MORE I	[baɪt]	Biss; beißen	
bleed C/p.141	[bliːd]	bluten	
block U11/6	[blɒk]	Block, Klotz	
blog U3/6	[blɒg]	Blog	
blonde U10/NYC2	[blɒnd]	blond	
blood U2/2	[blʌd]	Blut	
blue whale U5/10	[bluː weɪl]	Blauwal	
blue-ringed U1/7	[bluːrɪŋd]	blau beringt	
board MORE 1	[bɔːd]	an Bord gehen	
apple bobbing U4/1	['æpl ˌbɒbɪŋ]	Apfeltauchen (traditionelles Halloween-Spiel)	
body MORE 1	['bɒdi]	Körper	
bone U4/F	[bəʊn]	Knochen	
book U17/DSC6	[bʊk]	buchen	
bookshop U15/2	['bʊkʃɒp]	Buchhandlung	
(car) boot U13/6	['kɑː buːt]	Kofferraum	
bored MORE 1	[bɔːd]	gelangweilt	
(be) born MORE 1	[bɔːn]	geboren	
borrow (from) U4/4	['bɒrəʊ]	ausleihen (von)	
both MORE 1	[bəʊθ]	beide	
bother U6/DSC2	['bɒðə]	stören	
Botswana U12/9	[bɒt'swɑːnə]	Botswana	

bottle MORE 1	['bɒtl]	Flasche
bottom U7/2	['bɒtəm]	untere/r/s
bowl U4/3	[bəʊl]	Schüssel
boyfriend MORE 1	[bɔi:frend]	fester Freund
branch MORE 1	[brɑːntʃ]	Zweig; Ast
brave U4/2	[breɪv]	tapfer
Brazil U17/11	[brə'zɪl]	Brasilien
break MORE 1	[breɪk]	(zer-)brechen
break U1/2	[breɪk]	Pause
break into U2/2	['breɪk͵ɪntə]	einbrechen in
breathe U12/5	[briːð]	atmen
bridge MORE 1	[brɪdʒ]	Brücke
bright U1/9	[braɪt]	hell, leuchtend
brilliant MORE 1	['brɪliənt]	genial, toll
bring MORE 1	[brɪŋ]	(mit-)bringen
Britain MORE 1	['brɪtən]	Großbritannien
British MORE 1	['brɪtɪʃ]	britisch
brochure C/p.141	['brəʊʃə]	Broschüre, Prospekt
broom U9/1	[bruːm]	Besen
brush U18/1	[brʌʃ]	(ab-)bürsten
budgie MORE 1	[bʌdʒi]	Wellensittich
build U7/3	[bɪld]	bauen
building MORE 1	['bɪldɪŋ]	Gebäude
bully U3/7	['bʊli]	tyrannisieren, mobben
bumblebee bat U5/10	['bʌmblbiː bæt]	Hummelfledermaus
bun U5/16	[bʌn]	Semmel, Brötchen
burn U12/5	[bɜːn]	(ver-)brennen
on business U6/7	[ɒn 'bɪznɪs]	geschäftlich, auf Dienstreise
busy MORE 1	['bɪzi]	beschäftigt
button MORE 1	['bʌtn]	Knopf, Taste
buy MORE 1	[baɪ]	kaufen
by MORE 1	[baɪ]	an; bei; mit
by U12/12	[baɪ]	bis (spätestens)
by accident U2/3	[baɪ 'æksɪdnt]	versehentlich, zufällig
by the way U10/NYC2	[baɪ ðə weɪ]	übrigens
bye MORE 1	[baɪ]	tschüss, tschau

C

cabbage U10/1	['kæbɪdʒ]	Kohl, Kraut
cabin C/p.139	['kæbɪn]	Hütte
cache U7/7	[kæʃ]	Versteck
cage MORE 1	[keɪdʒ]	Käfig
cake MORE 1	[keik]	Kuchen
California U17/4	[kælɪ'fɔːnjə]	Kalifornien
call MORE 1	[kɔːl]	(an-)rufen
call U18/10	[kɔːl]	nennen

call back U15/1	[kɔːl bæk]	zurückrufen
called MORE 1	[kɔːld]	genannt
calm U2/7	[kɑːm]	ruhig
calm down U9/S4	[kɑːm 'daʊn]	sich beruhigen
Cambodia U12/3	[kæm'bəʊdiə]	Kambodscha
camera MORE 1	['kæmərə]	Kamera, Fotoapparat
camp U7/3	[kæmp]	Zeltlager
canary U11/8	[kə'neəri]	Kanarienvogel
cancer U15/10	['kænsə]	Krebs (Krankheit)
candle U4/3	['kændl]	Kerze
canoeing U7/3	[kə'nuːɪŋ]	Paddeln, Kanufahren
capital MORE 1	['kæpɪtl]	Hauptstadt
care about U11/3	['keər͵ə'baʊt]	sich aus … etw. machen
care for somebody U18	['keə fə 'sʌmbədi]	sich um jemanden kümmern
I don't care. U2/2	[aɪ dəʊnt 'keə]	Ist mir egal.
careful MORE 1	['keəfl]	vorsichtig
carpet U14/3	['kɑːpɪt]	Teppich
carry U5/10	['kæri]	(über-)tragen
carry U9/1	['kærɪ]	befördern, transportieren
case MORE 1	[keɪs]	Fall; Hülle
castle MORE 1	[kɑːsl]	Schloss, Burg
catch MORE 1	[kætʃ]	fangen, festnehmen
cathedral U11/2	[kə'θiːdrəl]	Kathedrale, Dom
cattle U11/3	['kætl]	Vieh
ceiling C/p.141	['siːlɪŋ]	(Zimmer-)Decke
cell phone U18/NYC4	[sel fəʊn]	Handy
cellar U14/1	['selə]	Keller
centimetre U5/10	['sentɪ͵miːtə]	Zentimeter
Central Asia U14/1	['sentrəl 'eɪʒə]	Zentralasien
certain U14/DSC5	['sɜːtn]	sicher, gewiss
certainly MORE 1	['sɜːtnli]	sicherlich, bestimmt
chain U13/1	[tʃeɪn]	Kette
challenge U17/10	['tʃælɪndʒ]	Herausforderung
chance U2/S1	[tʃɑːnts]	Chance
change MORE 1	[tʃeɪndʒ]	(sich) (ver-)ändern
change trains U6/6	[tʃeɪndʒ treɪns]	umsteigen
change one's mind U12/DSC4	[tʃeɪndʒ wʌnz maɪnd]	seine Meinung ändern
character U2/2	['kærɪktə]	Charakter; hier: Person
chase MORE 1	[tʃeɪs]	verfolgen, jagen
chaser C/p.141	['tʃeɪsə]	Jäger/in
chart U15/1	[tʃɑːt]	Tabelle, Karte
charter school C/p.138	['tʃɑːtə ͵skuːl]	Charterschule
chat U12/5	[tʃæt]	plaudern, chatten; Unterhaltung, Plauderei
cheap MORE 1	[tʃiːp]	billig
cheek U11/8	[tʃiːk]	Wange, Backe
cheesecake U10/1	['tʃiːzkeɪk]	Käsekuchen
cheetah U5/10	['tʃiːtə]	Gepard

chef U10/7	[ʃef]	Koch, Köchin	
chemist's U6/2	['kemɪsts]	Apotheke, Drogerie	
chess EU/1	[tʃes]	Schach(spiel)	
chief U4/9	[tʃiːf]	Haupt-, Chef-	
child (pl **children**) MORE 1	[tʃaɪld, 'tʃɪldrən]	Kind	
chimpanzee U5/6	[tʃɪmpæn'ziː]	Schimpanse	
chips MORE 1	[tʃɪps]	Pommes	
chocolates U3/1	['tʃɒkləts]	Pralinen	
choose MORE 1	[tʃuːz]	(aus-)wählen	
chop U10/7	[tʃɒp]	Kotelett	
(household) chores U1/2	['haʊshəʊld ˌtʃɔː]	Aufgaben im Haushalt	
church U6/2	[tʃɜːtʃ]	Kirche	
cigar U13/7	[sɪ'gɑː]	Zigarre	
city MORE 1	[sɪti]	Stadt	
class MORE 1	[klɑːs]	(Schul-)Klasse	
classmate U18/5	['klɑːsmeɪt]	Klassenkamerad/in, Mitschüler/in	
clean (up) MORE 1	[kliːn ʌp]	sauber machen; putzen	
clean U2/2	[kliːn]	sauber	
cleaning lady U3/3	['kliːnɪŋ 'leɪdi]	Putzfrau	
clear U16/10	[klɪər]	hier: wolkenlos	
clear away U15/10	[klɪər ə'weɪ]	wegräumen, entfernen	
clear up U16/3	[klɪər 'ʌp]	(auf-)klären; hier: sich aufhellen	
cliff U17/10	[klɪf]	Klippe, Felsen	
climb MORE 1	[klaɪm]	(hinauf-)steigen; klettern	
climber U17/4	['klaɪmə]	Kletterer/in	
clock tower U6/DSC2	[klɒk taʊə]	Uhrturm	
close MORE 1	[kləʊz]	schließen, zumachen	
closed U9/DSC3	[kləʊzd]	geschlossen, zu	
clothes (no pl) MORE 1	['kləʊðz]	Kleider, Kleidung	
cloud U9/9	[klaʊd]	Wolke	
cloudy U16/2	['klaʊdi]	bewölkt	
clue MORE 1	[kluː]	Hinweis, Tipp	
I have no clue. U15/NYC3	[aɪ həv nəʊ 'kluː]	Ich habe keine Ahnung.	
coast U16/1	[kəʊst]	Küste	
coat U8/G	[kəʊt]	Mantel	
coffee MORE 1	['kɒfi]	Kaffee	
coin U7/7	[kɔɪn]	Münze, Geldstück	
coke U12/DCS4	[kəʊk]	Cola	
collect MORE 1	[kə'lekt]	sammeln	
come after U4/2	[kʌm 'ɑːftə]	jagen, verfolgen	
come along U7/3	[kʌm ə'lɒŋ]	mitkommen	
come over MORE 1	[kʌm 'əʊvə]	vorbeikommen	
comfortable U9/11	['kʌmftəbl]	bequem	
command U2/2	[kə'mɑːnd]	Befehl	
comment U8/7	['kɒment]	kommentieren	
communication U8/7	[kəˌmjuːnɪ'keɪʃn]	Kommunikation	

company U15/10	['kʌmpəni]	Firma, Unternehmen	
company U18/7	['kʌmpəni]	Gesellschaft	
compare U5	[kəm'peər]	vergleichen	
competition U17/5	[ˌkɒmpə'tɪʃn]	Wettbewerb	
complain U13/8	[kəm'pleɪn]	sich beschweren	
complete MORE 1	[kəm'pliːt]	vervollständigen	
complicated EU/1	['kɒmplɪkeɪtɪd]	kompliziert; schwierig	
compliment U10/F	['kɒmplɪmənt]	Kompliment	
conference U6/6	['kɒnfrnts]	Konferenz, Tagung	
confused U3/1	[kən'fjuːzd]	verwirrt	
confusing U3/8	[kən'fjuːzɪŋ]	verwirrend	
connect U14/1	[kə'nekt]	anschließen; verbinden	
consequence U15/11	['kɒntsɪkwənts]	Folge, Konsequenz	
contact MORE 1	['kɒntækt]	kontaktieren	
continue U16/1	[kən'tɪnjuː]	andauern; weitergehen	
conversation MORE 1	[kɒnvə'seɪʃn]	Gespräch, Unterhaltung	
convert U16/10	[kən'vɜːt]	umwandeln	
cook MORE 1	[kʊk]	Koch, Köchin; kochen	
cooker U13/6	['kʊkə]	Herd	
cool U11/10	[kuːl]	kühl	
coordinate U7/7	[kəʊ'ɔːdɪnət]	Koordinate	
corner MORE 1	[kɔːnər]	Ecke	
corridor U11/11	['kɒrɪdɔː]	Flur, Gang, Korridor	
cost C/p.138	[kɒst]	kosten	
Costa Rica U14/2	[ˌkɒstə 'riːkə]	Costa Rica	
Costa Rican U14/1	[ˌkɒstə 'riːkən]	costa-ricanisch	
costume U4/1	['kɒstjuːm]	Tracht; Kostüm	
cotton U14/DSC5	['kɒtn]	Baumwolle	
could MORE 1	[kʊd]	könnte/n, könntest	
couldn't (could not) U2/G	['kʊdnt]	könnte/n nicht; konnte/n nicht	
count MORE 1	[kaʊnt]	zählen	
count to MORE 1	[kaʊnt 'ʌp]	hochzählen, zusammenzählen	
country MORE 1	['kʌntri]	Land; Staat	
countryside U12/5	['kʌntrɪsaɪd]	Land, Landschaft	
couple U10/8	['kʌpl]	Paar	
courage U13/S6	['kʌrɪdʒ]	Mut, Tapferkeit	
course U12/5	[kɔːs]	Kurs, Lehrgang	
main course U10/7	['meɪn kɔːs]	Hauptgericht, Hauptgang	
cousin U12/1	['kʌzn]	Cousin/e	
cover MORE 1	[kʌvər]	bedecken, verdecken	
cover U6/6	[kræk]	hier: Titelseite	
Crack! U9/1	[kræk]	Knack!	
crash U8/10	[kræʃ]	zu Bruch fahren	
crazy MORE 1	['kreɪzi]	verrückt	
create MORE 1	[kri'eɪt]	erstellen, entwerfen	
creature U5/18	['kriːtʃə]	Kreatur, Lebewesen	
cricket U17/DSC6	['krɪkɪt]	Kricket	
crocodile MORE 1	['krɒkədaɪl]	Krokodil	

cross U6/1	[krɒs]	durchqueren, überqueren
cross U11/2	[krɒs]	Kreuz
cruise (ship) U1/1	[kru:z ʃɪp]	Kreuzfahrt(schiff)
cry MORE 1	[kraɪ]	weinen; schreien
cry U7/S3	[kraɪ]	Schrei
cup U5/15	[kʌp]	Tasse
cupboard U14/3	[ˈkʌbəd]	Schrank
curse U11/1	[kɜ:s]	Fluch
curtain U14/3	[ˈkɜ:tən]	Vorhang
customer MORE 1	[kʌstəmər]	Kunde, Kundin
cut MORE 1	[kʌt]	schneiden
cut down U15/10	[kʌt daʊn]	fällen
cycle U3/DSC1	[ˈsaɪkl]	Rad fahren

D

daily U1/3	[ˈdeɪli]	täglich
damn (informal) U12/15	[dæm]	verdammt
dance MORE 1	[dɑ:nts]	tanzen
dancer U11/3	[ˈdɑ:nsə]	Tänzer/in
danger U4/S2	[ˈdeɪndʒə]	Gefahr
dangerous MORE 1	[ˈdeɪndʒərəs]	gefährlich
dark MORE 1	[dɑ:k]	dunkel, finster
dark U4/3	[dɑ:k]	Dunkelheit
date C/p.138	[deɪt]	Verabredung
daughter MORE 1	[ˈdɔ:tə]	Tochter
dead U2/S1	[ded]	tot
decide MORE 1	[dɪˈsaɪd]	entscheiden
decision U12/5	[dɪˈsɪʒən]	Entscheidung
deckchair U13/6	[ˈdektʃeə]	Liegestuhl
deep MORE 1	[di:p]	tief
definitely U13/10	[ˈdefənətli]	eindeutig, definitiv; auf jeden Fall
degree (°) U16/3	[dɪˈgri:]	Grad (°)
delete U12/13	[dɪˈli:t]	streichen, löschen
delicious U3/DSC1	[dɪˈlɪʃəs]	köstlich
delta U11/2	[ˈdeltə]	Delta, Flussmündung
demon U4/S2	[ˈdi:mən]	Dämon
depend U5/NYC1	[dɪˈpend]	abhängen von
describe MORE 1	[dɪˈskraɪb]	beschreiben
desert U5/10	[ˈdezət]	Wüste
design U5/18	[dɪˈzaɪn]	gestalten, entwerfen
design and technology U1/4	[dɪˈzaɪn ənd tekˈnɒlədʒi]	Design und technisches Zeichnen
desk MORE 1	[desk]	Schreibtisch
dessert MORE 1	[dɪˈzɜ:t]	Nachtisch, Dessert
destroy U9/10	[dɪˈstrɔɪ]	zerstören
detail U6/11	[ˈdi:teɪl]	Detail, Einzelheit

diamond U11/14	[ˈdaɪəmənd]	Diamant
diary MORE 1	[ˈdaɪəri]	Tagebuch
dictionary U14/8	[ˈdɪkʃənəri]	Wörterbuch
die (from) MORE 1	[daɪ]	sterben (an/von)
difference MORE 1	[ˈdɪfərənts]	Unterschied
different MORE 1	[ˈdɪfrənt]	verschieden/e; anders
difficult U3/8	[ˈdɪfɪklt]	schwierig, schwer
dinner lady MORE 1	[ˈdɪnə ˈleɪdi]	Mitarbeiterin einer Schulkantine
directions U6/5	[dɪˈrekʃns]	Anweisungen
director U3/2	[daɪˈrektə]	Direktor/in
dirty U2/2	[ˈdɜ:ti]	dreckig, schmutzig
disagree with sb U18	[dɪsəˈgri:]	jmd nicht zustimmen, nicht übereinstimmen
disappear U4/7	[dɪsəˈpɪə]	verschwinden
disappointment U9/DSC3	[ˌdɪsəˈpɔɪntmənt]	Enttäuschung
disaster C/p.138	[dɪˈzɑːstə]	Katastrophe, Desaster
discover U11/8	[dɪˈskʌvə]	herausfinden, entdecken
discuss MORE 1	[dɪˈskʌs]	besprechen
the dishes (pl) U2/5	[ðə ˈdɪʃɪz]	das Geschirr
disk U9/9	[dɪsk]	Scheibe
dismay U3/DSC1	[dɪˈsmeɪ]	Bestürzung
doctor U2/2	[ˈdɒktə]	Arzt, Ärztin
document U11/3	[ˈdɒkjʊmənt]	Dokument
dollar U12/3	[ˈdɒlə]	Dollar
dolphin U5/11	[ˈdɒlfɪn]	Delphin
done MORE 1	[dʌn]	fertig
doorbell U13/7	[ˈdɔ:bel]	Türklingel
dos and don'ts U3/6	[du:z ænd dəʊnts]	was man tun und nicht tun sollte
down MORE 1	[daʊn]	hinunter, hinab
down the road U12/9	[daʊn ðə rəʊd]	in/von unserer Straße
Down Under U1/1	[daʊn ˈʌndə]	Australien und Neuseeland
dragon U5/6	[ˈdrægən]	Drache
draw MORE 1	[drɔ:]	malen; zeichnen
dream MORE 1	[dri:m]	Traum; träumen
dress MORE 1	[dres]	Kleid
drink MORE 1	[drɪŋk]	trinken; Getränk
drive MORE 1	[draɪv]	fahren; führen; Fahrt
drive U4/5	[draɪv]	Auffahrt, Einfahrt
driveway C/p.138	[ˈdraɪvweɪ]	Auffahrt, Einfahrt
driving test U8/10	[ˈdraɪvɪŋ test]	Fahrprüfung
drop MORE 1	[drɒp]	fallen lassen
drop U16/7	[drɒp]	sinken
dry U16/1	[draɪ]	trocken
dry U18/1	[draɪ]	(ab-)trocknen
duck U11/3	[dʌk]	Ente
during U1/9	[ˈdjʊərɪŋ]	während
dustbin U9/1	[ˈdʌstbɪn]	Mülleimer

E

each other U14/4	[iːtʃ 'ʌðə]	einander, gegenseitig
eagle MORE 1	['iːgl]	Adler
earache U15/3	['ɪəreɪk]	Ohrenschmerzen
early MORE 1	['ɜːli]	früh
earth MORE 1	[ɜːθ]	Erde
easily U11/12	['iːzɪli]	leicht, einfach
easy MORE 1	['iːzi]	einfach
east U5/10	[iːst]	östlich, Ost-; Osten
eat in U12/DSC4	[iːt ɪn]	hier essen
education U17/10	[edjʊ'keɪʃn]	(Aus-)Bildung
Egypt MORE 1	['iːdʒɪpt]	Ägypten
Egyptian U11/2	[ɪ'dʒɪpʃən]	Ägypter/in; ägyptisch
(not) either of them U15/1	['aɪðə əv ðəm]	keine/r/s von beiden
electricity U14/1	[ɪlek'trɪsəti]	Elektrizität, Strom
elementary school C/p.138	[elɪ'mentəri ˌskuːl]	Volksschule
something else U7/7	[sʌmθɪŋ'els]	noch etwas
embarrassed U3/1	[ɪm'bærəst]	verlegen
embarrassing U3	[ɪm'bærəsɪŋ]	peinlich, unangenehm
emergency MORE 1	[ɪ'mɜːdʒənsi]	Notfall, Notdienst
emperor U11/2	['empərə]	Kaiser
emperor penguin U18/10	['empərə ˌpeŋgwɪn]	Kaiserpinguin
empty MORE 1	['empti]	leer
in the end U3/DSC1	[ɪn ðiː end]	schließlich, am Ende
ending MORE 1	['endɪŋ]	Ende, Schluss
Englishman (pl -men) U11/8	['ɪŋglɪʃmən]	Engländer
enjoy MORE 1	[ɪn'dʒɔɪ]	genießen
enough MORE 1	[ɪ'nʌf]	genügend, genug
entrance U11/12	['entrəns]	Eingang
equipment U17/DSC6	[ɪ'kwɪpmənt]	Ausrüstung
erupt C/p.140	[ɪ'rʌpt]	ausbrechen
(volcanic) eruption C/p.140	[vɒlˌkænɪk ɪ'rʌpʃən]	(Vulkan-)Ausbruch
escape U9/S4	[ɪ'skeɪp]	(ent-)fliehen; entkommen
especially U7/7	[ɪ'speʃli]	besonders
Estuarine crocodile U5/10	['estjʊəriːn 'krɒkədaɪl]	Salzwasserkrokodil
etc. (et cetera) U4/3	[et 'setərə]	usw., etc.
Ethiopia U12/3	[ˌiːθi'əʊpiə]	Äthiopien
even U9/9	['iːvən]	sogar
even U16/10	['iːvən]	noch
ever MORE 1	['evə]	je
evergreen C/p.140	['evəgriːn]	immergrün
every MORE 1	['evri]	jede/r/s
everybody U6/6	['evribɒdi]	jede/r; alle
everyone U1/6	['evriwʌn]	jede/r; alle
everything MORE 1	['evriθɪŋ]	alles
everywhere MORE 1	['evriweə]	überall
evil U4/S2	['iːvəl]	das Böse
exactly U7/7	[ɪg'zæktli]	genau
for example U7/7	[fər ɪg'zɑːmpl]	zum Beispiel
excellent MORE 1	['eksələnt]	ausgezeichnet
excited MORE 1	[ɪk'saɪtɪd]	aufgeregt
exciting MORE 1	[ɪk'saɪtɪŋ]	aufregend; spannend
excuse U8/7	[ɪk'skjuːz]	Ausrede
(do) exercise U14/DSC5	['eksəsaɪz]	trainieren
exotic U5/6	[ɪg'zɒtɪk]	exotisch; fremdländisch
expectation U16	[ˌekspek'teɪʃən]	Erwartung
expensive U2/7	[ɪk'spensɪv]	teuer
experience C/p.141	[ɪk'spɪəriənts]	Erfahrung
experiment U2/2	[ɪk'sperɪmənt]	Experiment, Versuch
expert U9/9	['ekspɜːt]	Experte, Expertin
explain U3/1	[ɪk'spleɪn]	erklären
explode U9/1	[ɪk'spləʊd]	explodieren
expression U7/S3	[ɪk'spreʃn]	Ausdruck
extend U3/DSC1	[ɪk'stend]	erweitern
extra U3/1	['ekstrə]	mehr; besonders; Extra
extreme U17/10	[ɪk'striːm]	extrem

F

face MORE 1	[feɪs]	Gesicht
face U17/10	[feɪs]	sich etwas aussetzen; sich zuwenden
face U14/DSC5	[feɪs]	Ziffernblatt
fact U2/2	[fækt]	Tatsache, Fakt; Wirklichkeit
fail somebody U2/S1	['feɪl ˌsʌmbədi]	jemanden enttäuschen
(it isn't) fair U10/NYC2	[ɪt iznt feə]	(es ist nicht) fair
fake U9/9	[feɪk]	Fälschung
fall asleep U17/7	[fɔːl ə'sliːp]	einschlafen
fall off U8/11	[fɔːl ɒf]	herunterfallen
fall over U11/12	[fɔːl 'əʊvə]	hinfallen; umfallen
false MORE 1	[fɒls]	falsch
famous MORE 1	['feɪməs]	berühmt
fancy dress U8/13	[ˌfænsi 'dres]	Verkleidung, Kostüm
far away U4/5	[fɑːr ə'weɪ]	weit weg, fern
farewell U13/S6	[feə'wel]	Abschied
farm MORE 1	[fɑːm]	Bauernhof
farmer U11/3	['fɑːmə]	Bauer, Bäuerin
fast MORE 1	[faːst]	schnell
fat U5/G	[fæt]	dick, fett
fat U11/3	[fæt]	Fett
fault MORE 1	[fɔːlt]	Schuld

favour, favor (AE) U5/NYC1	['feɪvə]	Gefallen
favourite MORE 1	['feɪvrɪt]	Lieblings-
fear U4/2	[fɪə]	fürchten
fear U17/10	[fɪə]	Furcht, Angst
feather U13/6	['feðə]	Feder
feed MORE 1	[fiːd]	zu essen geben, füttern
fence U13/6	[fens]	Zaun
(a) few U3/1	[ə fjuː]	ein paar; einige
field U7/1	[fiːld]	Feld; Spielfeld
fight MORE 1	[faɪt]	kämpfen; Kampf
file U12/13	[faɪl]	Ordner; (Akten-)Hefter
fill U11/10	[fɪl]	füllen
final U13/S6	['faɪnəl]	letzte/r/s, End-
finally MORE 1	['faɪnəli]	schließlich; endlich
find out U7/8	[faɪnd 'aʊt]	herausfinden
fingerprint U2/2	['fɪŋgəprɪnt]	Fingerabdruck
finish U1/2	['fɪnɪʃ]	aufhören; beenden; vervollständigen
fire MORE 1	['faɪə]	Feuer
first name U12/1	['fɜːst ˌneɪm]	Vorname
first thing U14/DSC5	['fɜːst θɪŋ]	gleich als erstes
fishing rod MORE 1	['fɪʃɪŋ rɒd]	Angelrute
get fit EU/1	[get 'fɪt]	sich fit machen
fix U18/10	[fɪks]	befestigen
flag U10/7	[flæg]	Flagge, Fähnchen
flat MORE 1	[flæt]	Wohnung
flight U2/2	[flaɪt]	Flug
float U13/1	[fləʊt]	schweben
float U14/1	[fləʊt]	schwimmen, oben bleiben
floor MORE 1	[flɔː]	Boden; Stockwerk
flower C/p.138	['flaʊə]	Blume
fly MORE 1	[flaɪ]	fliegen
fog U16/3	[fɒg]	Nebel
foggy U16/2	['fɒgi]	neblig
follow MORE 1	['fɒləʊ]	folgen
following MORE 1	['fɒləʊɪŋ]	folgende/r/s
food MORE 1	[fuːd]	Essen
fool U3/DSC1	[fuːl]	Dummkopf, Narr
fool U9/9	[fuːl]	hereinlegen, täuschen
foot (pl. feet) MORE 1	[fʊt]	Fuß
footprint U2/2	['fʊtprɪnt]	Fußabdruck
for example U7/7	[fə ɪg'zɑːmpl]	zum Beispiel
for sure (informal) U11/S5	[fə 'ʃɔː]	bestimmt, ganz sicher
forecast U16/3	[fɔːkaːst]	Vorhersage
foreign language U12/5	['fɒrən ˈlæŋgwɪdʒ]	Fremdsprache
forest U6/1	['fɒrɪst]	Wald
forever U4/S2	[fə'revə]	für immer
forget MORE 1	[fə'get]	vergessen

forgive U2/S1	[fə'gɪv]	vergeben
former U17/10	['fɔːmə]	ehemalig, früher
formula U16/1	['fɔːmjələ]	Formel
foundation U12/3	[faʊn'deɪʃən]	Stiftung
fountain U6/DSC2	['faʊntɪn]	Springbrunnen
free MORE 1	[friː]	befreien; frei, kostenlos
free climbing U17/10	['friː ˌklaɪmɪŋ]	Freiklettern
freedom U17/10	['friːdəm]	Freiheit, Unabhängigkeit
French MORE 1	[frentʃ]	französisch; Französisch
fridge U10/7	[frɪdʒ]	Kühlschrank
friendly U5/6	['frendli]	freundlich
front MORE 1	[frʌnt]	vorder-
front door MORE 1	[frʌnt 'dɔː]	Vordertür; Haustür
full U11/8	[fʊl]	voll
full U17/10	[fʊl]	erfüllt
funny MORE 1	['fʌni]	lustig, komisch
furious U1/11	['fjʊəriəs]	wütend
furniture U14	['fɜːnɪtʃə]	Möbel
future U17/10	['fjuːtʃə]	Zukunft

G

galaxy U9/4	['gæləksi]	Galaxie
gaming cards U5/6	['geɪmɪŋ kaːds]	Spielkarten
garage MORE 1	['gærɑːʒ]	Garage
garden shed 13/7	['gɑːdən ʃed]	Gartenhäuschen
gas U9/S4	[gæs]	Gas
gasoline C/p.138	['gæsəliːn]	Benzin
gate U4/5	[geɪt]	Tor
generally U16/10	['dʒenrli]	im Allgemeinen
genius U12/15	['dʒiːniəs]	Genie
gentleman (pl gentlemen) U2/2	['dʒentlmən, 'dʒentlmən]	Gentleman; Herr
geo-caching U7/7	['dʒiːəʊkæʃɪŋ]	Geo-caching, GPS-Schnitzeljagd
geography U1/4	['dʒɒgrəfi]	Erdkunde, Geografie
German U9/DSC3	['dʒɜːmən]	deutsch; Deutsch
get MORE 1	[get]	erhalten, bekommen; holen
get dressed U1/2	[get drest]	sich anziehen
get home U1/2	[get həʊm]	nach Hause kommen
I don't get it. U4/S2	[aɪ dəʊnt get ɪt]	Verstehe ich nicht.
get in touch U2/S1	[get ɪn tʌtʃ]	kontaktieren, sich in Verbindung setzen
get into trouble U5/2	[get 'ɪntuː 'trʌbl]	in Schwierigkeiten geraten
get lost U6/7	[get 'lɒst]	sich verirren; sich verlaufen haben
get on U12/5	[get ɒn]	ein-/zusteigen
get out (of) MORE 1	[get 'aʊt əv]	hinauskommen, herauskommen (aus)

get stuck U13/2	[get 'stʌk]	festsitzen
get up MORE 1	[get 'ʌp]	aufstehen
ghost U4/1	[gəʊst]	Geist
giant U17/G	['dʒaɪnt]	Riesen-, riesig
giraffe U5/11	[dʒə'rɑːf]	Giraffe
girlfriend U2/2	['gɜːlfrend]	Freundin
give MORE 1	[gɪv]	geben
give directions U6/5	[gɪv daɪ'rekʃəns]	den Weg beschreiben
give up MORE 1	[gɪv ʌp]	aufgeben
give way to U16/1	[gɪv weɪ tu]	in etwas übergehen
glad U1/1	[glæd]	froh
glass U7/7	[glɑːs]	Glas
glasses U11/2	['glɑːsəz]	Brille
global U17/10	['gləʊbl]	weltweit, global
Go ahead! U6/9	[gəʊ ə'hed]	Komm schon!
go along U7/7	[gəʊ ə'lɒŋ]	mitgehen
go for a run U2/5	[gəʊ fɔː ə rʌn]	laufen gehen
go for a walk U16/5	[gəʊ fɔː ə wɔːk]	spazieren gehen
go off U2/2	[gəʊ 'ɒf]	losgehen, weggehen; abgehen; ausgehen
go past U6/1	[gəʊ pɑːst]	vorbeigehen
go red EU/1	[gəʊ 'red]	rot werden
go to sleep MORE 1	[gəʊ tə 'sliːp]	einschlafen
go up U16/4	[gəʊ 'ʌp]	steigen
go wrong U3/6	[gəʊ rɒŋ]	schief gehen
goal U15/G	[gəʊl]	Tor; Ziel
goalie (informal) U17/8	['gəʊli]	Tormann, Torfrau
goat U11/3	[gəʊt]	Ziege
god U11/8	[gɒd]	Gott
go-kart EU/1	['gəʊkɑːt]	Gokart
gold MORE 1	[gəʊld]	Gold; golden
goldfish U18/7	['gəʊldfɪʃ]	Goldfisch
golf U1/9	[gɒlf]	Golf
Good luck! U6/1	[gʊd lʌk]	Viel Glück!
Goodness me! U2/2	['gʊdnəs 'miː]	Du lieber Himmel!
Oh, my goodness! U11/S5	[əʊ maɪ 'gʊdnəss]	Ach du meine Güte!
goose (pl geese) U11/2	[guːs, giːs]	Gans
Got you! U18/NYC4	[gɒt jʊ]	Hab' dich!
grab U18/NYC4	[græb]	greifen, nehmen
gram U5/10	[græm]	Gramm
grandfather U12/1	['grændfɑːðə]	Großvater
grandmother U12/1	['grændmʌðə]	Großmutter
grandparents (pl) MORE 1	['grænpeərənts]	Großeltern
grade (AE) C/p.138	[greɪd]	Jahrgangsstufe
grape U10/1	[greɪp]	Traube
grilled U15/NYC3	[grɪld]	gegrillt
grizzly bear C/p.140	[ˌgrɪzli 'beə]	Grizzlybär

ground MORE 1	[graʊnd]	(Erd-)Boden, Erde
group MORE 1	[gruːp]	Gruppe
grow U5/14	[grəʊ]	wachsen; hier: werden
grow up U17/4	[grəʊ 'ʌp]	aufwachsen
guard U2/2	[gɑːd]	Wache, Wachposten
guard U11/8	[gɑːd]	bewachen
guess MORE 1	[ges]	(er-)raten
guide U7/3	[gaɪd]	(Reise-)Führer, Reiseleiter
guinea pig MORE 1	['gɪni pig]	Meerschweinchen
guys (informal) MORE 1	[gaɪz]	Leute
gym U14/DSC5	[dʒɪm]	Turnsaal; Fitnesscenter

H

hairdresser C/p.138	['heəˌdresə]	Friseur/in
hairy U5/4	['heəri]	haarig, stark behaart
half (pl halves) MORE 1	[hɑːf, hɑːvz]	Hälfte
half an hour MORE 1	[hɑːf ən aʊə]	eine halbe Stunde
Halloween U4/1	[hæləʊiːn]	Halloween
ham MORE 1	[hæm]	Schinken
handful U7/7	['hændfʊl]	eine Hand voll
hang around U12/5	[hæŋ ə'raʊnd]	herumlungern
hang on U3/DSC1	[hæŋ 'ɒn]	durchhalten; hier: warten
happen U2/2	[hæpən]	geschehen
happy MORE 1	['hæpi]	glücklich, fröhlich
hard MORE 1	[hɑːd]	schwierig
hard U7/3	[hɑːd]	hart
hard hat U7/3	['hɑːd hæt]	Schutzhelm
harm U10/NYC2	[hɑːm]	Schaden, Unheil
haunted U4/1	['hɔːntɪd]	heimgesucht; Spuk-
have (food/drinks) MORE 1	[hæv]	zu sich nehmen
Have fun! U15/NYC3	[hæv 'fʌn]	Viel Spaß!
head MORE 1	[hed]	Kopf
headache U15/3	['hedeɪk]	Kopfschmerzen
headmaster EU/1	[hed'mɑːstə]	Schulleiter, Direktor
hear MORE 1	[hɪə]	hören
heavy MORE 1	['hevi]	schwer
heavy U16/4	['hevi]	stark
height C/p.141	[haɪt]	Höhe
helmet U3/DSC1	['helmət]	Helm
help MORE 1	[help]	helfen; Hilfe
Here we go! MORE 1	[hɪə wiː 'gəʊ]	Jetzt geht's los!
Here you are. MORE 1	[hɪə juː 'ɑː]	Hier, bitte!, Bitte schön!
hers U14/7	[hɜːz]	ihre/r/s

Hi there! MORE 1	[haɪ ðeə]	Hallo!	
hide MORE 1	[haɪd]	(sich) verstecken	
hieroglyphics U11/1	[haɪrə'glɪfɪks]	Hieroglyphen	
high MORE 1	[haɪ]	hoch	
high school C/p.138	['haɪ ˌskuːl]	höhere Schule, Highschool	
hiking U16/5	['haɪkɪŋ]	Wander-; Wandern	
hill U6/1	[hɪl]	Hügel; Anhöhe	
hire MORE 1	['haɪə]	mieten, ausleihen	
history U1/4	['hɪstəri]	Geschichte	
hit U1/6	[hɪt]	schlagen	
hoax U9/9	[həʊks]	Streich, Trick	
hobby U12/7	['hɒbi]	Hobby, Freizeitbeschäftigung	
hold U18/5	[həʊld]	abhalten	
hole MORE 1	[həʊl]	Loch	
holiday camp U7/7	['hɒlɪdeɪ]	Ferienlager	
home MORE 1	[həʊm]	Zuhause; zu Hause	
home run C/p.139	[ˌhəʊm 'run]	Homerun (Baseball)	
home schooling C/p.138	['həʊm 'skuːlɪŋ]	Unterricht zu Hause	
honestly MORE 1	['ɒnɪstli]	ehrlich; wirklich	
hop U2/2	[hɒp]	hüpfen	
hope MORE 1	[həʊp]	hoffen	
hope U16	[həʊp]	Hoffnung	
hopefully U11/S5	['həʊpfli]	hoffnungsvoll; hoffentlich	
horn U11/3	[hɔːn]	Horn	
horrible U12/18	['hɒrɪbl]	schrecklich	
horse MORE 1	[hɔːs]	Pferd	
hospital MORE 1	['hɒspɪtəl]	Krankenhaus	
hot U1/2	[hɒt]	heiß	
hot springs C/p.140	[ˌhɒt 'sprɪŋz]	heiße Quellen	
household U1/2	['haʊshəʊld]	Haushalt	
how MORE 1	[haʊ]	wie	
how about ... U11/S5	[haʊ ə'baʊt]	wie wär's mit ...	
how to U4/12	['haʊ tə]	wie man	
however U9/DSC3	[ˌhaʊ'evə]	aber; jedoch, allerdings	
hug U1/11	[hʌg]	umarmen	
huge MORE 1	[hjuːdʒ]	riesig, riesengroß	
human U11/2	['hjuːmən]	Mensch; menschlich	
hunt U1/9	[hʌnt]	jagen; Jagd	
hurray U13/2	[hʊ'reɪ]	hurra	
hurricane U17/10	['hʌrɪkən]	Orkan; Hurrikan	
hurry MORE 1	['hʌri]	sich beeilen	
hurt MORE 1	[hɜːt]	wehtun, schmerzen	
husband MORE 1	['hʌzbənd]	Ehemann	
hypnosis U2/G	[hɪp'nəʊsɪs]	Hypnose	
hypnotise U2/1	['hɪpnətaɪz]	hypnotisieren	
hypnotist U2/1	['hɪpnətɪst]	Hypnotiseur, Hypnotisiererin	

I

ice skating U17/1	['aɪsskeɪtɪŋ]	Schlittschuh laufen	
I'd like MORE 1	[aɪd laɪk]	ich möchte	
if MORE 1	[ɪf]	wenn	
ill MORE 1	[ɪl]	krank	
illness U15/10	['ɪlnəs]	Krankheit	
imagine U7/10	[ɪ'mædʒɪn]	sich vorstellen	
imaginary U5	[ɪ'mædʒɪnəri]	erfunden	
immediately U3/1	[ɪ'miːdiətli]	sofort	
important MORE 1	[ɪm'pɔːtənt]	wichtig	
in fact U4/2	[ɪn 'fækt]	genau genommen	
in one go MORE 1	[ɪn wʌn 'gəʊ]	auf einmal	
in this way U9/1	[ɪn ðɪs 'weɪ]	dadurch, auf diese Weise	
inch (pl inches) U16/10	[ɪntʃ, 'ɪntʃɪz]	Zoll (2,54 cm)	
indeed U9/S4	[ɪn'diːd]	in der Tat, wirklich	
India MORE 1	['ɪndiə]	Indien	
Indians U15/10	['ɪndiənz]	Indios (Ureinwohner Südamerikas)	
American Indian C/p.140	[ə,merɪkən 'ɪndiən]	Indianer/in	
information U1/2	[ˌɪnfə'meɪʃn]	Information, Auskunft	
information technology (IT) U1/4	[ɪnfə'meɪʃn tek'nɒlədʒi]	Informatik	
injure U15/14	['ɪndʒə]	verletzen	
ink U1/11	[ɪŋk]	Tinte	
inside U1/6	[ɪn'saɪd]	innen; hinein	
instead U8/4	[ɪn'sted]	stattdessen	
intelligent U5/13	[ɪn'telɪdʒənt]	intelligent	
intention U8/1	[ɪn'tenʃn]	Vorhaben, Absicht	
interested (in) MORE 1	['ɪntrəstɪd]	interessiert (an)	
interesting MORE 1	['ɪntrəstɪŋ]	interessant	
interrupt U6/DSC2	[ˌɪntə'rʌpt]	unterbrechen	
intersect U15/NYC3	[ˌɪntə'sekt]	(sich) (über-)kreuzen	
interview MORE 1	['ɪntəvjuː]	Interview	
into MORE 1	['ɪntʊ]	in	
invent U11/2	[ɪn'vent]	erfinden	
invention U11/2	[ɪn'venʃn]	Erfindung	
investigation U9/9	[ɪn,vestɪ'geɪʃn]	Untersuchung, Ermittlung	
invitation MORE 1	[ɪnvɪ'teɪʃən]	Einladung	
invite MORE 1	[ɪn'vaɪt]	einladen	
Italy U11/2	['ɪtəli]	Italien	
Italian U6/4	[ɪ'tæljən]	italienisch/e/r/s	
item U6/DSC2	['aɪtəm]	Punkt, Objekt	

J

jam U11/9	[dʒæm]	Marmelade
Japan U1/6	[dʒəˈpæn]	Japan
jewel U2/2	[ˈdʒuːəl]	Juwel
jewellery U11/2	[ˈdʒuːəlri]	Schmuck
job MORE 1	[dʒɒb]	Arbeit; Aufgabe
join U3/DSC1	[dʒɔɪn]	sich anschließen/treffen
join (in) MORE 1	[dʒɔɪn ˈɪn]	teilnehmen (an), mitmachen (bei)
joke U7/7	[dʒəʊk]	Witz
journey U9/1	[ˈdʒɜːni]	Reise
juggle U11/9	[dʒʌgl]	jonglieren
juggler U11/3	[ˈdʒʌglə]	Jongleur/in
juice MORE 1	[dʒuːs]	Saft
jump MORE 1	[dʒʌmp]	hüpfen; springen
jungle U1/1	[ˈdʒʌŋgl]	Dschungel
junior U17/6	[ˈdʒuːniə]	Junioren-, Jugend-
junior prom C/p.138	[ˌdʒuːniə ˈprɒm]	Unterstufenabschlussball
just U8/7	[dʒʌst]	gerade eben

K

karate EU/1	[kəˈrɑːti]	Karate
(be) keen on U4/13	[bi kiːn ɒn]	sich begeistern für
keep MORE 1	[kiːp]	(be-)halten
keep calm U12/5	[kiːp ˈkɑːm]	ruhig bleiben
keep safe U18/7	[kiːp seɪf]	(ab-)sichern, sicher machen
keep someone company U18/7	[kiːp ˈsʌmwʌn ˈkʌmpəni]	jdm. Gesellschaft leisten
keep watch U7/S3	[kiːp ˈwɒtʃ]	Ausschau/Wache halten
key MORE 1	[kiː]	Schlüssel
kick U4/13	[kɪk]	Tritt, Stoß; treten, kicken
kidnap U9/10	[ˈkɪdnæp]	entführen
kill MORE 1	[kɪl]	töten
kilogram U5/13	[ˈkɪləgræm]	Kilogramm
what kind (of) MORE 1	[wɒt ˈkaɪnd]	was für
kiss U2/2	[kɪs]	küssen
kitchen MORE 1	[ˈkɪtʃən]	Küche
kitty U18/NYC4	[ˈkɪti]	Kätzchen
knife (pl knives) U4/4	[naɪf, naɪvz]	Messer
knight U4/S2	[naɪt]	Ritter
knock MORE 1	[nɒk]	Klopfen; klopfen
know MORE 1	[nəʊ]	wissen; kennen
kph (kilometres per hour) U5/8	[ˈkɪləˌmiːtəs pə aʊə]	Kilometer pro Stunde

L

lab (informal) U14/DSC5	[læb]	Labor
lake U7/1	[leɪk]	See
lamb U10/1	[læm]	Lamm
lamp U14/3	[læmp]	Lampe
lamp post U6/F	[ˈlæmp pəʊst]	Laternenmast
land U5/6	[lænd]	Land
land U9/1	[lænd]	landen
language MORE 1	[ˈlæŋgwɪdʒ]	Sprache
large U2/7	[lɑːdʒ]	groß
late MORE 1	[leɪt]	(zu) spät
later MORE 1	[ˈleɪtə]	später
laugh MORE 1	[lɑːf]	lachen
laughter U2/2	[ˈlɑːftə]	Gelächter
lay off sb (informal) U10/NYC2	[leɪ ˈɒf ˌsʌmbədi]	jemanden in Ruhe lassen
lead U13/10	[liːd]	(an-)führen
leaf (pl leaves) MORE 1	[liːf, liːvz]	Blatt
leaflet U12/18	[ˈliːflət]	Broschüre
learn MORE 1	[lɜːn]	lernen; herausfinden
at least U13/12	[ət ˈliːst]	mindestens, wenigstens
leather U11/3	[ˈleðə]	Leder
leave MORE 1	[liːv]	verlassen, weggehen
leave behind U12/DSC4	[ˌliːv bɪˈhaɪnd]	zurücklassen
left U6/6	[left]	übrig
left-hand U7/2	[ˈlefthænd]	linke/r/s
less (than) U15/10	[les]	weniger (als)
lesson MORE 1	[ˈlesən]	Unterrichtsstunde
letter MORE 1	[ˈletə]	Brief; Buchstabe
Let's see. U15/NYC3	[lets siː]	Schauen wir mal.
librarian U14/DSC5	[laɪˈbreəriən]	Bibliothekar/in
library MORE 1	[ˈlaɪbrəri]	Bibliothek, Bücherei
lie MORE 1	[laɪ]	liegen; sich legen
lie U8/7	[laɪ]	Lüge
life (pl lives) MORE 1	[laɪf, laɪvz]	Leben
life jacket U7/3	[ˈlaɪf dʒækɪt]	Schwimmweste
lift (up) MORE 1	[lɪft]	(hoch-)heben
light U9/6	[laɪt]	Licht
light U11/3	[laɪt]	leicht
lights U6/9	[laɪts]	Ampel
(be) like 1/12	[laɪk]	wie etwas sein, ähnlich sein
limo (informal) C/p.138	[ˈlɪməʊ]	Limousine
line MORE 1	[laɪn]	Linie
lion MORE 1	[ˈlaɪən]	Löwe
Lisbon U1/1	[ˈlɪzbən]	Lissabon
list U4/10	[lɪst]	Liste
Listen up here. U15/NYC3	[ˌlɪsən ˈʌp hɪə]	Hör(t) mal zu.

litter tray U18/1	['lɪtə treɪ]	Katzenklo
live MORE 1	[lɪv]	leben
lobby U16/11	['lɒbi]	Eingangshalle, Foyer
(door) lock U4/5	['dɔ: lɒk]	(Tür-)Schloss
lock U13/2	[lɒk]	abschließen
look U11/3	[lʊk]	Aussehen; Blick
look after MORE 1	[lʊk 'a:ftə]	sich kümmern um
look at MORE 1	['lʊk ət]	betrachten, sehen
look for MORE 1	['lʊk fɔ:]	suchen nach
look forward to U9/DSC3	[lʊk fɔ:wəd tu]	sich freuen auf
look like U7/7	[lʊk laɪk]	aussehen wie
lose U3/DSC1	[lu:z]	verlieren
(get) lost U6/7	[get 'lɒst]	sich verirrt haben
lost and found office U14/DSC5	[lɒst ənd faʊnd 'ɒfɪs]	Fundbüro
a lot (of) MORE 1	[ə 'lɒt]	viel/e
lots of MORE 1	['lɒts,əv]	viel, jede Menge
lots of love U3/1	[ˌlɒts əv 'lʌv]	alles Liebe, liebe Grüße
loud MORE 1	[laʊd]	laut
lovely U16/5	['lʌvli]	schön
low U16/1	[ləʊ]	niedrig, schwach
luck MORE 1	[lʌk]	Glück
bad luck U14/DSC5	[ˌbæd 'lʌk]	Pech, Unglück
luckily U3/1	['lʌkli]	glücklicherweise
be lucky MORE 1	[bi: 'lʌki]	Glück haben

M

machine U3/4	[mə'ʃi:n]	Maschine
madam MORE 1	['mædəm]	gnädige Frau (Anrede)
made of MORE 1	[meɪd əv]	aus … gemacht
magic U13	['mædʒɪk]	Magie, Zauber
main U10/7	[meɪn]	Haupt-
main course U10/7	[meɪn kɔ:s]	Hauptgang
make friends U17/11	[meɪk frendz]	Freundschaft schließen
make sure U6/DSC2	[meɪk 'ʃɔ:]	sich versichern, darauf achten
make up U5/18	[meɪk ʌp]	erfinden
malaria U5/10	[mə'leəriə]	Malaria
mammal U5/10	['mæml]	Säugetier
man (pl men) MORE 1	[mæn, men]	Mann
manage sth. U17/10	['mænɪdʒ]	etwas schaffen
many MORE 1	['meni]	viele
map U6/3	[mæp]	(Land-)Karte
marble U15/NYC3	['ma:bl]	aus Marmor
market U18/NYC4	['ma:kɪt]	Markt
market square U6/9	[ˌma:kɪt skweə]	Marktplatz
married U12/9	['mærɪd]	verheiratet

mask U4/3	[ma:sk]	Maske
master U2/S1	['ma:stə]	Meister
match MORE 1	[mætʃ]	zuordnen
material U14/DSC5	[mə'tɪəriəl]	Stoff, Material
mathematician U12/15	['mæθəmə'tɪʃn]	Mathematiker/in
It doesn't matter. MORE 1	[ɪt dʌznt 'mætə]	Das ist nicht wichtig.
maximum U16/4	['mæksɪməm]	Maximum
maybe U2/2	['meɪbi]	vielleicht
mean U4/5	[mi:n]	gemein
mean MORE 1	[mi:n]	bedeuten; meinen
meat U10/2	[mi:t]	Fleisch
medal U2/1	['medl]	Medaille
medical science U15/10	['medɪkl saɪəns]	medizinische Wissenschaft
medicine (no pl) U1/9	['medsən]	Medizin, Medikament/e
medicine man U15/10	['medsən mæn]	Medizinmann
meet up U8/7	[mi:t ʌp]	(sich) treffen
melt U11/3	[melt]	schmelzen
memory MORE 1	['memri]	Gedächtnis; Erinnerung
mention MORE 1	['mentʃən]	erwähnen
menu U10/7	['menju:]	Speisekarte
mess U2/2	[mes]	Unordnung, Durcheinander
metal U14/DSC5	['metl]	Metall
metallic U9/9	[mə'tælɪk]	metallisch
metre MORE 1	['mi:tə]	Meter
middle MORE 1	['mɪdl]	Mitte
midnight MORE 1	['mɪdnaɪt]	Mitternacht
might U8	[maɪt]	könnte; vielleicht (tun, sein)
mild U16/10	[maɪld]	sanft; mild
mile U16/10	[maɪl]	Meile
million MORE 1	['mɪljən]	Million
mine U14/7	[maɪn]	meine/r/s
mineral water MORE 1	['mɪnərəl 'wɔ:tə]	Mineralwasser
miss U8/10	[mɪs]	verpassen
miss U12/5	[mɪs]	vermissen
missing MORE 1	['mɪsɪŋ]	vermisst
mission U13/S6	['mɪʃən]	Auftrag, Mission
mixed-up U8/7	[ˌmɪkst'ʌp]	durcheinander
mobile (phone) MORE 1	[məʊbaɪl fəʊn]	Handy
modern U3/2	['mɒdn]	modern
mom (AE) C/p.138	[mɒm]	Mama, Mutti
Mongolian 14/1	[mɒŋ'gəʊliən]	mongolisch
monster U4/2	['mɒnstə]	Monster, Ungeheuer
monument U11/2	['mɒnjʊmənt]	Denkmal, Monument
moon U7/1	[mu:n]	Mond

morph MORE 1	[mɔːf]	morphen, sich verwandeln	
mosquito (pl -es or -s) U5/10	[mɒˈskiːtəʊ]	Stechmücke, Moskito	
(the) most MORE 1	[ðə ˈməʊst]	am meisten; die meisten	
most of the time U6/6	[ˈməʊst əv ðə taɪm]	meistens	
mostly U11/2	[ˈməʊstli]	hauptsächlich	
motorway U7/1	[ˈməʊtəweɪ]	Autobahn	
mountain MORE 1	[ˈmaʊntɪn]	Berg	
mountain biking U17/1	[ˈmaʊntɪn ˌbaɪkɪŋ]	Mountainbiken	
mountain climbing U17/1	[ˈmaʊntɪn ˌklaɪmɪŋ]	Bergsteigen	
mountain climber U17/4	[ˈmaʊntɪn ˌklaɪmə]	Bergsteiger/in	
mouse (pl mice) MORE 1	[maʊs, maɪs]	Maus	
move U7/5	[muːv]	übersiedeln; (sich) bewegen	
move house U15/G	[muːv haʊs]	umziehen	
move in U12/9	[ˈmuːv ɪn]	einziehen	
moveable U14/1	[ˈmuːvəbl]	beweglich, transportierbar	
movie U16/11	[ˈmuːvi]	Film	
mph (miles per hour) U16/3	[ˌmaɪlz pə ˈaʊə]	Meilen pro Stunde	
Ms U5/NYC1	[məz]	Frau (Anrede)	
mummy U11/1	[ˈmʌmi]	Mumie	
museum U2/2	[mjuːˈziːəm]	Museum	
mushroom U10/4	[ˈmʌʃruːm]	Pilz	
music shop U6/2	[ˈmjuːzɪk ˌʃɒp]	Musikladen	
musician MORE 1	[mjuːˈzɪʃn]	Musiker/in	
must MORE 1	[mʌst]	müssen	
mustn't U11/10	[ˈmʌsənt]	nicht dürfen	
myself U12/5	[maɪˈself]	mir, mich; hier: selbst	
mystery U18/NYC4	[ˈmɪstəri]	Rätsel; Geheimnis	

N

nail U13/6	[neɪl]	Nagel	
naked U11/3	[ˈneɪkɪd]	nackt, unbekleidet	
national park U17/4	[ˈnæʃnl pɑːk]	Nationalpark	
nearly MORE 1	[ˈnɪəli]	fast; beinahe	
need MORE 1	[niːd]	brauchen	
need to U6/9	[niːd tuː]	müssen	
neighbour MORE 1	[ˈneɪbə]	Nachbar/in	
Neither do I. U18/7	[ˈnaɪðə dʊ ˈaɪ]	Ich auch nicht.	
nervous MORE 1	[ˈnɜːvəs]	nervös	
network U13/10	[ˈnetwɜːk]	Netzwerk	

never MORE 1	[ˈnevə]	nie(mals)	
news (pl) MORE 1	[njuːz]	Nachrichten	
newspaper MORE 1	[ˈnjuːzpeɪpə]	Zeitung	
next door U14/7	[nekst ˈdɔː]	nebenan	
New Zealand U1/2	[ˌnjuːˈziːlənd]	Neuseeland	
nice MORE 1	[naɪs]	nett; schön, angenehm	
nightmare C/p.138	[ˈnaɪtmeə]	Alptraum	
nil U17/8	[nɪl]	nichts, null	
Nile U11/2	[naɪl]	Nil	
no longer U9/9	[ˈnəʊ lɒŋə]	nicht mehr	
No way! MORE 1	[nəʊ weɪ]	Auf keinen Fall!	
nobody MORE 1	[ˈnəʊbədi]	niemand	
noise MORE 1	[nɔɪz]	Lärm, Krach; Geräusch	
none U13/S6	[nʌn]	keine/r/s	
nonsense U9/10	[ˈnɒnsns]	Unsinn	
normally U18/10	[ˈnɔːməli]	normalerweise	
north U1/6	[nɔːθ]	nördlich, Nord-; Norden	
North Pole U1/1	[nɔːθ pəʊl]	Nordpol	
Northern Ireland U16/4	[ˈnɔːðən ˈaɪələnd]	Nordirland	
northwest C/p.141	[ˌnɔːθˈwest]	nordwestlich, Nordwest-; Nordwesten	
not any longer U13/S6	[nɒt ˈeni ˈlɒŋgə]	nicht mehr	
not any more U7/7	[nɒt ˈeni mɔː]	nicht mehr	
Not at all. U6/3	[nɒt æt ɔːl]	Nichts zu danken.	
no longer U13/S6	[nəʊ ˈlɒŋgə]	nicht mehr	
not feel well U8/7	[nɒt fiːl wel]	sich unwohl fühlen	
not only … but also U3/6	[nɒt ˈəʊnli bʌt ˈɔːlsəʊ]	nicht nur … sondern auch	
not that difficult U12/5	[nət ðæt ˈdɪfɪklt]	nicht so schwer	
not until U9/DSC3	[nɒt ənˈtɪl]	erst	
not yet U13/S6	[nɒt jet]	noch nicht	
note MORE 1	[nəʊt]	Notiz; Ankündigung	
notebook U12/13	[ˈnəʊtbʊk]	Notebook(-Computer)	
nothing MORE 1	[ˈnʌθɪŋ]	nichts	
notice MORE 1	[ˈnəʊtɪs]	bemerken	
number C/p.140	[ˈnʌmbər]	Anzahl	

O

object U7/8	[ˈɒbdʒɪkt]	Objekt, Gegenstand, Sache	
obsessed U17/10	[əbˈsest]	besessen	
ocean U17/10	[ˈəʊʃn]	Meer, Ozean	
octopus (pl -es) U1/6	[ˈɒktəpəs]	Tintenfisch	
the odd one out U9/5	[ði ɒd wʌn ˈaʊt]	das fünfte Rad am Wagen; hier: das Wort, das nicht dazugehört	

of course MORE 1	[əv ˈkɔːs]	natürlich
off MORE 1	[ɒf]	aus; weg
be off U7/S3	[biː ɒf]	fortgehen, weggehen
Off you go. U2/2	[ˌɒf juː ˈgəʊ]	Geh(t) schon., Gehen Sie schon.
offer U5/16	[ˈɒfə]	Angebot
office U2/2	[ˈɒfɪs]	Büro
officer U7/7	[ˈɒfɪsə]	Offizier/in; Beamter, Beamtin
often MORE 1	[ˈɒftən]	oft, häufig
older U1/2	[ˈəʊldə]	älter
olive U10/4	[ˈɒlɪv]	Olive
the Olympic Games C/p.139	[ði əʊˌlɪmpɪk ˈgeɪmz]	die Olympischen Spiele
on his own U1/6	[ɒn hɪs ˈəʊn]	allein, auf sich gestellt
on my own U17/8	[ɒn maɪ ˈəʊn]	alleine
on time U9/DSC3	[ɒn ˈtaɪm]	pünktlich
once MORE 1	[wʌns]	einmal
once upon a time U4/S2	[ˈwʌns əpɒn ə ˈtaɪm]	es war einmal
one by one U9/1	[wʌn baɪ wʌn]	nacheinander
onto MORE 1	[ˈɒntə]	auf
operation U3/1	[ˌɒprˈeɪʃn]	Operation
opposite U6/4	[ˈɒpəzɪt]	gegenüber
order MORE 1	[ˈɔːdə]	Reihenfolge
order U10/5	[ˈɔːdə]	bestellen
order U12/DSC4	[ˈɔːdə]	Bestellung
organise U3/1	[ˈɔːgnaɪz]	organisieren
organisation C/p.138	[ˌɔːgənaɪˈzeɪʃən]	Einrichtung, Organisation
ostrich U5/11	[ˈɒstrɪtʃ]	(Vogel) Strauß
other U1/6	[ˈʌðər]	andere/r/s
ours U14/7	[ˈaʊəz]	unsere/r/s
outdoor U7/1	[ˈaʊtˌdɔː]	im Freien
out loud U3/1	[aʊt laʊd]	laut, lauthals
out of MORE 1	[ˈaʊt əv]	aus
outlook U16/3	[ˈaʊtlʊk]	Aussicht
outside MORE 1	[aʊtˈsaɪd]	außen, außerhalb
out there U9/8	[aʊt ðeə]	da draußen
over MORE 1	[ˈəʊvə]	über, herüber
own MORE 1	[əʊn]	eigene/r/s
owner MORE 1	[ˈəʊnə]	Besitzer/in, Eigentümer/in
ox (pl oxen) U11/3	[ɒks, ˈɒksən]	Ochse
oxygen U15/10	[ˈɒksɪdʒən]	Sauerstoff

P

pack U16/7	[pæk]	packen
pain U15/1	[peɪn]	Schmerz
paint EU/1	[peɪnt]	malen, streichen
painting U11/3	[ˈpeɪntɪŋ]	Bild, Gemälde
pair MORE 1	[peər]	Paar
palm leaves U11/3	[ˈpɑːm liːvz]	Palmenblätter
pancakes U10/1	[ˈpænkeɪkz]	Palatschinken, Pfannkuchen
panic U12/5	[ˈpænɪk]	in Panik geraten
paper MORE 1	[ˈpeɪpər]	Papier; Zeitung
papyrus U11/1	[pəˈpaɪrəs]	Papyrus
paragraph MORE 1	[ˈpærəgrɑːf]	Absatz, Abschnitt
parents MORE 1	[ˈpeərənts]	Eltern
part MORE 1	[pɑːt]	Teil
partner U1/2	[ˈpɑːtnə]	Partner/in
party MORE 1	[ˈpɑːti]	Party
pass (a test) U15/G	[pɑːs]	(eine Prüfung) bestehen
pass on U3/6	[pɑːs ɒn]	weitergeben
pass through U13/1	[pɑːs ˈθruː]	durchlaufen; hier: durchgehen durch
passenger C/p.141	[ˈpæsəndʒə]	Passagier-
password U3/6	[ˈpɑːswɜːd]	Passwort
past U6/1	[pɑːst]	nach; vorbei an
path U6/1	[pɑːθ]	Weg, Pfad
patient U15/1	[ˈpeɪʃnt]	Patient/in
pattern U14/DSC5	[ˈpætn]	Muster
pay MORE 1	[peɪ]	bezahlen
peas MORE 1	[piː]	Erbsen
peach U10/1	[piːtʃ]	Pfirsich
peak U16/10	[piːk]	Gipfel, Bergspitze
pear U10/1	[peə]	Birne
penguin U18/10	[ˈpeŋgwɪn]	Pinguin
pennant C/p.139	[ˈpenənt]	Wimpel (dreieckige Flagge)
people (pl) MORE 1	[ˈpiːpl]	Leute, Menschen
people person U17/10	[ˈpiːpl pɜːsən]	geselliger Mensch
pepperoni U12/DSC4	[ˌpepəˈrəʊni]	(scharfe) Salami
per U5/8	[pɜː]	pro
per cent (%) U11/2	[pəˈsent]	Prozent (%)
perfect U1/12	[ˈpɜːfekt]	perfekt
perfume U11/3	[ˈpɜːfjuːm]	Parfüm
perfumed U11/3	[ˈpɜːfjuːmd]	parfümiert
person U1/7	[ˈpɜːsn]	Person, Mensch
Peru U14/1	[pəˈruː]	Peru
pet shop U18/7	[ˈpet ˌʃɒp]	Tierhandlung
pharaoh U11/2	[ˈfeərəʊ]	Pharaoh
photo U3/DSC1	[ˈfəʊtəʊ]	Foto
photograph U9/9	[ˈfəʊtəgrɑːf]	Foto(grafie)
physical education (PE) U1/4	[ˈfɪzɪkl ˌedjʊˈkeɪʃn]	Sport(unterricht)
picture MORE 1	[ˈpɪktʃə]	Bild
pick up MORE 1	[pɪk ˈʌp]	aufheben, abholen
picnic U3/DSC1	[ˈpɪknɪk]	Picknick

pie U10/1	[paɪ]	Kuchen; Pastete
piece MORE 1	[piːs]	Stück
pig U5/1	[pɪg]	Schwein
pineapple U12/DSC4	[ˈpaɪnˌæpl]	Ananas
pitch (AE) U10/NYC2	[pɪtʃ]	werfen
pitcher (AE) C/p.139	[ˈpɪtʃə]	(Ball-)Werfer
pity U9/DSC3	[ˈpɪti]	hier: schade, dass
plain U14/DSC5	[pleɪn]	einfarbig, ungemustert; einheitlich
plan U3/1	[plæn]	planen
plan U14/6	[plæn]	(Lage-)Plan
plane U2/2	[pleɪn]	Flugzeug
planet U9/1	[ˈplænɪt]	Planet
plant U11/2	[plɑːnt]	Pflanze
plastic U14/DSC5	[ˈplæstɪk]	Plastik, Kunststoff
play MORE 1	[pleɪ]	Theaterstück; Spiel
play a trick/tricks on somebody U4/3	[pleɪ ə ˈtrɪk ɒn]	jemanden einen Streich spielen
player MORE 1	[ˈpleɪər]	Spieler/in
plenty of U4/12	[ˈplenti əv]	eine Menge von
plum U10/1	[plʌm]	Zwetschke, Pflaume
pocket U4/7	[ˈpɒkɪt]	(Hosen-)Tasche
point (at) U7/7	[pɔɪnt]	zeigen (auf)
point U15/14	[pɔɪnt]	Punkt; Argument
poison U1/9	[ˈpɔɪzn]	Gift
poisonous U1/6	[ˈpɔɪznəs]	giftig
police (no pl) MORE 1	[pəˈliːs]	Polizei
police station U2/2	[pəˈliːs ˌsteɪʃn]	Polizeiwache
policeman (pl -men) MORE 1	[pəˈliːsmən]	Polizist
policewoman (pl -women) U6/7	[pəˈliːsˌwʊmən]	Polizistin
politely U6/DSC2	[pəˈlaɪtli]	höflich
poor MORE 1	[pɔːr]	arm
Poor you! U7/S3	[pɔːr juː]	Du Armer/Arme!
pond U7/7	[pɒnd]	Teich
popular U5/6	[ˈpɒpjʊlə]	beliebt
pork U10/1	[pɔːk]	Schweinefleisch
Portuguese U12/9	[ˌpɔːtʃʊˈgiːz]	Portugiesisch
possible U16/12	[ˈpɒsɪbl]	möglich
post U3/6	[pəʊst]	posten, einen Beitrag verfassen (online)
posting U3/6	[ˈpəʊstɪŋ]	Posting, Beitrag (online)
post office U6/2	[ˈpəʊst ɒfɪs]	Postamt
pot U13/7	[pɒt]	Topf
pound (£) MORE 1	[paʊnd]	Pfund
power MORE 1	[ˈpaʊər]	Kraft; Macht
powerful U4/S2	[ˈpaʊəfəl]	mächtig
practice MORE 1	[ˈpræktɪs]	Übung
practise MORE 1	[ˈpræktɪs]	üben; Übung

prayer U1/2	[preə]	Gebet
prepare U1/2	[prɪˈpeə]	(vor-/zu-)bereiten
(be) prepared U17/8	[biː prɪˈpeəd]	vorbereitet sein
present MORE 1	[ˈpreznt]	Geschenk
presentation U8/2	[ˌprezənˈteɪʃən]	Präsentation
president MORE 1	[ˈprezɪdənt]	Präsident/in
press MORE 1	[pres]	drücken; klicken
pretty MORE 1	[ˈprɪti]	hübsch
pretty U7/7	[ˈprɪti]	ziemlich
priest U11/8	[priːst]	Priester/in
print out U12/13	[ˈprɪnt aʊt]	ausdrucken
prison U13/6	[ˈprɪzn]	Gefängnis
private U1/2	[ˈpraɪvət]	privat, Privat-
prize MORE 1	[praɪz]	Preis, Auszeichnung
probably U9/S4	[ˈprɒbəbli]	wahrscheinlich
produce U15/10	[prəˈdjuːs]	erzeugen
professional U17/6	[prəˈfeʃnl]	professionell, hauptberuflich
professor U11/7	[prəˈfesə]	Professor/in
profile U17/4	[ˈprəʊfaɪl]	Profil
project U8/2	[ˈprɒdʒekt]	Projekt
prom C/p.138	[prɒm]	(Abschluss-)Ball
promise MORE 1	[ˈprɒmɪs]	versprechen; Versprechen
prompt U6/DSC2	[prɒmt]	Hinweis
pronto (informal) U2/2	[ˈprɒntəʊ]	sofort
protect U4/S2	[prəˈtekt]	schützen
proud (of) U7/7	[praʊd]	stolz sein (auf)
public U15/NYC3	[ˈpʌblɪk]	öffentlich, staatlich
pull MORE 1	[pʊl]	ziehen
pumpkin U4/1	[ˈpʌmpkɪn]	Kürbis
push MORE 1	[pʊʃ]	schieben
push U9/11	[pʊʃ]	drücken
push yourself U17/10	[pʊʃ jɔːˈself]	sich selbst motivieren, anspornen
put MORE 1	[pʊt]	setzen, legen, stellen
put a spell on sb U13/6	[pʊt ə ˈspel ɒn ˈsʌmbədi]	jemanden verzaubern
put on U1/2	[pʊt ɒn]	anziehen
put out U13/7	[pʊt aʊt]	löschen
pyjamas (no pl) U18/13	[pəˈdʒɑːməz]	Pyjama, Schlafanzug
pyramid U11/1	[ˈpɪrəmɪd]	Pyramide

Q

quarter MORE 1	[ˈkwɔːtə]	Viertel(stunde)
quick MORE 1	[kwɪk]	schnell; kurz
quiet MORE 1	[ˈkwaɪət]	leise, ruhig
quite U1/11	[kwaɪt]	ziemlich

R

race U17/10	[reɪs]	Wettfahrt; Wettkampf
radiator U14/3	['reɪdɪeɪtə]	Heizkörper
railway U6/2	['reɪlweɪ]	Gleise, Schienen; (Eisen)bahn
railway station U6/2	['reɪlweɪ 'steɪʃn]	Bahnhof
rain MORE 1	[reɪn]	Regen; regnen
raincoat U16/7	['reɪnkəʊt]	Regenmantel
rainfall U16/10	['reɪnfɔːl]	Niederschlag
rainforest U15/10	['reɪnfɒrɪst]	Regenwald
rainy U16/2	['reɪni]	regnerisch
range C/p.140	[reɪndʒ]	hier: Gebirgskette
rattle U13/1	['rætl]	klappern, rasseln
reach U17/G	[riːtʃ]	erreichen, ankommen
react U9/DSC3	[ri'ækt]	reagieren
ready MORE 1	['redi]	fertig, bereit
real MORE 1	[rɪəl]	wirklich; echt, real
really MORE 1	['rɪəli]	wirklich
reason U3/8	['riːzn]	Grund
receptionist U16/5	[rɪ'sepʃənɪst]	Rezeptionist/in
recipe U10/7	['resəpi]	Rezept
record U16/10	['rekɔːd]	Rekord
record EU/1	[rɪ'kɔːd]	aufzeichnen
the Red Cross U12/9	[ðə ˌred 'krɒs]	das Rote Kreuz
reddish U10/NYC2	['redɪʃ]	rötlich
reed U14/1	[riːd]	Schilf(rohr)
refugee U12/3	[ˌrefjʊ'dʒiː]	Flüchtling
refugee camp U12/3	[refjʊ'dʒiː kæmp]	Flüchtlingslager
region C/p.140	['riːdʒən]	Region, Gegend
religion U11/2	[rɪ'lɪdʒən]	Religion
religious C/p.138	[rɪ'lɪdʒəs]	religiös; Religions-
remember MORE 1	[rɪ'membər]	sich erinnern (an)
remind U12/DSC4	[rɪ'maɪnd]	erinnern
repeat MORE 1	[rɪ'piːt]	wiederholen
reply MORE 1	[rɪ'plaɪ]	antworten
report U16/4	[rɪ'pɔːt]	Bericht
reptile U5/6	['reptaɪl]	Reptil
request U17/DSC6	[rɪ'kwest]	Bitte
rescue MORE 1	['reskjuː]	Rettung; retten
reservation C/p.140	[ˌrezə'veɪʃən]	Reservat
respond MORE 1	[rɪ'spɒnd]	antworten
response MORE 1	[rɪ'spɒns]	Antwort
responsibly U3	[rɪ'spɒnsɪbli]	verantwortungsvoll
rest U13/7	[rest]	Rest
rest U17/8	[rest]	Ruhe; Pause
result EU/1	[rɪ'zʌlt]	Folge; Ergebnis
return MORE 1	[rɪ'tɜːn]	zurückkehren
revenge U9/DSC3	[rɪ'vendʒ]	Rache
revision U1	[rɪ'vɪʒən]	Wiederholung

reward U18/NYC4	[rɪ'wɔːd]	Belohnung
rhino (=rhinoceros) U5/13	['raɪnəʊ]	Nashorn, Rhinozeros
rhyme MORE 1	[raɪm]	Reim
rice pudding U10/1	[raɪs 'pudɪŋ]	Milchreis
rich MORE 1	[rɪtʃ]	reich
right away U1/2	[raɪt əweɪ]	sofort
right-hand U7/2	['raɪthænd]	rechte/r/s
Right here. U18/NYC4	[raɪt hɪə]	Hab' ich hier.
right now U13/8	[raɪt naʊ]	jetzt gerade
ring MORE 1	[rɪŋ]	anrufen
ring U1/9	[rɪŋ]	Kreis
rise U16/4	[raɪz]	steigen
river MORE 1	['rɪvər]	Fluss
road MORE 1	[rəʊd]	Straße
roam U9/8	[rəʊm]	wandern
roast U13/7	[rəʊst]	rösten
roast potato U13/6	[rəʊst pə'teɪtəʊ]	Ofenkartoffel
robber MORE 1	['rɒbər]	Räuber/in
role U3/DSC1	[rəʊl]	Rolle
roll U11/12	[rəʊl]	rollen
roller-skating U12/G	['rəʊləskeɪtɪŋ]	inlineskaten
Roman U7/7	['rəʊmən]	römisch
Romania U6/6	[rʊ'meɪnɪə]	Rumänien
Romanian U6/6	[rʊ'meɪnɪən]	rumänisch
Rome U1/1	[rəʊm]	Rom
roof MORE 1	[ruːf]	Dach
room U9/1	[ruːm]	Platz
rope U2/S1	[rəʊp]	Seil
rose U3/2	[rəʊz]	Rose
rotten U13/7	['rɒtən]	verfault, verdorben
round U6/4	[raʊnd]	um … herum
round U9/1	[raʊnd]	rund
rounders C/p.139	['raʊndəz]	Schlagball (Sportart)
routine U1/3	[ruː'tiːn]	Routine
row U9/DSC3	[rəʊ]	(Sitz-)Reihe
rubbish (informal) U9/DSC3	['rʌbɪʃ]	mies, schlecht
rug U14/3	[rʌg]	Teppich
rugby practice U1/2	['rʌgbi 'præktɪs]	Rugbytraining
rule MORE 1	[ruːl]	Regel; beherrschen
runaway U18/NYC4	['rʌnəweɪ]	entlaufen
running U17/1	['rʌnɪŋ]	Laufen

S

sacred U11/2	['seɪkrəd]	heilig
safe U5/1	[seɪf]	sicher
sail U16/G	[seɪl]	Segeln
salad MORE 1	['sæləd]	Salat
salt MORE 1	[sɔːlt]	Salz
the same MORE 1	[ðə 'seɪm]	der-/die-/dasselbe
sand U1/6	[sænd]	Sand
sandal U11/3	['sændl]	Sandale
sausage MORE 1	['sɒsɪdʒ]	Wurst, Würstchen
save MORE 1	[seɪv]	retten
say sorry U3/1	[seɪ 'sɒri]	sich entschuldigen
scale U16/1	[skeɪl]	Skala, Maßstab
scare U4/13	[skeə]	Angst machen, erschrecken
be scared (of) MORE 1	[biː 'skeəd əv]	Angst haben (vor)
scary U3/8	['skeəri]	furchterregend; unheimlich
scene MORE 1	[siːn]	Szene
science MORE 1	['saɪəns]	Naturwissenschaft
scientist U9/9	['saɪəntɪst]	Wissenschaftler/in
scooter MORE 1	['skuːtə]	Roller
score U15/G	[skɔː]	erreichen, erzielen (Tore)
score U15/1	[skɔː]	Punktestand, Spielstand
Scotland U16/4	['skɒtlənd]	Schottland
scream U13/1	[skriːm]	schreien; kreischen
screen MORE 1	[skriːn]	Leinwand; Bildschirm
sculpture U3/2	['skʌlptʃə]	Bildhauerei; Skulptur, Plastik
sea MORE 1	[siː]	Meer
sea level U16/10	['siː ˌlevel]	Meeresspiegel
seat U2/2	[siːt]	(Sitz-)Platz
second U9/10	['sekənd]	Sekunde
secret U2/2	['siːkrət]	geheim
secretary U14/DSC5	['sekrətri]	Sekretär/in
security U2/2	[sɪ'kjʊərəti]	Sicherheit
seed U9/1	[siːd]	Same/n
seem U10/NYC2	[siːm]	scheinen
sell MORE 1	[sel]	verkaufen
send MORE 1	[send]	senden, schicken
senior prom C/p.138	[ˌsiːniə 'prɒm]	Maturaball
sergeant U2/2	['sɑːdʒənt]	Sergeant; hier: Polizeimeister
series MORE 1	['sɪəriːz]	Serie; Reihe
serious U10/NYC2	['sɪəriəs]	ernst(haft)
servant MORE 1	['sɜːvənt]	Diener/in
serve U10/10	[sɜːv]	servieren
several U7/7	['sevərəl]	einige, mehrere
shall U3/DSC1	[ʃæl]	sollen; wollen
shake U1/11	[ʃeɪk]	schütteln
What a shame! U9/DSC3	[wɒt ə 'ʃeɪm]	Wie schade!
That's a shame. U15/6	[ðæts ə 'ʃeɪm]	Wie schade! So ein Jammer!
share U9/DSC3	[ʃeə]	teilen
shed MORE 1	[ʃed]	Schuppen, Stall
sheep (pl sheep) U11/3	[ʃiːp]	Schaf
shell U1/6	[ʃel]	Schale; Muschel
(animal) shelter U18/7	['ænɪməl ˌʃeltə]	Tierheim
shock U2/2	[ʃɒk]	Schock
shocked U11/11	[ʃɒkt]	schockiert, entsetzt
shopping centre U6/6	['ʃɒpɪŋ 'sentə]	Einkaufszentrum
short for U5/8	[ʃɔːt fɔːr]	kurz, kurz für
should U4/5	[ʃʊd]	sollte/n, solltest
show MORE 1	[ʃəʊ]	zeigen
shower U16/7	['ʃaʊə]	Regenschauer
showing U9/DSC3	['ʃəʊɪŋ]	Vorführung
sick U15/10	[sɪk]	krank
feel sick MORE 1	[fiːl 'sɪk]	sich schlecht fühlen
side U4/5	[saɪd]	Seite
sight U1/11	[saɪt]	Anblick
go sightseeing C/p.141	[gəʊ 'saɪtˌsiːɪŋ]	Sehenswürdigkeiten besichtigen
sign U6/3	[saɪn]	Zeichen, Schild
signal U18/10	['sɪgnəl]	Signal; Zeichen
silly MORE 1	['sɪli]	dumm, albern
similar (to) MORE 1	['sɪmɪlə tʊ]	ähnlich (wie)
simple U5/G	['sɪmpl]	einfach
simply U6/9	['sɪmpli]	einfach
since U15/14	[sɪnts]	seit
sing MORE 1	[sɪŋ]	singen
Singapore U2/2	[ˌsɪŋə'pɔː]	Singapur
single parent U12/9	['sɪŋgl 'peərənt]	Alleinerziehende/r
sink U14/3	[sɪŋk]	Waschbecken, Spüle
sister MORE 1	['sɪstər]	Schwester
sit up U2/2	[sɪt 'ʌp]	sich aufsetzen
situation MORE 1	[sɪtʃu'eɪʃn]	Situation, Lage
size U1/9	[saɪz]	Größe
ski MORE 1	[skiː]	Skifahren
sky U9/1	[skaɪ]	Himmel
slave U11/3	[sleɪv]	Sklave, Sklavin
sleep U9/11	[sliːp]	Schlaf
slice U10/3	[slaɪs]	Scheibe
slippers U3/9	['slɪpərs]	Hausschuhe
slow MORE 1	[sləʊ]	langsam
small talk U16/5	['smɔːl ˌtɔːk]	Small Talk, Plauderei
smart EU/1	[smɑːt]	schlau
smart phone U12/DSC4	['smɑːt ˌfəʊn]	Smartphone

smell MORE 1	[smel]	riechen	**sports centre** U17/DSC6	[spɔts 'sentə]	Sportzentrum
smelly C/p.138	['smeli]	übelriechend	**sportsman (pl -men)** U17/3	['spɔːtsmən, spɔːtsmən]	Sportler
smile MORE 1	[smaɪl]	lächeln	**sportswoman (pl -women)** U17/3	['spɔːtswʊmən, 'spɔːtswɪmɪn]	Sportlerin
smoke MORE 1	[sməʊk]	Rauch; rauchen	**spotted** U14/DSC5	['spɒtɪd]	gepunktet
snack U7/7	[snæk]	Snack, Imbiss	**sprinkle** U13/6	['sprɪŋkl]	sprenkeln, sprengen
snow U18/10	[snəʊ]	Schnee	**square** U6/8	[skweə]	Quadrat, Platz
snowy U16/2	['snəʊi]	verschneit	**stage** MORE 1	[steɪdʒ]	Bühne
so-called U7/7	[ˌsəʊ'kɔːld]	sogenannt	**stain** U13/1	[steɪn]	Fleck
So do I. U18/7	[səʊ du aɪ]	Ich auch.	**staircase** U14/1	['steəkeɪs]	Treppe
So what? U1/6	[səʊ 'wɒt]	Na und?	**stairs** U4/3	[steəz]	Treppe
sofa U5/15	['səʊfə]	Sofa	**stand up** MORE 1	[stænd 'ʌp]	aufstehen
soil C/p.141	[sɔɪl]	Erde, Boden	**stand up (for)** MORE 1	[stænd 'ʌp]	sich einsetzen (für)
soldier U11/8	['səʊldʒə]	Soldat/in	**star** MORE 1	[stɑː]	Stern
sold out U9/DSC3	[səʊld aʊt]	ausverkauft	**starter** U10/7	['stɑːtə]	Vorspeise
solo U17/10	['səʊləʊ]	Solo-	**starting point** U16/10	['stɒːtɪŋ pɔɪnt]	Ausgangspunkt
solve MORE I	[sɒlv]	lösen	**station** U2/2	['steɪʃn]	Bahnhof; Station
somebody MORE 1	['sʌmbədi]	jemand	**statue** U6/DSC2	['stætʃuː]	Statue, Standbild
someone MORE 1	['sʌmwən]	jemand	**stay** MORE 1	[steɪ]	bleiben
something MORE 1	['sʌmθɪŋ]	etwas	**stay (at)** U8/1	[steɪ]	übernachten (bei)
something else U7/7	['sʌmθɪŋ els]	sonst etwas	**stay calm** U12/5	['steɪ kɑːm]	ruhig bleiben
sometimes MORE 1	['sʌmtaɪmz]	manchmal	**steal** U2/3	[stiːl]	stehlen
somewhere U1/6	['sʌmweər]	irgendwo	**step** U6/9	[step]	Schritt
son MORE 1	[sʌn]	Sohn	**step** U11/8	[step]	Stufe
soon MORE 1	[suːn]	bald	**stew** U10/10	[stjuː]	Eintopf
sort MORE 1	[sɔːt]	Sorte, Art	**sticker** U4/3	['stɪkə]	Sticker
sound U4/4	[saʊnd]	Geräusch	**stiff** U2/2	[stɪf]	steif
sound U8/5	[saʊnd]	klingen	**still** MORE 1	[stɪl]	(immer) noch
south U1/2	[saʊθ]	südlich, Süd-; Süden	**stilts** U14/1	[stɪlts]	Stelzen
South East Asia U5/10	[saʊθ iːst 'eɪʒə]	Südostasien	**stolen** U13/7	['stəʊlən]	gestohlen
South Island U1/2	[saʊθ 'aɪlənd]	Südinsel	**stomach** U15/3	['stʌmək]	Magen
southern U17/10	['sʌðən]	südlich, Süd-	**stomachache** U15/3	['stʌmək ˌeɪk]	Magen-/Bauchschmerzen
Southern Ocean U17/10	['sʌðən 'əʊʃn]	Südmeer, südlicher Ozean	**storey** C/p.141	['stɔːri]	Stockwerk
spa U1/1	[spɑː]	Kurort	**storm** C/p.141	[stɔːm]	Sturm
space U9	[speɪs]	Weltall	**straight ahead** U6/1	[streɪt ə'hed]	genau vor, geradeaus
space U18/7	[speɪs]	Platz, Raum	**straight on** U6/3	[streɪt ɒn]	geradeaus
spaceship U4/S2	['speɪsʃɪp]	Raumschiff	**straightaway** U10/7	[streɪtə'weɪ]	sofort
space station U9/4	['speɪs ˌsteɪʃən]	Raumstation	**strange** MORE 1	[streɪndʒ]	sonderbar
speak MORE 1	[spiːk]	sprechen	**strap** U14/DSC5	[stræp]	Band
speed U17/10	[spiːd]	Geschwindigkeit, Tempo	**strawberry** U10/1	['strɔːbəri]	Erdbeere
spell MORE 1	[spel]	buchstabieren	**street** MORE 1	[striːt]	Straße
spell U13/7	[spel]	Zauber, Bann	**stretch (from)** C/p.140	['stretʃ frəm]	sich erstrecken (von)
put a spell on sb U13/6	[pʊt ə 'spel ɒn 'sʌmbədi]	jemanden verzaubern	**stripe** MORE 1	[straɪp]	Streifen
spend MORE 1	[spend]	ausgeben (Geld); verbringen (Zeit)	**striped** U14/DSC5	[straɪpt]	gestreift
sphinx U11/1	[sfɪŋks]	Sphinx	**stroke** U18/1	[strəʊk]	streicheln
spirit U11/8	['spɪrɪt]	Geist	**strong** MORE 1	[strɒŋ]	stark
spontaneous U16	[spɒn'teɪniəs]	spontan	**strongest** MORE 1	['strɒŋɡəst]	stärkste/r/s
spoon U15/1	[spuːn]	Löffel	**get stuck** U13/2	[get 'stʌk]	steckenbleiben

student U1/6	['stju:dnt]	Student/in; Schüler/in	
study U1/2	['stʌdi]	studieren; lernen	
stuff (informal) U13/7	[stʌf]	Zeug	
stupid MORE 1	['stju:pɪd]	dumm, blöd	
subject U1/4	['sʌbdʒekt]	(Schul-)Fach	
success U3/1	[sək'ses]	Erfolg	
such U3/6	[sʌtʃ]	solche/r/s	
suddenly MORE 1	['sʌdnli]	plötzlich, auf einmal	
suggest MORE 1	[sə'dʒest]	vorschlagen	
suggestion MORE 1	[sə'dʒestʃn]	Vorschlag	
summary U7/S3	['sʌmri]	Zusammenfassung	
sun MORE 1	[sʌn]	Sonne	
sunglasses U14/DSC5	['sʌŋ,glɑ:sɪz]	Sonnenbrille	
sunshine MORE 1	['sʌnʃaɪn]	Sonnenschein	
superglue U4/5	['su:pəglu:]	Superkleber	
supermarket U6/2	['su:pəmɑ:kɪt]	Supermarkt	
superstar U12/3	['su:pəstɑ:]	Superstar	
supper U1/2	['sʌpə]	Abendessen	
be supposed to U5/NYC1	[bi: sə'pəʊzd tʊ]	sollen	
(be) sure U6/DSC2	[ʃɔ:]	sicher (sein)	
surf (the net) U12/13	[sɜ:f ðə 'net]	surfen (im Internet)	
surfer U17/6	['sɜ:fə]	Surfer/in	
surprise MORE 1	[sə'praɪz]	Überraschung	
swallow U15/1	['swɒləʊ]	(hinunter-)schlucken	
swap U6/DSC2	[swɒp]	(ver-)tauschen	
sweep U1/2	[swi:p]	kehren, fegen	
sweet MORE 1	[swi:t]	süß	
sweets (pl) MORE 1	[swi:ts]	Süßigkeiten	
swim MORE 1	[swɪm]	schwimmen	
swimmer U5/1	['swɪmə]	Schwimmer/in	
swimming trunks U16/7	['swɪmɪŋ trʌŋks]	Badehose	
swing U2/2	[swɪŋ]	(hin- und her-)schwingen	
Swiss U17/6	[swɪs]	schweizerisch	
switch off U12/13	[swɪtʃ'ɒf]	abschalten	
symbol U16/3	['sɪmbəl]	Symbol, Zeichen	
system C/p.138	['sɪstəm]	System	

T

table MORE 1	['teɪbl]	Tisch	
tackle U17/18	['tækl]	attackieren (im Sport)	
taipan U5/10	['taɪpæn]	Taipan-Schlange	
take an order U12/DSC4	[teɪk ən 'ɔ:də]	eine Bestellung aufnehmen	
take away U12/DSC4	[teɪk ə'weɪ]	mitnehmen	
take down U14/1	[teɪk daʊn]	abbauen	
take it easy U8/4	[teɪk ɪt 'i:zi]	sich entspannen	

take off U9/1	[teɪk 'ɒf]	abheben, starten	
take off U13/1	[teɪk 'ɒf]	abnehmen	
take out MORE 1	[teɪk 'aʊt]	herausnehmen	
take over U9/10	[teɪk 'əʊvə]	übernehmen; erobern	
take (time) MORE 1	[teɪk 'taɪm]	(Zeit) brauchen/dauern	
take turns U8/12	[teɪk tɜ:ns]	sich abwechseln	
tall MORE 1	[tɔ:l]	groß	
tan U16/11	[tæn]	Bräune	
tar C/p.138	[tɑ:]	Teer	
task MORE 1	[tɑ:sk]	Aufgabe	
teach MORE 1	[ti:tʃ]	beibringen; unterrichten	
team U5/G	[ti:m]	Team	
teatime U5/15	['ti:taɪm]	Teestunde	
technology U9/9	[tek'nɒlədʒi]	Technologie	
teen U12/5	[ti:n]	Teenager, Teenie	
telegram U11/8	['telɪgræm]	Telegramm	
television MORE 1	['telɪvɪʒn]	Fernseher	
tell a lie U8/7	[tel ə laɪ]	lügen	
tell off EU/1	[tel 'ɒf]	ausschimpfen	
temperature U16/1	['temprɪtʃə]	Temperatur	
temple U11/1	['templ]	Tempel	
term EU/1	[tɜ:m]	Semester	
terrible MORE 1	['terəbl]	schrecklich, furchtbar	
be terrified C/p.141	[bi: 'terəfaɪd]	große Angst haben	
text U3/DSC1	[tekst]	eine SMS schicken, simsen	
text message MORE 1	['tekst 'mesɪdʒ]	Textnachricht, SMS	
Thailand U5/10	['taɪlænd]	Thailand	
(more) than U5/10	[ðæn]	(mehr) als	
thank God U11/S5	[θæŋk gɒd]	Gott sei Dank	
thank sb MORE 1	[θæŋk]	jemandem danken	
their MORE 1	[ðeə]	ihr/e	
theirs U14/7	[ðeəz]	ihre/r/s	
them MORE 1	[ðem]	sie, ihnen	
these MORE 1	[ði:z]	diese	
thick U16/3	[θɪk]	dicht; dick	
thief (pl thieves) U2/2	[θi:f, θi:vz]	Dieb/in	
though U10/NYC2	[ðəʊ]	aber, allerdings	
thrill U17/10	[θrɪl]	Nervenkitzel	
throat U15/3	[θrəʊt]	Hals	
through U6/1	[θru:]	durch	
throughout the year U16/10	[θru:'aʊt ðə 'jɪə]	das ganze Jahr (über)	
throw MORE 1	[θrəʊ]	werfen	
thunderstorm U16/2	['θʌndəstɔ:m]	Gewitter	
tidy (up) U8/1	['taɪdi ,ʌp]	aufräumen	
tight U1/11	[taɪt]	fest	
till U12/12	[tɪl]	bis	
time machine U9/4	['taɪm məʃi:n]	Zeitmaschine	

timetable U1/5	['taɪmteɪbl]	Stundenplan
tip U3/6	[tɪp]	Hinweis, Tipp
tired of U14/1	[taɪəd ɒv]	etwas satt haben; überdrüssig
today MORE 1	[tə'deɪ]	heute
to-do list U17/DSC6	[tə'du: ˌlɪst]	Aufgabenliste
toe U15/6	[təʊ]	Zeh/e
together MORE 1	[tə'geðə]	zusammen, gemeinsam
tomb U11/1	[tu:m]	Grab, Gruft
tomorrow MORE 1	[tə'mɒrəʊ]	morgen
ton U5/10	[tʌn]	Tonne (1000 kg)
tongue MORE 1	[tʌŋ]	Zunge
tongue-twister U11/9	[tʌŋ 'twɪstə]	Zungenbrecher
tonight MORE 1	[tə'naɪt]	heute Abend
too MORE 1; U1/11	[tu:]	auch; zu
tool U12/7	[tu:l]	Werkzeug
tooth (pl teeth) MORE 1	[tu:θ, ti:θ]	Zahn
toothache U15/3	['tu:θeɪk]	Zahnschmerzen
top U4/3	[tɒp]	ganz oben, Gipfel, Spitze
topic U15/1	['tɒpɪk]	Thema
topping U12/DSC4	['tɒpɪŋ]	Belag
torch U11/10	[tɔ:tʃ]	Taschenlampe
tornado C/p.140	[tɔ:'neɪdəʊ]	Wirbelsturm
total U12/DSC4	['təʊtl]	gesamt; völlig
touch MORE 1	[tʌtʃ]	berühren
touchdown C/p.139	['tʌtʃdaʊn]	Touchdown
tour U3/DSC1	[tʊə]	Tour
tourist MORE 1	['tʊərɪst]	Tourist/in
tourist centre U11/10	['tʊərɪst 'sentə]	Touristenzentrum
tourist office U6/2	['tʊərɪst 'ɒfɪs]	Fremdenverkehrsbüro
towards MORE 1	[tə'wɔ:dz]	in Richtung, auf … zu
towel U5/1	['taʊəl]	Handtuch
tower U6/DSC2	[taʊə]	Turm
town MORE 1	[taʊn]	Stadt
(running) track EU/1	[træk]	Anlage; Laufbahn
tractor U12/5	['træktə]	Traktor
tradition U4/3	[trə'dɪʃn]	Tradition
traditional U17/10	[trə'dɪʃnl]	traditionell
traffic lights U6/DSC2	['træfɪk laɪts]	Verkehrsampel
trailer U14/1	['treɪlə]	Anhänger, Wohnwagen
train U6/6	[treɪn]	Zug
train U17/6	[treɪn]	trainieren
trainer MORE 1	['treɪnə]	Turnschuh
trainer U17/8	['treɪnə]	Trainer/in
translate U12/9	[træns'leɪt]	übersetzen
transmitter U18/10	[trænz'mɪtə]	Sender
trap U7/S3	[træp]	fangen; in einer Falle
travel U1/1	['trævl]	reisen

tray U18/1	[treɪ]	Tablett
treasure MORE 1	['treʒə]	Schatz
treasure hunt U7/7	['treʒə ˌhʌnt]	Schatzsuche
treat U4/3	[tri:t]	Vergnügen, Belohnung
tree house U7/3	['tri: haʊs]	Baumhaus
trick or treat U4/3	['trɪk ə 'tri:t]	Süßes oder Saures (Frage beim Halloween-Umzug)
tricky U11/2	['trɪki]	betrügerisch; schwierig, kompliziert
trip MORE 1	[trɪp]	Ausflug, Reise
triplets U17/8	['trɪpləts]	Drillinge
(it's no) trouble U10/NYC2	[ɪts nəʊ 'trʌbl]	keine Ursache
get into trouble U5/1	[get 'ɪntu: 'trʌbl]	Probleme/Ärger bekommen
trust U9/S4	[trʌst]	Vertrauen
truth MORE 1	[tru:θ]	Wahrheit
try MORE 1	[traɪ]	versuchen
turkey U10/1	['tɜ:ki]	Truthahn
turn U1/9	[tɜ:n]	werden; abbiegen
turn off MORE 1	[tɜ:n 'ɒf]	abschalten
turn on MORE 1	[tɜ:n 'ɒn]	einschalten
turn up U3/6	[tɜ:n 'ʌp]	auftauchen
turn up/down U16/7	[tɜ:n 'ʌp/daʊn]	lauter/leiser stellen
TV MORE 1	[ˌti:'vi:]	Fernseher; Fernsehen
twice MORE 1	[twaɪs]	zweimal
twin U3/DSC1	[twɪn]	Zwilling, Zwillings-
type (of) MORE 1	[taɪp]	Art; Typ; Sorte

U

UFO (=unidentified flying object) U9/9	[jʊ:ef'əʊ]	Ufo (unbekanntes Flugobjekt)
ufologist U9/9	[ju:'fɒlədʒɪst]	Ufologe, Ufologin
ugly U5/6	['ʌgli]	hässlich
uncle U12/1	['ʌŋkl]	Onkel
unconscious U9/S4	[ʌn'kɒnʃəs]	bewusstlos
underground U6/6	['ʌndəgraʊnd]	U-Bahn
underline U10/11	[ˌʌndə'laɪn]	unterstreichen
underneath U14/1	[ˌʌndə'ni:θ]	unterhalb
understand MORE 1	[ʌndə'stænd]	verstehen
understanding U6/DSC2	[ˌʌndə'stændɪŋ]	Verständnis
unfair U4/4	[ʌn'feə]	unfair
unfortunately EU/1	[ʌn'fɔ:tʃənətli]	unglücklicherweise
unfriendly U13/7	[ʌn'frendli]	unfreundlich
unhappy MORE 1	[ʌn'hæpi]	unglücklich
unidentified U9/9	[ˌʌnaɪ'dentɪfaɪd]	unbekannt, nicht identifiziert

uniform U1/2	['ju:nifɔ:m]	Uniform	
unit U7/7	['ju:nɪt]	Gerät; Einheit	
universe U9/1	['ju:nɪvɜ:s]	Universum	
university U12/9	[ju:nɪ'vɜ:səti]	Universität	
unpack U16/7	[ʌn'pæk]	auspacken	
until MORE 1	[ən'tɪl]	bis	
unusual MORE 1	[ʌn'ju:ʒʋəl]	ungewöhnlich	
upload EU/1	[ʌp'ləʋd]	hochladen	
upset U3/1	[ʌp'set]	gestört, verärgert, böse	
upstairs U3/2	[ʌp'steəz]	oben	
up to U5/14	['ʌp ˌtu]	bis zu	
use MORE 1	[ju:z]	benutzen, verwenden	
useful MORE 1	['jusfəl]	nützlich	
usually MORE 1	['ju:ʒʋəli]	gewöhnlich, normalerweise	

V

valley U7/1	['væli]	Tal	
valuable U15/10	['væljʋbl]	wertvoll	
vampire U4/1	['væmpaɪə]	Vampir	
van C/p.141	[væn]	Kleinbus	
vegetable MORE 1	['vedʒtəbl]	Gemüse	
vet U18/1	[vet]	Tierarzt, Tierärztin	
video game U2/5	['vɪdiəʋ ˌgeɪm]	Videospiel	
Vietnam U12/3	[ˌvjet'næm]	Vietnam	
village MORE 1	['vɪlɪdʒ]	Dorf	
visit MORE 1	['vɪzɪt]	besuchen	
visit U7/7	['vɪzɪt]	Besuch	
voice MORE 1	[vɔɪs]	Stimme	
volcanic eruption C/p.139	[vɒl'kænɪk ɪˌrʌpʃən]	Vulkanausbruch	
volcano C/p.139	[vɒl'keɪnəʋ]	Vulkan	
volume U16/7	['vɒlju:m]	Lautstärke	
vote U15/1	[vəʋt]	wählen	

W

waiter, waitress U10/5	['weɪtə, 'weɪtrəs]	Bedienung, Kellner/in	
wake somebody up U2/2	[weɪk ˌsʌmbədi 'ʌp]	jemanden aufwecken	
walk a pet U18/1	[wɔ:k ə 'pet]	Gassi gehen	
walk up U4/3	[wɔk ʌp]	hinaufgehen	
wall U4/9	[wɔ:l]	Wand, Mauer	
wallet U2/1	['wɒlɪt]	Brieftasche	
war U9/10	[wɔ:r]	Krieg	
wardrobe U14/3	['wɔ:drəʋb]	Kleiderschrank	

warn U7/S3	[wɔ:n]	warnen	
wash up U7/10	[wɒʃ 'ʌp]	abspülen, abwaschen	
washing machine MORE 1	['wɒʃɪŋ məˌʃi:n]	Waschmaschine	
do the washing-up U2/2	['du: ðə wɒʃɪŋ 'ʌp]	abspülen	
waste of time U17/8	[weɪst əv taɪm]	Zeitverschwendung	
watch MORE 1	[wɒtʃ]	beobachten; zuschauen; Uhr	
watch TV MORE 1	[wɒtʃ ti:'vi:]	fernsehen	
waterfall U7/3	['wɔ:təfɔ:l]	Wasserfall	
give way U16/1	[gɪv 'weɪ]	Platz machen	
wear MORE 1	[weə]	tragen	
weather MORE 1	['weðə]	Wetter	
weather forecast U16/3	['weðər 'fɔ:ka:st]	Wettervorhersage	
weather report U16/4	['weðər rɪ'pɔ:t]	Wetterbericht	
weatherman U16/7	['weðəmæn]	Wettermann	
weaver U11/3	['wi:və]	Weber/in	
web U3/6	[web]	Netz, Internet	
webpage U1/9	['webpeɪdʒ]	Internetseite	
weigh U5/10	[weɪ]	wiegen	
Welcome! MORE 1	['welkəm]	Wilkommen!	
well U6/6	[wel]	gesund, wohlauf	
western U16/10	['westən]	westlich	
wet U4/4	[wet]	nass	
whale U5/10	[weɪl]	Wal	
whale shark U5/13	['weɪl ʃɒ:rk]	Walhai	
What about? MORE 1	[wɒtˌə'baʋt]	Worum geht's?	
What a shame! U9/DSC3	[wɒt ə ʃeɪm]	Wie schade!	
What else? MORE 1	[wɒt 'els]	Was noch?	
What for? U18/NYC4	[wɒt fɔ:]	Warum?, Wofür?	
What's going on? U2/2	[wɒts gəʋɪŋ 'ɒn]	Was ist los?	
what sort of U3/6	[wɒt sɔ:t ɒv]	welche Art	
What's the matter? MORE 1	[wɒts ðə 'mætə]	Was ist los?	
wherever U16/7	[weə'revə]	wo(hin) auch immer	
which MORE 1	[wɪtʃ]	welche/r/s	
while U3/DSC1	[waɪl]	Weile	
while U15/14	[waɪl]	während	
whisper MORE 1	['wɪspər]	flüstern	
who U4/13	[hu:]	der, die, das	
Who cares? U15/NYC3	[hʋ 'keəs]	Wen kümmert es?	
whole MORE 1	[həʋl]	ganz; voll	
whom U14	[hu:m]	wem, wen	
whose U5/11	[hu:z]	wessen	
wide MORE 1	[waɪd]	breit; weit	
wife (pl wives) MORE 1	[waɪf, waɪvz]	Ehefrau	

wild MORE 1	[waɪld]	wild	
wildlife U15/10	[ˈwaɪldlaɪf]	Tierwelt	
will MORE 1	[wɪl]	werden (Zukunft)	
win MORE 1	[wɪn]	gewinnen	
wind MORE 1	[wɪnd]	Wind	
windsurfing U17/1	[ˈwɪndsɜːfɪŋ]	Windsurfen	
windy U16/2	[ˈwɪndi]	windig	
winner U9/DSC3	[ˈwɪnə]	Gewinner/in	
wish MORE 1	[wɪʃ]	Wunsch	
witch U4/1	[wɪtʃ]	Hexe	
without U12/5	[wɪðˈaʊt]	ohne	
witness U2/7	[ˈwɪtnəs]	Zeuge, Zeugin	
wizard U4/2	[ˈwɪzəd]	Zauberer	
wolf (pl wolves) MORE 1	[wʊlf, wʊlvz]	Wolf	
woman (pl women) MORE 1	[ˈwʊmən, ˈwɪmɪn]	Frau	
(no) wonder U7/7	[ˈwʌndə]	(kein) Wunder	
wonderful MORE 1	[ˈwʌndəfəl]	wunderbar	
wood MORE 1	[wʊd]	Wald; Holz	
wooden MORE 1	[ˈwʊdn]	Holz-, hölzern	
wool U11/3	[ˈwʊl]	Wolle	
work U2/2	[wɜːk]	hier: funktionieren	
work out U12/G	[ˈwɜːk aʊt]	trainieren	
worker U11/3	[ˈwɜːkə]	Arbeiter/in	
workman (pl workmen) U11/8	[ˈwɜːkmən]	Handwerker	
worldwide U5/10	[ˈwɜːldˌwaɪd]	weltweit	
be worried U3/1	[bi ˈwʌrid]	besorgt sein	
worry about U16/7	[wʌri əˈbaʊt]	sich Sorgen machen	
worrier U8/10	[ˈwʌriə]	Schwarzmaler/in	
be worth U3/2	[biː ˈwɜːθ]	wert sein	
wound U11/8	[wuːnd]	Wunde	
write down U3/DSC1	[raɪt daʊn]	niederschreiben	
writer U15/14	[ˈraɪtə]	Verfasser/in	

Y

yacht U17/10	[jɒt]	Jacht	
yachtswoman U17/10	[ˈjɒtswʊmən]	Seglerin	
year MORE 1	[jɪə]	Jahr; Jahrgangsstufe	
not ... yet U13/S6	[nɒt ˈjet]	noch nicht	
yours U2/2	[jɔːz]	deine/r/s; Ihre/r/s; eure/r/s	
yourself MORE 1	[jɔːˈself]	du/Sie/ihr selbst	
youth U7/10	[juːθ]	Jugend	
youth camp U7/10	[juːθ kæmp]	Jugendlager	
yurt U14/1	[jʊət]	Jurte	

Z

zombie U4/2	[ˈzɒmbi]	Zombie	

Acknowledgements

This publication is in copyright.

All rights reserved; no part of this publication may be reproduced, stored in a retrieval system, or transmitted in any form or by any means, electronic, mechanical, photocopying, recording, or otherwise, without the prior written permission of the publishers.

The publishers would like to thank the following for their kind permission to reproduce the following photographs and other copyright material:

p70 (CD: Food Icons), p88 Granger Historical Picture Archive, p124 Aurora Photos (Tommy Caldwell) / **Alamy Stock Photo;** p40 Leslie Banks (kitchen), p44 Margie Hurwich (girl), p46 Warnerbroers (boy on the phone), p65 Elen (UFOs), p85 Auremar (father, mother, uncle) / Darren Baker (aunt) / Ruslan Huzau (grandmother) / Flair Images (grandfather) / Godfer (cousin) /Narimbur (Ben), p90 Lexx72 (pepperoni), p99 Kondratova (trailer), p116 Tracy Whiteside (girl), p120 Russ Ensley (skateboarding), p122 Tracy Whiteside, p128 Kalcutta (girl drying cat) / Wavebreakmedia Ltd (boy stroking dog), p129 Mimagephotography (boy), p133 Tamara Bauer, p136 Vlue, p137 Dmytro Surkov, p139 Mary Katherine Wynn (American football) / Americanspirit (baseball) / Photographerlondon (basketball), p140 Lane Erickson (Yellowstone) / Photographerlondon (grizzly bear) I **Dreamstime.com; James Lozeau** p99 (treehouse: Finca Bellavista, Costa Rica); p9 J and J Productions (Jacob), p58 Juice Images Ltd (children in tree), p65 Bettman/Kontributor (UFO photo), p80 Egyptian (tomb), p81 Hulton Archive, p128 Steve Teague (girl cleaning out cage), p141 Jim Reed (storm chasers) **/ Getty Images; Helbling** p23, p26, p48, p51 (waterfall), p68, p90, p104; p107, p126, p128 (children playing game); ©iStockphoto.com/ p19 Juanmonino, p26 ajphoto (boy with camera), p31 lisathephotographer, p34 aldomurillo (mother and son) / creatives (pig), p35 GlobalP (dog, fish, rabbit, horse) / mikheewnik (turtle) / viki2win (cat) / Laures (mouse) / tunart (hamster), p36 MR1805 (blue whale), p37 IMPALASTOCK (chimpanzee) / EMPPhotography (giraffe) / BrendanHunter (antilope) / JBryson (boy with white shirt, girl), p51 aabejon (picnic), p87 alynst (Les) / mtreasure (Lisa), p99 robas (houses in Vietnam), p102 pkline (math quiz), p114 mguttman (girl), p116 aabejon (boy) / spencerdare (map), p118 Yarinca (Carina), p121designsimply (Danni), p128 Andrew_Howe (girl feeding cat), p138 EHStock (Susannah); **Metro** p45 (http://metro.co.uk); p123 Roy Riley/EPA **/ picturedesk.com; pixabay** p130 (house, rat); p9 Anton_Ivanov (Abeeku), p10 Max Topchii, p12 YUSRAN ABDUL RAHMAN, p13 Max Topchii, p24 Antartstock (hand holding phone) / Cienpies Design (background) / lineartestpilot (face), p26 CREATISTA (girl phone) / Iakov Filimonov (girl looking for pen) / Celig (boy eating chocolate), p36 Darrenp (taipan snake) / Bullstar (Eustarine crocodile) / corlaffra (mosquito) / Maros Bauer (cheetah) / Wolfilser (cars), p37 Alberto Loyo (anaconda) / Stephanie Periquet (elephant) / Deborah Kolb (lion) / Andrey Burmakin (giraffe) / tratong (rhino) / A_Lesik (dolphin) / Jan-Nor Photography (ostrich) / Kalmatsuy (boy with red T-shirt), p40 Paul Matthew Photography (living room) / David Hughes (hall) / Photographee.eu (bedroom), p44 cristovao (boy), p46 MJTH (girl on the phone), p47 More Images, p48 1000 Words (traffic light) / chrisdorney (fountain) / Bikeworldtravel (statue) / Pete Spiro (clock tower) / Ron Ellis (bus stop) / Tupungato (bridge), p51 Richard Thornton (climber), p54 Olesia Bilkei, p58 Thomas Pajot (text bubbles) / Hilch (notes) / moosa art (invitation), p60 freesoulproduction, p68 Claudio Divizia (closed sign) / Lester Balajadia (ticket sign) / Carsten Reisinger (lift) / Macrovector (festival poster), p76 amstockphoto (bat) / Cheryl Ann Quigley (hit) / sonya etchison (pitch) / Dennis Debono (team), p80 Jaroslav Moravcik (Tutankhamun) / Waj (pyramid), p84 s_bukley (Angelina Jolie), p86 Olesia Bilkei (campfire) / Aleksey Oleynikov (Vicky) / Catalin Petolea (tractor), p87 Anton_Ivanov (Denise) / singh_lens (Amar), p90 Imageman (cheese) / Roxana Bashyrova (pineapple) / Hong Vo (mushrooms, tomatoes) / gosphotodesign (ham), p99 withGod (yurts) / Rafal Cichawa (Uros' houses), p102 Monkey Business Images (family) / Patricia Hofmeester (school bag) / Chimpinski (cap) / KKulikov (trainers) / Aleksander Krsmanovic (ruler) / Luchi_a (book), p104 OZaiachin (watch strap) / Aaron Amat (sunglasses) / Elnur (jacket), p105 Neamov (leather jacket) / koya979 (straw) / Khvost (socks), p106 Mettus, p109 Ammit Jack (Indian) / Fotos593 (Amazon jungle) / Andrzej Kubik (water lilies), p110 More Images, p112 DavidPinoPhotography (library) / rangizzz (prize) / zhu difeng (internet café), p114 RedKoala (weather symbols), p118 Mike Charles (Lake District), p120 l i g h t p o e t (swimming) / Kwanbenz (ice skating) / CandyBox Images (running) / maxpro (mountain biking) / matimix (football) / hektoR (climbing) / muzsy (volleyball) / Lucy Clark (tennis) / Tumar (basketball) / Dima Fadeev (windsurfing) / gorillaimages (skiing) / 2xSamara.com (snowboarding) / Verena Matthew (cycling) / trubavin (surfing) / Luckylmages (roller-skating), p121 Greg Epperson (Ricky), p126 Rosli Othman (cricket) / Maxisport (football, rugby) / bikeriderlondon (tennis, swimming) / Tony Bowler (golf), p128 sonya etchison (boys washing dog) / kurhan (cat vet) / racorn (girl brushing horse) / Catherine Murray (litter tray) / Sergey Novikov (girls walking dog) / trubitsyn (boy playing with dog), p129 Amazingmikael (girl), p130 Bborriss.67 (dogs) / keantian (cats) / Anton Gvozdikov (birds), p131 Phawat (snake), p132 Jan Martin Will (penguin) / deer boy (map), p134 Tupungato (market) / Africa Studio (money) / Maxx-Studio (phone), p138 Hdyma Natallia (flag) / Monkey Business Images (Mark) / Donna Ellen Coleman (prom couple), p139 sianc (girl) / sergios (boy), 140 welcomia (Redwood National Park) / Sarah Fields Photography (Rocky Mountains) / Everett Historical (Apache), p141 Minerva Studio (tornado) / Guido Amrein Switzerland (hurricane) **/ Shutterstock.com; Toonz Animation** p21, p33, p55, p67, p84, p98; **Wikimedia Commons** p36 Drahkrub (bumblebee bat, Creative Commons License 4.0, https://commons.wikimedia.org/wiki/File:Pipistrellus_female-1.jpg), p118 Wolfgangbeyer at the German language Wikipedia (Death Valley, Creative Commons License 3.0, https://de.wikipedia.org/wiki/Datei:Death_Valley_Zabriskie_Point.jpg), p124 Octagon (Dawn Wall, Creative Commons License 3.0, https://commons.wikimedia.org/wiki/File:El_Capitan_01.JPG), p141 (Hurricane Katrina) (United States Air Force); **cover image** ©iStockphoto.com/fstop123

Every effort has been made to trace the owners of any copyright material in this book. If notified, the publishers will be pleased to rectify any errors or omissions.